Special Edition

DEX

VARIATIONS AND VIGNETTES

ADVANCED
SINGLETAIL
PLAY

Copyright 2025 by Dex

All rights reserved. This book or any portion thereof may not be reproduced or used in any manner whatsoever without the express written permission of the author, except for the use of brief quotations in a book review.

Printed in the United States of America

Library of Congress Cataloging-in-Publication Data

Dex, 1955-

Variations and Vignettes: Advanced Singletail Whip Play

ISBN-13: 979-8-9922239-0-3 (paperback)

979-8-9922239-1-0 (paperback Special Edition)

979-8-9922239-2-7 (Kindle)

979-8-9922239-3-4 (ePub)

1. Sex and sexuality. 2. Alternative lifestyle. 3. BDSM. 4. Leather lifestyle. 5. Spirituality. 6. Healing energy. 7. Dungeon play. 8. Bullwhip.

Disclaimer: Readers attempting the techniques, variations, and vignettes described in this book do so at their own risk. Any play with a whip involving other persons carries a risk of physical injury. No one should undertake a whip scene unless they have reached a level of expertise with a whip that is consistent with the complexity and difficulty of the scene proposed. Results will vary tremendously depending upon the skill and expertise of the whip thrower. In no circumstances is the author liable for any injuries resulting from two consenting adults participating in a mutually agreed-upon scene gone bad.

First Edition

Joan's Books

Tampa, FL

Table of Contents

Introduction...ix
Beyond Whips in the Dungeon—Expanding the Play Repertoire........ix
Chapter 1: Variables in Whips that Result in Variations in Play...........1
Chapter 2: Variations in the Construction of a Whip: Whip Lasagna....31
Chapter 3: Variations in Crackers or Poppers......................47
Chapter 4: Variations in Static Throws............................65
Chapter 5: Variations in Dynamic Throws: Rhythm and Syncopation...69
Chapter 6: Variations in Footwork................................75
Chapter 7: Surface Targeting: Creating Variations in Sensations........83
Chapter 8: Variations in Play Environment........................89
Chapter 9: Music - the Greatest Variable of All....................95
Chapter 10: Mixing Play Genres to Create New Sensations..........103
Chapter 11: Two-handed Whip Work: Twice the Sensations........111
Chapter 12: Advanced Whip Catching: Variations for the Bottom.....139
Chapter 13: Crafting a Vignette.................................143
Chapter 14: Erotic Vignette....................................149
Chapter 15: Quiet Vignette....................................159
Chapter 16: Sensory Deprivation Vignette.......................163
Chapter 17: Blindfolded Whip Thrower Vignette..................169
Chapter 18: Creating a Canvas Vignette.........................173
Chapter 19: The Clothespin Vignette............................179
Chapter 20: Self-Flagellation Vignette...........................183
Chapter 21: Saline Genital Vignette.............................187
Chapter 22: The Moby Dick Vignette...........................191
Chapter 23: The Whip Flurry Vignette..........................195

Chapter 24: Games with Whips (Kinky of Course) 205
Chapter 25: Needle Play—Whip Play Combo Vignette 211
Chapter 26: Bullwhip Magick Vignette: Feathers Everywhere. 215
Chapter 27: Roses Roses: The Flower Vase Vignette 227
Chapter 28: Streamer Whip Strip Tease Vignette 233
Chapter 29: Bloody Mess Vignette: Blood Play with a Bullwhip 237
Chapter 30: Consent, Communication, and Safety 239
Epilogue: Qi Gong—Moving Energy with Your Mind 251
Conclusion: The Art of the Whip. 257
Appendix A: Care of a Kangaroo Whip 261
Appendix B: Carrying Cases for Whips 265
Appendix C: Top Space and Top Drop. 269
Appendix D: Bottom Space and Bottom Drop. 273
Appendix E: Signs That a Venue Is Not Whip Friendly 277
Appendix F: Breaking in a New Kangaroo Whip 281
Appendix G: Singletail Sheet Music 285
Appendix H: Extemporaneous Thoughts of a Seasoned Whip Thrower . 293

Preface

THIS BOOK IS a companion to *Whips in the Dungeon: Singletail Techniques for Play* (WITD), my first foray into writing a book focused solely on whips for BDSM play. WITD provides basic instructions and insights designed to bring the potential whip thrower up to speed quickly and efficiently enough that they can use their whip for safe, satisfactory play on an actual whip bottom.

My inspiration for this second whip book came from a reader's request for variations on the moves and scenes described in WITD. I knew that the first book was a starting point. This request got me thinking of the endless possibilities in the broad spectrum of dungeon whip play. Thus, this companion book was born. You will find that it builds on the techniques and ideas in WITD. There will be references to pictures and information in the first book.

Further companion material is available in the videos I created during the pandemic. In lockdown, I filmed a series of short videos to supplement WITD. Nine months later, with over 600 video shorts, the series includes whips and has expanded to canes, other impact play, and beyond. These videos naturally complement Variations and Vignettes. They are available at several places: on Fetlife for subscribers, on my YouTube channels: Whips in the Dungeon and The Leather Journey, and on the Whips in the Dungeon website [http://witd.houseofgraves.com].

The reader of this book should have a good working knowledge of whips and be an intermediate to advanced whip thrower. Terms introduced in WITD will not be redefined in depth here. Cross-references will be provided so it will be easy to look up a term or concept referring back to WITD. The cross-referencing nomenclature will be similar to this example - (WITD, p. 23). This will refer directly to the appropriate page in WITD. References to the video series will follow the nomenclature (WITD xxx.xx) to refer to the specific video short (note: this video nomenclature is only used on the **Whips in the Dungeon website**. (http://witd.houseofgraves.com)

Since whip enthusiasts in the BDSM lifestyle have many different identity preferences, this book will use the terms whip throwers or tops and whip catchers or bottoms.

For obvious reasons, this book is intended only for readers 18 years of age and older. As discussed in the previous book, adults learn differently than adolescents. In a nutshell, adults learn best by relating a new skill to a skill with which they already have proficiency, thereby acquiring proficiency with the new skill quicker.

I will take an approach grounded in my own background as a retired professor in the field of education. Learning about BDSM is an autodidactic activity and is largely a self-directed learning endeavor. Self-directed learning is an adult learning theory that begins with having the desire to learn about something new, taking the initiative to begin the learning process, applying resourcefulness to the learning process, and persistence to the completion of the learning task or project.

This book will begin from the premise that any adult reading the book has the desire to learn more about singletail whips and already has experience with singletails. They will take the initiative to read and practice some of the variations described within the book. They will then muster internal resources to locate, acquire, and create new variations with a singletail whip. Finally, they will persist in the learning process until they become proficient enough to use these whip variations in play in a dungeon and create their own vignettes.

Ultimately, I hope this book will speed up the learning process on some new techniques and encourage creativity with your whips in the dungeon. This is supposed to be fun!

Acknowledgments

No journey is ever made alone, and my journey with the whip is no different. There are many whip makers, whip enthusiasts, and leather folk to thank. I have been living this journey since 1999 when I entered the lifestyle.

Readers can explore acknowledgments in the first book to get to know my earliest whip influences. There are some I missed and many more recent people I want to thank.

I would like to extend my gratitude to k9blitz and Sidetrax for providing a wonderful space for whip throwing during my retirement years.

The Whips in the Dungeon Whip Practice group meets via Zoom each month, and I encourage readers to consider attending or finding something similar. We learn a great deal from each other, and we get to share our passion for whips. My teachers in this regard have been Robert (CA), Travis (ID), Mike (Lisbon, Portugal), and Leather Redux (IL), our group regulars. Many of the ideas in this book are a product of our friendships and discussions.

Thanks to my patrons at the WITD Patreon website for their feedback on drafts and advanced reader copies as they progressed.

Thanks to Tigrrrr for shooting the cover photo again, and for photographing whips for this book. And thank you budddd for once again modeling for the front cover. Blisfulpleasure's keen eye captured a memorable moment as Apex-S suspended Moodstone. Dean Rodgers at Knotty Photos provided a sweet surprise when MasoTendenceiz was caught reading my first book on whips using

PainSlut5000 as a footstool. David Weathersby masterfully captured the whips in motion for Master LeatherRedux's writing contributions. Thanks to Eric Draco for visualizing the outdoor trespassing scene that lead to the capture, bullwhipping and for contributing photographic evidence of the infraction. TheQuietMaster has contributed photos over half a decade and it was his watchful eye that captured the Beyond Leather showcase scene. Zark and Tigrrrr captured the Weekend of Wickedness scenes. Desert Minx stopped plaiting long enough to take a photo of her beautiful signal whips that became the back cover of the book.

A heartfelt thank you goes to my go-to whip maker, Peter Jack, "The Whip Man" from New Zealand, whose work is unmatched.

I am forever grateful to the late lady sally for creating and braiding the most wonderful crackers in the world. Lady sally was much more than an innovator with whip poppers. She was a fabulous whip bottom, supreme masochist, technical adviser, travel companion, workshop helper, demo bottom, and leather sister.

Finally, I want to express my love and gratitude and to my favorite whip catcher, Moodstone. Her contributions to my writing endeavors are invaluable.

This book is dedicated to the most beautiful being in the world . . . a whip catcher.

Introduction

Beyond Whips in the Dungeon— Expanding the Play Repertoire

THE LEARNING GOAL of my first book, Whips in the Dungeon (WITD), is to get the whip out of the toy bag and into active play within the dungeon. So now that the whip is in the dungeon and into a basic play repertoire, what are some of the variations and vignettes possible with whips?

The learning goal of this book is to take the intermediate whip thrower and expand their play repertoire to the point that each scene is even more satisfying for the top, the bottom, and perhaps anyone watching. I offer these insights with the caveat that one's skill with the whips is a reflection of the passion that one puts into throwing them.

Throwing a whip in the dungeon well and having successful scenes with my whip bottoms does not make me more worthy than others to teach about whips. However, I believe that I have something worth teaching others because of my many years of experience consistently throwing a whip. With this book, I hope to share some of that experience, with both successes and failures, along the journey.

This book will focus on singletail whips, but as with WITD, other classes of whips will be incorporated into the vignettes section. Thinking about and using different types of whips before and sometimes after using a singletail is integral to creating variations in sensations with surface skin play. Other implements will also be incorporated into the vignettes, as they create a variety of sensations when added to a singletail scene.

Part of becoming a master whip thrower is to move beyond simple play with a whip in the dungeon: to be able to throw fluidly with the music, to craft a scene, to read the bottom, and to be flexible enough with whip skills to vary sensations and adjust a whip scene to fit into the current orchestral set playing in a dungeon.

The first part of mastering all of those skill sets is to identify many of the possible variables that come into play in a whip scene. Will variables in whip construction make a difference in dungeon play? Will differences in cracker materials create a range of sensations, from feathering to leaving marks to commemorate the scene? Will different throwing techniques vary the sensation felt on the receiving end of the whip? Is there a different feel with static throws vs dynamic throws? Everyone settles on a favorite foot position, but does varying foot positions create a variation in the sensation the whip catcher feels?

The short answer to all of those questions is yes, yes, yes, yes, and definitely yes. This book will break down each of those variables, and the reader will begin to visualize the possibilities within a whip scene.

Considering the many variables available to the whip thrower, there are many ways to craft a whip vignette. The vignettes in this book cross a spectrum from erotic play to cathartic play. Hopefully, they will open the reader's eyes to seeing that infinite possibilities exist using even simple variations.

Finally, some of my most memorable real-life vignettes will be offered - scenes that will hopefully spark the reader's imagination and creativity to craft their own memorable vignettes.

An expansion and extended discussion of bullwhip magick will explore in more detail the reaction of the soma to the phenomenon of energy exchange through a bullwhip strike. More discussion about energy conversion and processing by the whip catcher will provide insight into the possibilities for variation created by the whip thrower.

Finally, I include a chapter on a place I had never envisioned traveling to—the erotic performance art in the form of bullwhip theater showcase scenes.

Chapter 1

Variables in Whips that Result in Variations in Play

WHILE THIS BOOK focuses on singletail whips, it is important to know about the different classes of whips. Variables in play apply to all classes of whips. I will necessarily touch on some of the same information found in WITD. This chapter will describe different types of whips and how to create variations in play with each type of whip.

Floggers. A flogger is the most common multi-tail whip seen in the dungeon. Almost every top owns one and knows how to throw it. It is a fairly easy whip to learn how to throw and will most likely not cause serious damage if a mistake is made when throwing.

Floggers can be made of many materials, but traditionally are made of some form of leather. Variables in traditional flogger construction can be narrowed down to the type of leather used, the tanning process used, the finishing cut on the end of the tails, the width and length of the tails, and the gender of the animal. (WITD, Photo 1).

Types of Leather Used for Floggers. A flogger can be made from almost any type of leather, but the most common are deer skin, lamb, goat, cowhide, bison, elk, and moose.

Floggers can also be made from string, rope, and other synthetic materials (rubber, for example). But I'm a leatherman, so let's focus on leather. Many exotic hides are available through small tanneries and small market custom flogger makers.

The weight of the leather, the tanning process used, the natural grain, or whether the natural grain has been removed (to create suede) all affect the various sensations that a flogger can create.

Floggers provide a range of sensations from sensuous and light to heavy and thuddy to sharp and painful. Floggers were my first toy that translated into a fetish. I collected many floggers for more than a decade. I had almost every exotic flogger imaginable, from kangaroo suede (the lightest leather) to alpaca.

Generally, floggers can be organized by weight into three groups: light, medium, and heavy-weight. Light-weight floggers are often used for erotic play. I recommend that bottoms who enjoy erotic flogger play have their own light-weight flogger to loan to the top they are playing with for use in genital play.

Light-weight floggers:

Rabbit – This is soft, fluffy, and erotic. (Flemish Giant hides make the longest tails)

Photo 1 Flemish Giant Rabbit Fur Flogger

Kangaroo suede - This is a kangaroo hide with the natural grain removed, turning it into suede. It is paper-thin, extremely light, and good for erotic and genital play.

Doeskin- Doeskin is female deerskin. It is light and soft.

Deerskin – Deerskin is light and soft, a good warmup flogger, and a must-have for the toy bag.

Lamb and goat skin – These are usually found in a light-weight flogger if they are vegetable tanned (veg tanned) or chrome tanned. Leathers that are oil-tanned are heavier.

Horsehair - This is made from horsetail. It is light-weight and airy but can be stingy and cause micro-abrasions. Note: Here, we have a light-weight flogger that can be stingy.

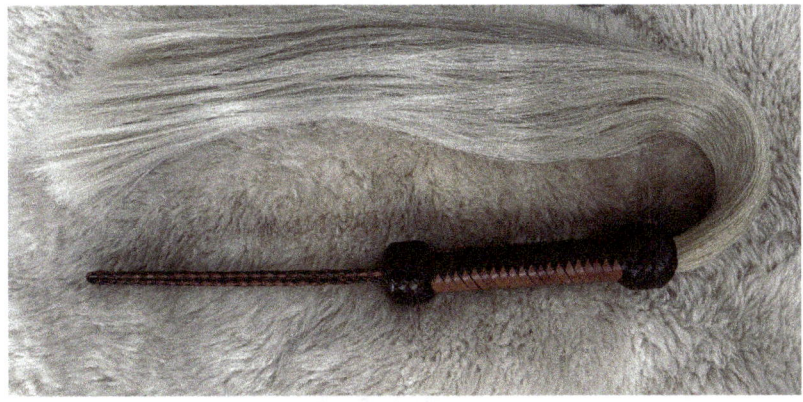

Photo 2 Palomino Horsehair Flogger

Medium-weight floggers:

Lamb and goat skin - If oil-tanned, floggers made from these skins tend to be medium-weight and stingier.

Elk – This is a buttery and soft skin but heavier and thuddier than deerskin.

Cowhide - If veg-tanned or chrome-tanned, cowhide is usually considered a medium-weight flogger material. Variables depend on the width and length of the tails and whether the tails are round cut.

Heavy-weight floggers:

Cowhide - If cowhide is oil-tanned (usually veg-tanned first and then oil-tanned in combination), it produces a heavier tail. When finished with a slant cut, it adds stinginess to the sensation.

Latigo – Latigo leather is cowhide leather made with a combination tanning process that begins with chrome tanning and is finished with vegetable tanning to add wax, fat, and oils to the leather. When finished with a slant cut, it adds stinginess to the sensation.

Moose – Moose hide is heavy and thuddy. If it is from a bull moose, it is even heavier and thuddier.

Bullhide - Bullhide makes heavy-weight leather. When placed side by side with bison or buffalo hides, it is hard to distinguish.

Bison or Buffalo – These have a heavy, thuddy weight.

When pursuing a flogger fetish, leathers and hides are often repeated and overlapped. At its height, my collection had 45 floggers, all made from different hides, with varying tail widths, lengths, and tail-cut finishes.

If I blindfolded a bottom and played the guessing game with them, most could not tell one light-weight flogger from another, a medium-weight flogger from another, or a heavy-weight flogger from another.

Photo 3 20" Elk Flogger with 1/2" tails compared to 26" Elk Supermop with 3/4" tails

Most bottoms cannot distinguish between the sensation created by a bison flogger as opposed to a bull leather flogger or a doe flogger from a deerskin flogger of similar tail length, width, and finish cut. A bottom won't be able to distinguish between a deerskin flogger cut out of white-tailed deer and mule deer skin. The leathers are too similar in weight and composition. These subtleties are indeed only for the top, who may also have a leather fetish.

For the average top, who might have limited toy-buying resources, I recommend settling on just one flogger in each weight – a light-weight, a medium-weight, and a heavy-weight. I prefer black or brown tails as both colors lend themselves to veg-tanned hides. Tails that are all the colors of the rainbow are usually chrome-tanned (sometimes called alum or syn-tanned) and will not have the natural oils that veg-tanned hides have.

There may be an occasion when the top cannot pass up a specialty flogger to add to their trio of floggers. For example, when I thinned my herd, I settled on deerskin, elk, and moose. For specialty floggers, I kept a Flemish giant rabbit flogger, a Palomino horsehair flogger, and an oil-tanned goat skin flogger. These six floggers each feel different and provide distinct sensations, and most bottoms can easily distinguish the differences when they are thrown in a scene.

Photo 4 Matched set of veg tanned goat skin floggers beside an oil tanned goat skinned flogger

The artistry and beauty of a flogger are certainly enhanced by how creatively the flogger maker constructs and adorns the handle. One should note how well the maker constructs the Turk's head and pineapple transition knot. Most of my flogger handles are kangaroo, as kangaroo lends itself to fancy plaiting and patterns and allows for a very consistent feel in the handle.

Balance of the flogger is important. Anyone who's thrown a well-balanced flogger knows that it is the hallmark of a good flogger. An unbalanced flogger will unnecessarily tire the arm and cause fatigue, perhaps causing the scene to be cut short.

Photo 5 Deerskin flogger perfectly balanced behind the pineapple knot.

Variations: Variation in flogger play is created by using different floggers made of various leathers, weights, and tail finishing cuts.

The weight of a flogger varies by the type of leather used, the length of the tails, the width of the tails, the number of tails, and the tanning process used. The longer the tails, the heavier the flogger will be.

It is possible to create a heavy flogger out of deerskin (a very light leather) if enough tails are used, but it would be more difficult to control the flow pattern of the "supermop" created as a finished product.

I prefer floggers with 80-120 tails, which are sometimes called mops. Many floggers are made with 45-80 tails, which tend to be lighter and stingier than the mops. There is nothing wrong with that. These provide another possible variation.

My goal in using a mop-style flogger is to warm up the bottom. The wider the tails, the heavier the flogger. The more tails a flogger has, the more evenly the skin will be warmed. This larger target area is evenly hit with thuddy sensations that help drive the bottom into subspace and prepare the skin for the singletail. A singletail is less likely to mark the skin if the skin is evenly warmed up first by flogger play.

A flogger is a good starting place for any scene that involves impact play because it is an excellent way to warm up the skin and prepare it for heavier play.

Quirts or Viper Tongues. Quirts are similar in construction to snake whips but only have two tails, which are shaped into a viper tongue form and are stingy.

With skill, quirts can be feathered and used to warm up the skin for other types of play. They can easily leave a mark, and light bottoms will probably not enjoy them. Heavier bottoms will most likely embrace the sting and burning sensations they can provide.

A short quirt, often called a Western quirt, can be found in most tack shops. They are fairly inexpensive and most often made out of cowhide. Longer quirts, like a dog signal quirt, mirror the construction of a signal whip or a pocket snake whip, but instead of ending with a cracker or fall/cracker, the long quirt is finished with a wider fall cut in the shape of a viper tongue (Compare Western quirt with long quirt in WITD, Photo 2).

Types of Leather used in Quirts. The quirt tails, or viper tongues, are usually made of cowhide and most often are either latigo or red hide (red hide is a tanning process that leaves cowhide a deep red color). However, they could be made with any leather used to craft a flogger. Using different leathers would create a broader range of sensations. I prefer to stay with a latigo or red hide tongue, as the quirt's nature tends towards heavier, stingier play than with a flogger.

If the top wants to experiment with different viper tongues made out of a range of leathers, I recommend the quirt be finished with an English eye. Some whip makers use the English eye instead of a fall hitch to finish their singletails. The English eye allows one tail section to be interchanged to create multiple whips and variations just by exchanging the tail selection.

Photo 6 English eye used instead of a fall hitch

How the quirt tail is attached to the thong (the plaited part of the whip forming the belly) varies between whip makers and can provide another throwing variable. One of the quirts in Photo 7 is finished with a slightly wider fall split down the middle. This provides a wide range of sensations, from feathering to a heavy bite. The other quirt is designed with a swivel and is a wider, heavier leather, resulting in the quirt balance being tip-heavy. This tip heaviness results in a heavy, thuddy finish. Thus, the quirts vary because two different whip makers build their quirts slightly differently.

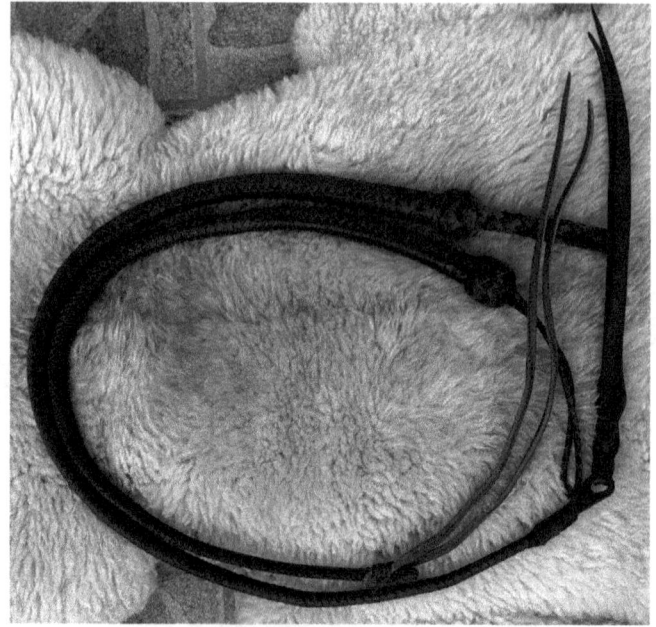

Photo 7 Happy Tails quirt compared to a Peter Jack quirt

Variations with Quirts. The quirt adds many possible variables to a whip scene. It can provide a quicker warmup of the skin in preparation for play with a singletail. It can also add intensity during an in-between (transition time, usually the moments between songs). For example, let's assume the warmup is accomplished with a quirt. The skin is brought up to a nice, even warm temperature. The scene progresses to a cat o' nine, which produces a thuddier but still stingy sensation. After the next in-between, one can return to the quirt but throw it harder to create more intensity, building the endorphins and preparing the whip catcher for the singletail.

Sometimes there is limited time in play because of the size of the crowd or limited equipment, so etiquette dictates not hogging equipment. The quirt is an excellent toy to start with because it can speed up the warmup process and then be used to ramp up a scene to the point that singletail play can be engaged in much quicker. This allows time/space compression when it is done with intentionality.

Cat O' Nine Tails. The cat o' nine is synonymous with corporal punishment whippings and is the implement often used in movies and historical accounts for that purpose.

Cat o' nine tails are characterized by nine plaited or braided tails. They can be made out of almost any of the wide variety of materials a flogger can be made out of, but traditionally, they are made out of leather. From a material construction perspective, they provide a broad range of sensations.

Sometimes, objects are tied to the end of the tails to cut, dig, or leave marks (WITD, Photo 3).

Types of Leather used in Cat O' Nine Tails. Traditional cats can be made out of any of the leathers a flogger is made out of. The difference is that there are just nine tails instead of a larger number of flat tails.

Hybrid or whip-like cats have a short thong that resembles a snake whip. The thong is approximately half the length of the cat, with the nine tails making up the other half of the implement. Hybrid cats are almost always kangaroo but could be made out of cowhide.

More About Traditional Cats. A traditional cat o' nine has a short, stiff handle like a flogger handle. It should be counter-balanced against the weight of the tails just as a flogger handle is balanced. Traditional cat o' nine tails offer a broad range of sensations.

One cat maker I am familiar with makes a soft goat skin cat o' nine that has round plaited tails and is finished with a "leaf" shaped tip. No knots on the end of this cat translates to very consistent light to medium-weight play. The same cat maker also makes a flat braided cat o' nine out of cowhide that has a flat leaf tip. It is quite heavy and shows how a round braided tail (the goat skin cat) compared to a flat braided tail (cowhide cat) finished with the same leaf tip can produce such a wide variety of sensations.

When looking for a cat o' nine tails to add to the dungeon toy bag, consider what toys are already in your collection and carefully examine the leather a cat is made from, the type of tails the cat has, and how the tips are finished. Ask yourself whether this cat will create a significantly different sensation from the cats one already owns.

As a general rule, flogger makers make flogger handle style cat o' nine tails, and singletail whip makers make hybrid whip-like cat o' nine tails.[1]

More About Whip-like Cats. Hybrid cat o' nines are more single-tail-like in that they have a shot-loaded thong. They can be a variety of lengths, but typically, the thong will be approximately the same length as the length of the nine tails. Half of the whip is built like a signal whip or snake whip, and the half beyond the transition knot is plaited like a cat o' nine.

These whip-like cats come with various "trade" names. It seems craftsmen who make these coin names from various cat species for the different variants of this type of whip, such as tomcat, cougar, whiskers, black panther, wildcat, etc. Compare in WITD Photo 3 (p. 3) a traditional cat with a flogger style handle to a hybrid cat o' nine. The tomcat in the photo has about an 18-inch thong and 18-inch tails.[2]

Similar hybrid cats are made by other whip makers; Examples of this are the Wildcat, which was made by Victor Tella (R.I.P.), and Whiskers, made by Matt Welsby. Welsby makes a "Cougar," which is a hybrid cat made from a tapered cane handle. Each of these cats has

---

1 As an aside, one clue that I have noticed as to whether a whip maker might be kink-friendly is if they offer a cat o' nine in their order gallery. Vanilla whip makers typically do not make a cat o' nine tails as they have no practical application in western or ranch settings.

2 Before I became addicted to bullwhip play, I often said that if the house was burning down and I only had time to grab one whip, I would grab my tomcat (a cat made by John - an Australian plaiter-who plaited for Happy Tails) and run out of the house screaming. That tomcat is a medium-weight hybrid cat with an 18-inch thong and 18-inch tails that are plaited in three-millimeter kangaroo (roo) strands and finished with a soap knot or crown knot, with about a four-inch tassel following the knot.

slightly different characteristics, which translate to different variations in play. Tella's Wildcat has wider cut strands, about six mm, and a larger finishing knot. Welsby's Whiskers has an extremely heavy shot load and packs a higher impact punch. Meanwhile, the Cougar, with a tapered cane handle, throws almost like a nun-chuck. Skip San Soucie (R.I.P.) also made a hybrid cat, and while I've never owned or thrown a San Soucie version, I'm convinced it would have a different sensation. I recently acquired a matched set of cat o' nine by Abraided Leather that is made with six-mm roo strands. I can tell you the difference between throwing a three-mm strand Tomcat and a six-mm strand cat is huge. The six-mm strand cats catch more air and have a louder swish going through the air but cannot be thrown with the finesse and wider variation in sensations that the three-mm strand cats can make. The three-mm cats fly through the air, and the six-mm cats swoosh through the air and finish thuddier.

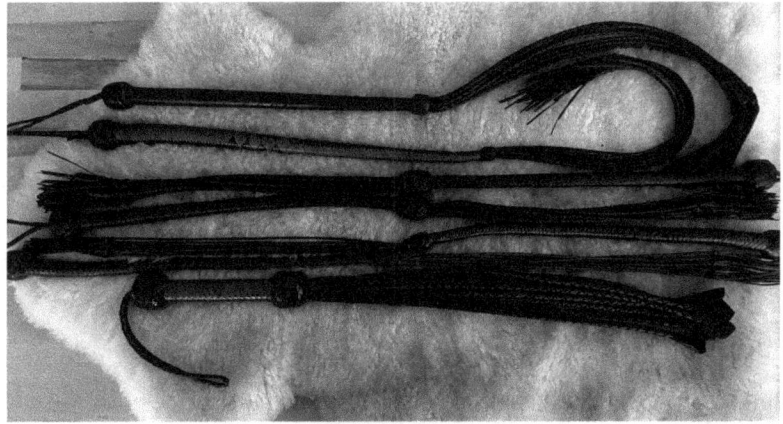

Photo 8 Cat o' Nine Tails comparison: Traditional cat with leaf tip finish, Happy Tails Tomcat, Abraided Leather cat, Matt Welsby's Whiskers and Cougar

Variations in Cats. Variations in cats are primarily created by two factors, which, when combined with variations in technique, provide almost infinite possibilities. The first is the type of leather the cat is made out of, which will directly impact the weight of the tails. The second is the way the tip of each tail is finished, which will impact the bite the tail takes as it strikes the skin.

Is it finished with a leaf shape? Is it finished with a soap knot? Is it finished with a crown knot? Is it finished with multiple half-hitches? Or are beads or stones tied into the tips? The force of the whips' swing, throwing style, and techniques used to impact the bottom all add variations to exponentially expand the results.

Galley Whips. Galley whips are shorter multi-tail whips traditionally made of leather. The one in WITD, Photo 4, has an approximately 18-inch-long thong with multi-tails made of 16-plait kangaroo. This short whip was originally designed to be used in close quarters and, as such, is a wonderful whip for use in a dungeon or house party.

Types of Leather. Galley whips in modern times are made with kangaroo. I suppose they could be made with red hide or calfskin, and that would be wonderful too.

Variations in Galley Whips. Galley whips can be of different lengths and can be shot-loaded or natural-belly. Obviously, the longer shot-loaded galley whips will deliver a heavier impact than a shorter unloaded version. Crafting them longer than described would defeat their usefulness in tight spaces.

The length and width of the tails create additional variations. The galley whip is an easy whip to use and a great whip with which to warm up the whip catcher.

Galley whips have become my preferred implement for warming up the skin over a flogger. They are lighter and do not tire the arm out as much as a flogger. They are also more whip-like and warm up the top in a sense as they feel and throw more like a singletail than a traditionally handled flogger. Refer to WITD Photo 4, p. 5. This cannot be overemphasized. In advanced whip play, the ultimate focus is on the singletails used to build and climax the scene, not on the warmup whips. So, warming up the skin with a whip that does not tire out the arm leaves the arm fresh to throw a singletail with the finesse and accuracy that an advanced play scene requires.

Throwing two-handed double-ended floggers in six-count Florentine might be flashy, but it can tire the arms to the point the bullwhip is not accurate. It is better to use galley whips that will get the skin warm with a lot less wear on the whip thrower's arms.

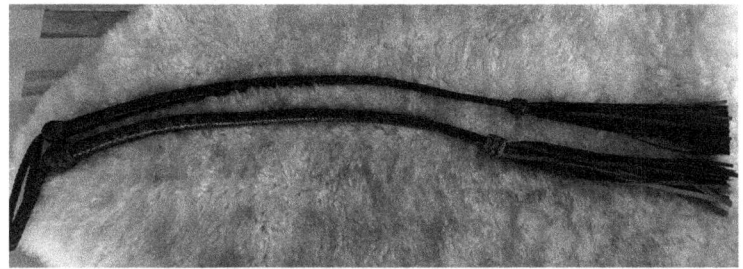

Photo 9 "Sister" galley whips by _Maker_. Same exact length, but one has heavier shot load and wider tails. When thrown two handed provide variations in sensations.

Singletail Whips

Dragontail. A dragontail is a piece of leather that ends in a point and is tightly rolled around some sort of handle. A dragon tongue is a piece of leather that is tightly rolled around some sort of handle and after a few inches the leather opens up into a tongue shape that widens then quickly tapers to a single point or tongue tip.

Types of Materials Used. Leather is the typical material used to make a dragontail, but they can be made from other materials as well.[3]

---

3 Leather crafters have turned many of their dragontails into works of art, but you can make your own, too. The dragontail depicted in WITD, Photo 5, is a fairly simple design but illustrates that a handy top could take a piece of leather and a piece of wooden dowel or a piece of a broomstick handle and easily make their

Mini dragontails can be as short as 12 inches long, while full-sized versions are three to four feet long. Most folks may not think of the dragontail as a singletail, but under the broader definition of any whip ending in one tail, it is most certainly a type of singletail. Dragontails are one of the simplest singletails not only to make but also to throw. They can be thuddy but also stingy and evil.

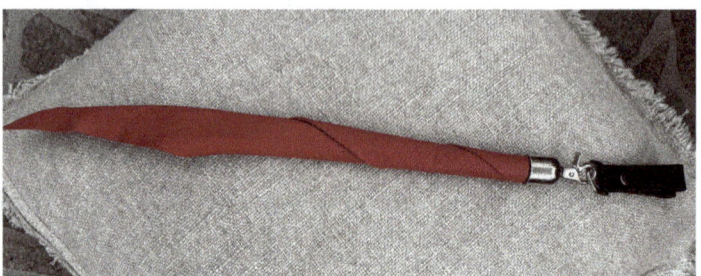

Photo 10 Mini-dragontail

When someone asks me which singletail should be their first purchase, I usually say a dragontail because a dragontail can be thrown using all four techniques taught in *Whips in the Dungeon*. Both of the static techniques and all of the dynamic techniques will work.

Dragontails are not as expensive as a plaited whip. While a new whip thrower is figuring out which style they prefer to throw, they can get mileage in both styles of dynamic throwing with a singletail that is fairly easy to manage and master.

Variations. Variations with a dragontail can be felt in the weight of the leather used to make the tail. Different leathers, even in the garment grade range, have different thicknesses.

One indication of thickness is the size of the handle. Thicker

---

own. This is a great thrift store or garage sale project. Buy a used garment-grade leather jacket or skirt at a rummage sale. The garment can be cut into a large rectangular piece of leather to craft a homemade dragontail. There is a video in my instructional series on how to make a homemade dragontail (WITD 101.60).

leather will result in a thicker handle. Heavier leather will be thuddier and less stingy. Thinner leather will flow better, be easier to crack, and, of course, will be stingier. Often, a crafter/vendor will color code their tails. In this photo, the black tail (thicker handle) is the heaviest, followed by blue, red, and, finally, a green tail that ends with a viper tongue.

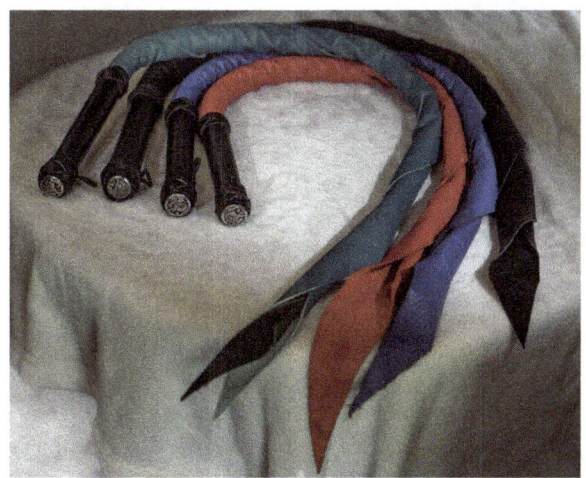

Photo 11 Dragontails compared

Dog Signal Whip or Signal Whip (Commonly called a "singletail" in the scene). As the story goes, dog signal whips (WITD, Photo 6, p. 6) are short pocket whips used to signal sled dogs in the cold reaches of Alaska and Canada.

Signal whips are possibly the most accurate whip used in the dungeon. This is primarily because of their construction. The signal whip design eliminates the fall and creates a cracker point at the end of the thong so that where the whip is pointed, the cracker strike will occur accurately.

Signal whips are measured by total length (heel knot to end of cracker). Signal whips are traditionally finished with a black braided cracker plaited into the tip end of the roo thong.

In more modern times in the kink community, signal whips are finished with an English eye so the cracker can easily be changed out.

This is ideal as it solves the problem of having to make modifications just to change out the cracker. Those modifications were discussed in WITD p. 29 and illustrated in WITD photo 31.

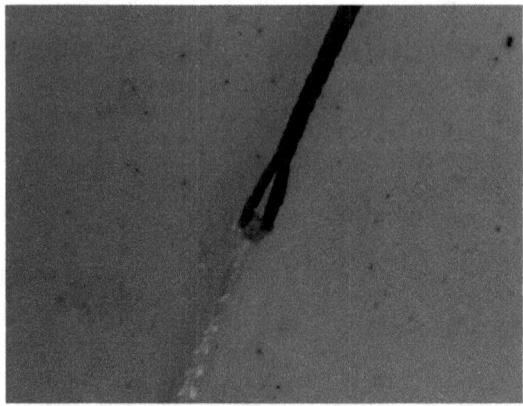

Photo 12 Signal whip finished with an English eye

Anyone planning on using a signal in dungeon play should ask the whip maker to finish their signal with an English eye. Most scene-friendly whip makers will do this. Otherwise, WITD p. 29 and photo 31 still apply and are good alternative modifications to a signal instead of an English eye.

Any length of whip could be finished as a signal whip by a whip maker, but typically, signal lengths are three feet, three and a half feet, and four feet. I personally own a four-foot, a three-foot matched set, a four-foot matched set, and a five-foot signal whip. I can tell you that three-foot and four-foot signal whips throw like one would expect a signal whip to throw.

A five-foot signal whip begins to act more like a long whip, and some precise accuracy is lost. For dungeon play, that is the entire reason why signal whips have come into such common scene use - their dead-on accuracy. They are also easier for the novice or occasional whip thrower to use accurately.

Horizontal signal whip throwers have probably influenced whip makers to craft what I call a hybrid bullwhip. Many whip makers call this a hybrid signal whip. The reason I call these whips hybrid bullwhips is because I'm using the handle construction to define the class of whip. Since the whip has a stiff handle, it is a type of bullwhip, but since it is finished with a signal-like cracker, it is a hybrid bullwhip.

However, if you are defining classes of whips by the way a whip is finished, it is finished like a signal whip and, therefore, could be called a hybrid signal whip. I would argue that this is flawed logic because bullwhips and snake whips are finished with fall hitch/fall/cracker arrangements, and if they were "named" by the way they are finished, there would be no way to distinguish between the whips.

Hence, bullwhips and snake whips are named by the way their handles are crafted, not the way the whips are finished. Just communicate clearly with a whip maker to ensure you both are on the same page and the finished whip is what you were expecting and what you ordered.

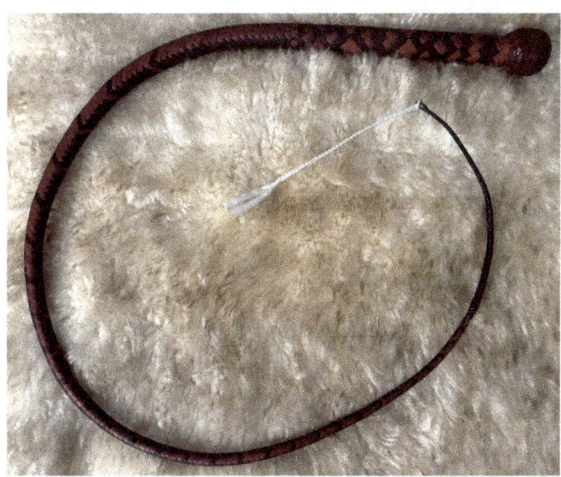

Photo 13 Hybrid Signal whip by Mojave Outliers

What I really like about the hybrid signal whip for horizontal throwing is the stiff handle allows the whip to be slowed down and controlled at slow speeds at or just above the whip's stall speed.[4] This

---

4 Stall speed is the speed at which gravity overcomes a whip's ability to fly and finish on target.

design, in my opinion, gives the beginning and novice whip throwers more control at slower speeds and allows them to learn finesse.

A traditional signal whip thrown horizontally has to be fairly stiff in the handle area and have agility down the thong. This is a difficult build for a whip maker to figure out. Then, if you add the variable of shot load - how much and where to put it to balance the weight of the shot down the thong, signals are not easy to build for someone dedicated to horizontal throwing.[5]

Types of Leather used in Signal Whips. Signals are primarily made out of kangaroo. Grey kangaroo is preferred over red kangaroo for whip making. Veg-tanned hides are preferred over chrom or alum-tanned hides. While not leather, a paracord whip from a quality paracord plaiter can provide a good alternative to the more expensive leather whips.

Variations. The main variation found in kangaroo singletail builds is whether they are shot-loaded or natural belly (meaning not shot-loaded). This is true of all three of the traditional types of singletails: signals, snakes, and bullwhips. Snake whips and signals customarily have shot, but they can be built with a natural belly. Bullwhips are built either way, with loaded and unloaded bellies being equally as common.

Going beyond the loaded or unloaded belly variation, the cracker or popper selection creates a variation that is felt by the whip catcher. Cracker selection and the sensations felt by the whip catchers will be discussed in detail later in the book. But variations are also created by cracker selection on the throwing end. A fluffy cracker will act as an air brake on the end of a whip and slow the action down as the whip finishes. A thinner cracker will be more streamlined and achieve its crack easier.

The build of the signal will create variations and often affect the

---

[5] I throw primarily overhand and love Peter Jack's signal's agility and natural rollout, but it is too loosey-goosey to throw horizontally. It took several builds and many conversations with Desert Minx at Mojave Outliers to fine-tune a build I like for horizontal throwing.

technique and style in which the whip can be thrown. Plait count creates yet another variation. 12 and 16-plait count whips are considered working plait counts. 20-plait count and higher are considered collector's grade whips and allow whip makers to plait with fancy and patterned plaiting. Higher plait counts do not equate to better whips for dungeon play. In a dimly lit dungeon, no one sees the fancy whip plaiting. They see only the rollout of the whip, how it finishes on target, and the resulting effects on the skin.

For three-foot signal whips, eight-plait and 12-plait whips can be made with no drops[6], depending upon the skill of the whip maker. These are adequate for dungeon play. The advanced whip thrower will notice better articulation and rollout in a 16 or 20-plait whip as compared to an eight or 12-plait whip.

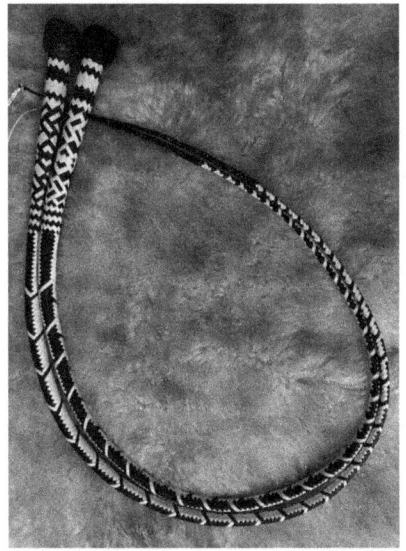

Photo 14 Matched set of 4' 20 plait red & white signal whips by Mojave Outliers

---

[6] During plaiting, as the whip thins, the whip maker will occasionally drop a strand underneath the overlay so the whip taper can be maintained.

Snake Whips. Snake whips are flexible down the length of the thong from heel knot to keeper or fall hitch. This flexibility allows for different throwing styles and artistic expression in a scene that a signal whip does not allow. Snake whips have better flow than a signal, and they roll out with a grace that signal whips cannot achieve. Most snake whips are shot-loaded. They are measured by their plaited length (heel knot to fall hitch). The measurement does not include the fall and cracker.

Pocket Snake Whips (WITD, Photo 7, p. 7). Pocket snake whips are the short version of a snake whip, so named because, in the Wild West, they were easily rolled up and put into a duster pocket. Typically, they are three to four feet long. They can be longer, but they are all under six feet long. Most often in the dungeon, if you see someone throwing a snake whip, it is a pocket snake whip.

Snake Whips. Snake whips are the full-sized version of a pocket snake whip. They are at least six feet or longer. They are typically shot-loaded, though they can be natural belly.

It is uncommon to see a snake whip (as opposed to the smaller pocket whip) used in the dungeon, usually because of space constraints. Many dungeons do not have the square footage and ceiling height needed to throw a snake whip. It is more common to see snake whips used in play in camping style or outdoor lifestyle events.

Pocket snake whips can easily be used in dungeon play. The longer snake whip has more limited uses. I find that a snake that is six feet or longer does not have the accuracy required for direct contact play in the dungeon. In comparison, a longer bullwhip in skilled hands does have this accuracy. This is because the bullwhip has a stiff handle.

However, longer snakes are a lot of fun to throw and are great for doing wraps on arms, legs, and torsos. Wraps can be a scene in themselves.

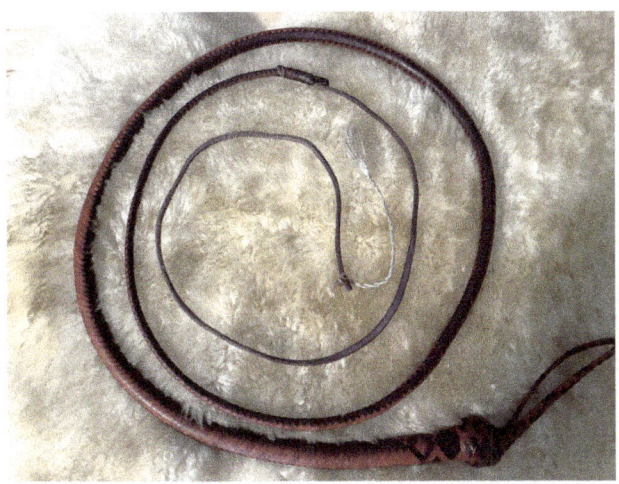

Photo 15 Peter Jack 6' snake

Black Snake Whips. These snake whips did not get their name from being plaited with black leather. Rather, they got their name because of their heavy shot load and often heavily weighted heel knot, which provided the ability to turn the handle area around and use it in a self-defense setting as a blackjack (Edwards, 1997).

Black snake whips have a heavy shot bag, are usually much thicker in the handle area than a snake whip, and are a lot of fun to crack. They go off like a cannon because of the added mass and energy transferred down the thong of the whip when cracked.

Photo 16 Happy Tails 8' black snake

Types of Leather used in Snake Whips. Veg-tanned kangaroo is the primary type of leather used. Snakes can be made out of cowhide and other leathers such as deerskin, but those are less desirable. Roo, baby! That's what you want.

Variations. Snake whips are not quite as accurate as signal whips, but they provide a wider variety of throwing possibilities and creative uses in a scene. Snake whips have better flow than signal whips. Most of this is due to construction (WITD, Chapter 2). They can consistently hit a three-inch circular or square target and hence are more than accurate enough to throw at someone's butt, shoulder, or breast.

Not every whip maker can make a great pocket snake. There are several reasons for this. One reason is some whip makers may think a pocket snake whip is simply a signal whip with a fall hitch and fall added. However, signal whips built for horizontal style often do not have good natural rollout. This is because they are braided tightly, often have a heavier heel-loaded shot bag, and may have extra binding in the handle area. This makes their core stiffer and able to be thrown horizontally at slower speeds under control without adverse effects from gravity. The result is a lower stall speed.

Pocket snake whips built like this often act like a wiggle stick. Overhand throwers might say the whip will never break in properly. It *will* break in, but it will never achieve the good natural rollout an overhand thrower is seeking.

The type of leather used for the shot bag affects the rollout of the snake whip. Many whip makers are dead set on using cowhide for their shot bags. The result will be a stiffer upper thong, and the whip will not have good rollout the entire length of the thong. The whip will arc to the end of the shot bag and then have a rollout with the remaining length of the thong.

Shot bags can be made out of cowhide if the cowhide is thin enough and flexible enough, but they can be disasters too.

Whip makers use a wide variety of techniques to build shot bags. Some do not even actually use a shot bag but, instead, use fabric embedded with shot. Some even use duct tape to craft a shot bag.

The whip makers who seem to have great snakes with good natural rollout are using a softer, flexible hide like a pigskin, deerskin, or even kangaroo to fabricate the shot bag. It is helpful if you can throw a snake made by a particular whip maker before you order a snake from that whip maker so you get an idea if the whip build is going to work for you.

Bullwhips. A bullwhip is one of the edgiest implements in BDSM (WITD, Photo 8, p. 9). The bullwhip's stiff handle gives added leverage when throwing. This makes them the easiest of all whips to break the sound barrier.

A bullwhip is measured from the heel knot to the fall hitch (also known as a keeper) of the whip, and not by total length.

Types of Leather used in Bullwhips. Working-class bullwhips for farm and ranch use are often made out of cowhide or red hide, but for advanced-level dungeon play, bullwhips should all be made out of kangaroo. If your budget can't afford kangaroo, then you can go with a paracord bullwhip.

Variations. Bullwhips may be shot-loaded (traditional American bullwhips) or naturally loaded, also called natural belly or unloaded (traditional Australian bullwhips).

Bullwhips that are four feet and shorter are considered mini-bullwhips. Bullwhips longer than four feet normally do not carry the mini-bull label. The most common bullwhips that I have seen in the dungeon are four-foot bullwhips, though three-foot bullwhips are popular as well.

A well-made bullwhip will have a balanced handle, meaning the heel knot will be counterweighted so that the balance point is where the end of the handle is (often marked by a pineapple knot) and where the thong begins. This balance point becomes a pivot point of sorts as the thong starts the rollout of the whip. The weight of the thong and fall will balance in a teeter-totter style at the pineapple knot with the counterweight of the handle and the heel knot.

Further fine-tuning of a bullwhip's balance can be achieved by adjusting the length of the fall. The length of the fall will vary as the fall balances the whip and the weight of the thong. I caution you to make fall adjustments in small increments, as once a piece of fall is cut off, it cannot be put back on. A quarter inch to a half inch at a time is recommended if the whip feels tip-heavy until you find that sweet spot where the whip finishes as it ends its rollout.

The craftsmanship of the plaiter and the type of leather used for the fall all factor into how long a whip maker will cut the fall for a bullwhip. As a general rule of thumb, the fall for a four-foot bullwhip will be at least 18-24 inches long. Fall materials that are good are latigo, red hide, and water buffalo.

The length of the cracker is a personal preference of the whip thrower, but an additional four to six inches will be added to the total length of the whip. A four-foot bullwhip will be at least six feet in total length. Thus, seeing a bullwhip longer than four feet in a dungeon is rare. It is not because longer whips cannot be thrown accurately but because most dungeon indoor spaces are not large enough to accommodate longer whips and, at the same time, allow other play to go on.

When a whip gets longer than eight feet, it takes an extreme amount of skill, muscle memory, and finesse to throw the whip, to consistently throw it accurately, and to craft a good scene with direct contact. It is more common to see long whips used for wraps and mind fuck type play.

Three-foot bullwhips are not very common. There are several reasons for this. A three-foot bullwhip will typically have a five-inch handle that leaves 31 inches of thong to plait an adequate taper to the fall hitch. This is difficult plaiting over a shorter run and often has more drops than would occur in a four-foot bullwhip. A lot of whip makers can make a nice four-foot bullwhip; fewer can achieve the scaling needed, and the taper required for a three-foot bullwhip.

Now, if the whip thrower wants a seven-inch handle, the thong would be 29", and the problem is amplified. Not every whip maker can plait a concentric tapering cylinder over a run that short and keep all the drops smooth and seamless. It is more difficult to scale and plait a three-foot bullwhip than to plait a six-foot bullwhip. I have a list of about 12 quality bullwhip makers I am comfortable ordering and referring whip throwers to for a four-foot bullwhip. When a three-foot bullwhip is considered, my reference list goes down to three whip makers. A three-foot bullwhip with the fall will be four and a half to five feet total length.

Five-foot bullwhips are also not as common. This is not because they cannot be thrown accurately and with finesse, but again, because most dungeons cannot accommodate the space required to throw a scene using a whip that is seven to eight feet in total length. Any whip less than six feet, I consider a short whip, and all of the WITD throwing techniques apply and can be used. When a whip moves into the long whip category (greater than six feet), basic whip throwing techniques apply as the whip is too long to utilize common dungeon short whip techniques.

Stock whips. Stock whips are the working whips of the Australian and New Zealand ranchers. They are single tails because they end in a single lash; hence, they are mentioned in this book.

A mini-stock whip, which in Australia would be used by youth to begin to learn basic cracking and sport cracking, could be used in the dungeon for play, with some caveats. The knuckle at the end of the handle provides a swivel for the thong. This knuckle reduces accuracy and, as a result, makes the stock whip almost impossible to accurately target for the type of play done in a dungeon. A stock whip can, however, be used for wraps in the dungeon, and it can be a lot of fun doing that type of sensation play.

With a well-made stock whip that has a tight knuckle and a whip thrower patient enough to put in the hours of practice needed to learn to control and feather it, no doubt that whip thrower could learn to throw it accurately in contact dungeon play.

Mini-Zenith Bullwhips. A zenith bullwhip has a tapered box knot between the end of the handle and the thong to allow it to be thrown on any 360-degree vector from the zenith knot. and cracked. It provides the flexibility in a bullwhip that stock whip throwers enjoy from the knuckle at the end of the handle but adds a degree of control and accuracy that is not normally found in a stock whip. It is an interesting design and variation.

Zenith bullwhips are normally 16 feet and longer. I once owned a 22-foot zenith bullwhip made by Peter Jack, which I liked to crack outdoors. Jack makes a scaled-down version of this whip and can make them as short as four feet. I own a five-foot mini-zenith and matched sets of four-foot mini-zenith bullwhips.

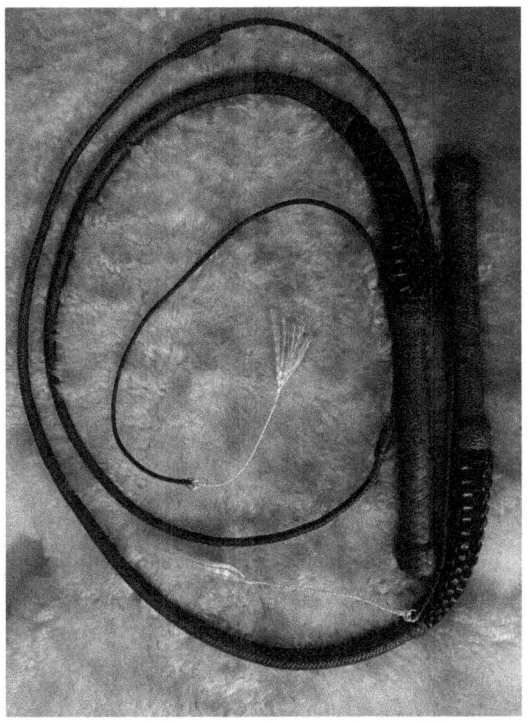

Photo 17 Matched set of 4' mini-zenith bullwhips by Peter Jack.

Chapter 2

Variations in the Construction of a Whip: Whip Lasagna

IN THIS CHAPTER, we learn more about how different whips are made and what variables in play are created through different changes in the whip's build. But first, what are the components of a whip build, or, as I like to say, whip lasagna?

Components in the lasagna build are the core, belly, bolster[7], binding, and overlay. Other possible components are a second belly, a second bolster/binding, and if a whip is shot-loaded, a shot bag is thrown into the lasagna. In bullwhips, handle material and length add another element to the lasagna.

Whip makers all make their lasagna differently, just as different chefs in the kitchen do. Some use a bolster between every belly; others do not use any bolsters and plait belly on belly. Some will put a bolster between the first and second bellies but no bolster between the second belly and the overlay. Some use a thick cane or exotic

---

7 A bolster is a piece of leather that is wrapped around the belly and bound in place to provide a smooth layer for the next belly to be plaited over.

hardwood for a handle, while others build their handle around a nail spike or a length of spring steel.

The only constant, regardless of the lasagna layers, is that the plaiting has to be tensioned straight as an arrow to the fall hitch; otherwise, the whip will not land on the target where it is pointed. When you are throwing at a nipple you do not want the whip to hit an underarm.

Signal Whips. Signal whips, like most whips, can be built in different ways. Different builds will, of course, create variations when used in play. So, how does one decide what type of build is best for them?

One of the first things to consider when buying a signal whip is what type of signal whip would work best with the primary throwing style that is going to be used with the whip: horizontal versus overhand. An overhand style requires a signal whip that achieves a good natural rollout. Horizontal works better with a stiffer build that achieves rollout but isn't loosey-goosey. A stiffer build for horizontal throwing minimizes the effect of gravity and allows a slower, more controlled pace of the whip while maintaining the throw above stall speed. Often, a heavier shot load weighted toward the heel knot will aid horizontal throwers in easily achieving a crack. Heavier binding in the handle area, but leaving the rest of the thong agile, will also aid horizontal throwers.

The Budget Build. Many whip makers will offer a budget signal whip build. This is done to offer a singletail to dungeon players at a better price point and allows the whip maker to do "production" work and crank out whips in a shorter amount of time.

Generally, this type of build will have a core, shot bag, bolster, and plaited overlay (eight or twelve plait). Some whip makers do not even do a bolster but will just plait a tight overlay. Usually, a budget signal will not have a belly. What, then, is the result? Though the budget signal whip may break in quickly and achieve a good rollout, after a year or so of throwing, it will end up throwing like a wet noodle. Many would say at that point, the whip is broken.

So why consider a budget build? If you are a beginner, it is a less expensive way to experience a roo whip, and in your first year of throwing will be adequate while you save up your pennies for a better whip.

If you are not sure that you are going to have the eye/hand coordination to throw a whip, then this is a less expensive investment. If you are a dungeon player who enjoys many types of play and only occasionally throws a whip, then a budget signal will be a welcomed addition to your toy bag and will not break the bank. If you enjoy throwing a whip but do not consider yourself a "whip thrower," then a budget whip might be what works for you. If you throw two-handed and don't want to invest or can't afford two signal whips, then a matched pair of budget signals might suit your needs.

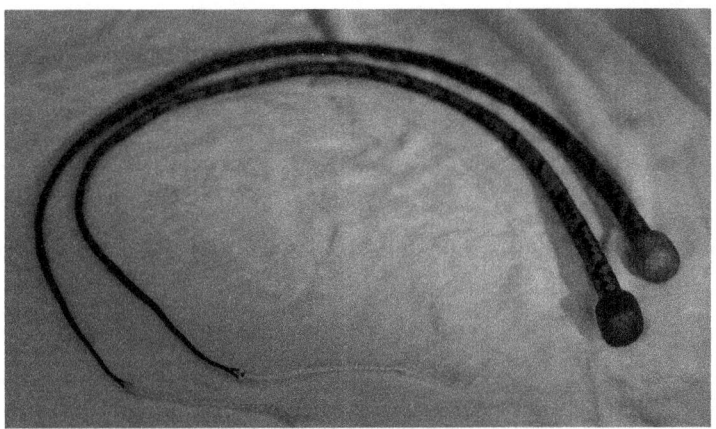

Photo 18 Matched set of 3' budget signal whips by Mojave Outliers.

I will add a personal note here. Because of its shorter length, a three-foot budget signal is a better option than a four-foot budget signal. In my opinion, the longer signal does better if it has a belly, which the budget one does not have.

I occasionally need a three-foot signal when playing in smaller spaces, such as at a house party or in a small dungeon. A three-foot signal has a place in a whip thrower's whip bag if only for the occasions where it is the only whip that can be used.

For two-handed whip throwing, a matched set of three-foot budget signal whips, given the number of times and occasions they will be used, fits my budget and whip bag needs. When the move is made to a four-foot signal whip, in my opinion, a budget four-foot signal will break down and become too loosey-goosey after six months to one year of throwing, and an experienced whip thrower will NOT be happy with its performance.

Quality Signal Whip. For intermediate to advanced whip throwers, whip enthusiasts, whip collectors, and whip people who throw regularly in the dungeon, I recommend a quality signal build as opposed to a budget signal build. For the quality signal whip build, the lasagna requirements and articulation needs also change. The length of the signal whip affects what should be done with the lasagna.

A well-made eight-plait, three-foot signal whip will perform better than a 12-plait budget build. In a three-foot signal whip, an eight-plait or 12-plait results in adequate articulation as the whip is so short there is not time for much flow.

When the signal moves to four feet, that extra foot results in better articulation and flow with a higher plait count. There is little notable difference with higher plait counts in a three-foot signal, while in a four-foot signal whip, 16 and 20 plait counts result in noticeably better articulation and flow.

A quality signal whip build will have a core, shot bag, bolster, belly, bolster, and overlay. (Some whip makers will not put the second bolster in but plait the overlay directly over the belly for yet another variation in the whip lasagna, and some will leave the first bolster out and plait belly on belly with only a bolster between the second belly and the overlay). Leaving one of the bolsters out, generally speaking, gives the whip better agility, but only time will tell if that added early agility results in the "loosey-goosey" effect once the whip is fully broken in.

As with any lasagna, there are tradeoffs, and it takes many miles of leather and plaiting for each whip maker to find out what works best for their whip builds. My preference is as follows: The belly will be four-plait or eight-plait, or sometimes 12, depending upon the whip maker. The overlay should be 12, 16, or 20-plait. My favorite is a four-foot signal with a 16-plait overlay, but a 20-plait overlay will give slightly better articulation. I'm not happy with the articulation a 12-plait build gives in a four-foot signal, but then I'm extremely picky.

A signal whip for advanced dungeon play should be finished with an English eye to allow cracker change-out between bottoms. Again, some modifications can be done to a traditional signal cracker that is plaited into the thong to allow the cracker to be easily changed. This is described in *Whips in the Dungeon*, p. 29 and Photo 31.

Snake Whips. For snake whips in dungeon play, we are only talking about pocket snake whips five feet long or less. In my own throwing experience, I find that with a snake whip longer than four feet, it is not possible to maintain the level of accuracy needed for quality dungeon play.

Types of Leather for Snake Whips. At this level of advanced throwing, only kangaroo will do. 12 or 16-plait are adequate, 20-plait will provide slightly better articulation. Higher than 20-plait in a snake this short is unnecessary and actually adds unneeded complications in figuring out the taper and the correct strand drops.

Variations. The most common variation and the most obvious is the length of the snake whip you are throwing. A three-foot is what I throw in the dungeon every scene.

While I can throw a four-foot snake accurately, the total length of the whip is six to seven feet long, and most dungeons cannot accommodate a whip this long for indoor play. Also, because a snake whip does not have a stiff handle, it does not provide the same intensity possible as a bullwhip. I find the snake whip is a good whip to introduce the whip catcher to a singletail when crafting a vignette or sequence of whips for play.

I sequence a snake whip in a progressive vignette between cat o' nine play and bullwhip play. If the ultimate goal is to warm the whip catcher up and segue to bullwhip play, then the snake whip is the logical whip to use. Given indoor dungeon limitations, a two-foot or three-foot pocket snake is the most common addition to the toy bag. I prefer the three-foot because, in my opinion, the two-foot snake whip is very much like a toy or child's whip. I own one, and it easily cracks, but it is not as much fun to throw.

Photo 19 2' 16 plait snake whip by Peter Jack.

Logic has narrowed the choice for a pocket snake whip to a three-foot snake, which will be approximately four to five feet in total length. A snake whip that is four to five feet in total length throws like a whip, has flow, provides a graceful rollout, and can be as accurate as a signal whip, considering some variables—the quality of the snake whip build and the experience of the whip thrower.

I love a snake whip. I love its graceful rollout and the fun of finessing this whip to build from a butterfly kiss to a decent intensity as a prelude to the bullwhip. I do not throw a signal whip in dungeon play but always defer to a three-foot snake whip.

Snake whip lasagna has some critical variables. Not every whip maker can make a good snake whip. Just because a whip maker builds a great bullwhip does not mean he can make a good snake whip.[8]

A snake whip begins with a core, shot bag, bolster, belly, bolster, and overlay. Some variables might be omitting one or both bolsters, but the belly is essential. A snake built without a belly will quickly become loosey-goosey.

In summary, the only snake whips I recommend for someone's BDSM toy bag are a three-foot snake whip for inside dungeon play and a six-foot to eight-foot snake whip for doing wraps at outdoor events.

Bullwhips. This is such a fun topic because there are so many variables in construction that will change the way a bullwhip throws.

Handle. Handles can be made out of cane, a nail spike, a steel tube, or a spring steel rod. There are undoubtedly other materials that can be used.

---

8 Mike Murphy is recognized as one of the finest bullwhip makers who ever lived, yet his snake whips did not have a good natural rollout. The sticking point was how he made his shot bag and the materials he used to create the shot bag. The shot bag should be made out of flexible leather that is not too stiff to achieve a natural rollout. Many whip makers use pigskin, lambskin, kangaroo, or a lightweight cowhide.
Joe Strain was known for his bullwhips, yet his snake whips, in my opinion, were better than his bullwhip builds. I throw my Strain snake whip almost every dungeon set, and I sold my Strain bullwhip in one of my thinning-the-herd moments.

The Turk's head or heel knot forms the pommel.[9] Pommels can be round or sometimes oval (as is commonly found on a stock whip). The pommel acts as a counterbalance or counterweight to balance the handle with the whip's thong.

For dungeon play, a counterweight that is too heavy will result in a whip that will wear out the whip-throwing arm too quickly. In my opinion, lighter bullwhips are better than a heavy beast of a bullwhip that cracks loudly but quickly wears out the arm. Once the arm is tired, accuracy will be affected.

Another variable in the handle is the ratio between the length and weight of the handle. American bullwhips typically have shorter handles and heavier counterweights than their Australian counterparts, which typically have longer handles that are not as heavy a counterweight. I prefer a nine-inch handle for most of my bullwhips. This length of the handle seems to give me enough clearance that I can easily throw a forward figure eight without clipping my left ear on the backhand side with the whip.

The handle length will affect the whip thrower's release point. For example, my release point, after years of throwing bullwhips with a nine-inch handle, is cemented in muscle memory. If I throw a ten-inch handled bullwhip, my whip will find its target or whip catcher's shoulder high – consistently high. This does not mean the whip is bad. The added inch in the handle just changed the release point. A small change on the throwing end results in several inches of change on the receiving end after the whip has traveled six feet or so.

Thong. The construction of a thong also has several variables. The first variable to consider is whether the thong is loaded or unloaded (natural belly or shot loaded).

Traditionally, in my experience, American bullwhip makers used shot to load their whips. In recent times, more and more American

---

9 A pommel is the butt end of the whip. The terms "heel knot" and "Turk's head" are used interchangeably with the term pommel.

makers are making natural belly bullwhips. A natural belly bullwhip will begin with a core, usually made of green hide or rawhide. The leather is wetted, rolled tightly, and allowed to dry in that rolled tapered shape.

On top of that, a four-plait belly will be plaited with roo. Here is where another variable is introduced. Most whip makers I have encountered put a bolster on top of each belly, but some do not use bolsters and plait the second belly right on top of the first. Regardless of whether a bolster is put between the first belly and the second belly, the resultant second belly is almost always eight-plait. But again, some whip makers will plait a higher count first belly, and the first belly might be an eight plait, with a 12 or 16-plait second belly. This is especially true if the overlay is going to be 20 or 24-plait or higher.

Whip makers weigh trade-offs in the construction lasagna as they attempt builds that meet the whip thrower's expectations. Sometimes, this is hit or miss. Hits stay in my toy bag and misses end up being sold in thinning the herd sessions, but that does not mean the whips sold were not excellent whips. It just means that they did not meet my specific needs for my throwing style in the dungeon.

Here is another crossroad in construction. Many whip throwers and makers consider a three-belly bullwhip to be the ultimate quality bullwhip. In my opinion, adding another bolster and a third belly in 12-plait plus another bolster before the final overlay of roo (the outside finishing plaiting – the pretty part that is seen) adds a lot of weight to a bullwhip. It may also add extra Viagra to the whip so the thong will take much longer to break in. Realize we are talking about short whips. In my opinion, a three-belly whip build is only an improvement on a long whip six feet long or longer.

So . . . this may or may not be the ultimate whip for dungeon play. I will say the two belly whips Mike Murphy made are sought after years after he quit plaiting. When I compare the two-belly bullwhips that Peter Jack has made me with the three-belly Navy commemorative whip he made me, I much prefer throwing the two-belly whips in the dungeon. The three-belly whip is just too heavy for long play scenes. My point is that before someone pays more to have a three-belly whip made, one might consider saving their money and having a two-belly whip made because it is better suited to long dungeon play sets. Many people actually prefer Axel's whips, which are single-belly whips.

Photo 20 Three-belly Peter Jack Navy Commemorative 4' 32 plait target bullwhip in gold and blue.

For the final overlay, 12 or 16-plait is fine and provides an accurate rollout for dungeon play if the whip is otherwise quality plaited. These plaits are considered "working" plaits, not "collectible" level plaits. Higher plait counts in the final overlay can result in pretty patterns and work from an artistic and aesthetic perspective but do not contribute significantly to the accuracy of a whip.

Higher plait counts will contribute in an infinitesimal way to the whip's articulation. An advanced whip thrower will notice slightly better articulation of the whip with a 20 or 24-plait count whip. Many throwers may not be able to discern this improvement in articulation. Some people even contend that the higher plait count makes the whip more prone to damage as it gains mileage.

A trade-off for the whip enthusiast who wants a collectible whip is to ask the whip maker to do the thong in a 12 or 16-plait and to split the strands for the handle, doing it in a 24 or 32-plait count. This handle with the higher plait count will result in a fancier-looking handle. An example of this is my Peter Jack latigo y' dago 44 bullwhip. Jack plaited the thong in 16-plait, then split the plaiting to plait the handle in 32-plait. This allowed for fancy plaiting and for the addition of a 44 on the handle to commemorate his 44th year of plaiting whips.

Photo 21 Peter Jack latigo y' dago (No. 44): handle 24 plait, thong 16 plait, 3 oz heel counterweight.

A loaded whip will throw differently than an unloaded (natural belly) whip. Also, the way a shot bag is constructed, or the way the shot is added to the whip will affect how it is thrown. Peter Jack's target bullwhip utilizes a light shot bag, but his latigo y dago fighting whip has shot almost throughout the entire length of the thong. Both of these whips throw differently.

Natural belly whips will throw differently depending upon how many bellies they have. Remember, it is not the shot that makes a whip crack. It is the whip's taper, but the shot will affect the way a whip feels and throws both on the throwing end and the catching end (WITD 201.29). Finding the whip maker and specific lasagna you like that matches your style and the way you like a whip to throw in the dungeon is part of the leather journey.

Fall Hitch or Keeper. The fall hitch or keeper is what connects the fall to the thong, which is the plaited section of the whip. This is also a simple variable, but it can affect the way a whip rolls out.

The fall hitch needs to be tied in a streamlined manner and should not be too chunky. If it is too large, it will act as a windbreak and actually slow the whip down. It will slightly affect its finishing rollout and accuracy. On the other hand, if it is tied too tightly and is too streamlined, the average whip thrower will not be able to change out a fall, even if they are using a fid or marlin spike. [10]

Some whip makers do not use a fall hitch but plait an English eye into the end of their whips. As noted previously, this allows fairly quick change out of the fall to provide variation in the finishing end of the whip. Multiple tails, cat o' nine, fall/cracker, or even a quirt tail can be added to an English eye. A three-foot signal whip finished with this style of English eye could, in theory, become a three-foot snake whip if a slimline fall were added to the English eye instead of tying on a cracker.

Falls. Fall material and length will affect how a whip throws and how accurate it is.

Cutting a fall is also a work of art. Not all whip makers cut a nicely tapered and skived fall. How the tip of the fall is finished will determine which method can be used to tie on the cracker (WITD 101.16). Let the fall talk to the whip thrower when considering how

---

10 Mike Murphy was famous for tying his fall hitch so tightly that no mortal human could change out one of his falls. In all of the Murphy whips I have owned, I have never successfully changed out a fall. Both Casey Tyler and Joe Strain have repaired my Murphy whips, installing new falls on them. But both are world-class whip makers.

to tie the cracker onto the whip. I prefer water buffalo, red hide, or latigo falls for materials.

Many whip makers use white hide. However, white hide does not readily accept conditioner and seems dried out minutes after it has been conditioned. Without adequate conditioning, it will also dry rot. The only fall I have ever had that failed was a white hide fall on a Murphy whip that dry rotted at the eye cut for the fall hitch.

Fall length. Fall length is another obvious variable in whip construction.

Normally, the whip maker uses the fall length in fine-tuning the balance of the whip. Of course, the length, weight of the handle, and counter-balance of the heel knot affect the weight and length of the fall. In recent years (perhaps the last decade), fall lengths have gotten longer. A four-foot bullwhip might have a two to two-and-a-half-foot fall.

A good whip maker is going to balance the whip using the fall and establish a sweet spot for the tone and frequency of the whip to naturally crack with ease. But for every whip thrower, this might need tuning.

I again caution whip throwers about trimming too much of the fall too quickly. First, throw the whip extensively and get used to the natural frequency and tone of the whip directly from the whip maker's hands. If the whip never seems to have a sweet spot for the way you throw, then you can try trimming one-eighth of an inch at a time off of the fall (WITD 201.28). Realize that as the fall is trimmed, the taper of the fall and skiving may have to be adjusted. So, how much is too much to cut off?

I recommend the Mike Murphy standard bullwhip ratio as a prototype. Call it a formula if you want. Mike Murphy was a well-known and sought-after Australian whip maker. His natural two-belly build had a slim profile, but an exceptionally loud crack.

Murphy cut his falls to be about half of the length of the thong. Therefore, his fall was one-third of the total length of the whip. Modern whip makers tend to make their falls longer than this, and often, they need trimming to find the sweet spot where the whip cracks naturally and finishes point on the target. To reiterate, use the Murphy ratio as a guide to follow so as not to trim a fall shorter than one-third of the total length of the whip when fine-tuning it.

From the original fall length to this magic number, trim one-eighth inch at a time until you find your sweet spot, but don't go shorter than one-half the length of the thong. This is only if you were not able to find the natural frequency and balance of the whip from the whip maker's build. Of course, if you cut too much off, it cannot be made longer. You may end up needing to get a replacement fall.

Length of the Thong. A three-foot thong will throw differently than a four-foot thong, a five-foot thong, or a six-foot thong. This variable is present regardless of whether a whip is a signal whip, snake whip, or bullwhip.

The length of the thong is going to affect the repetition rate when throwing dynamically. A shorter whip will recover faster and be ready for the next strike sooner than a longer whip. Another way to view this might be to think of quickness. A shorter whip is quicker than a longer whip.

Length and Frequency. Frequency is the natural wave a whip makes as it rolls out without forcing it or muscling it. A shorter whip will have a higher frequency than a longer whip (WITD 301.02). Length is the single biggest influence on frequency, although the choice of natural belly or shot-loaded also has an influence on frequency.

The natural frequency of a whip is an important variable when throwing in a dungeon to music. Matching the natural frequency of the whip to the rhythm of the music playing is a key variable in connecting the energy of the dungeon to the whip catcher the whip thrower is playing with.

This is why no serious whip thrower only owns one single-tail. Each whip, regardless of whether signal whip, snake whip, or bullwhip, will have a different frequency. Each class of whip, depending on the build (loaded vs unloaded), will have a slightly different frequency. Each whip of the same length, depending upon the build, will have a slightly different frequency. Each whip, depending upon which whip maker crafted it, will have a slightly different frequency. Each whip, even built by the same whip maker, and the same length will have a slightly different frequency. This is redundant but important. To digress, a whip's build lasagna will affect its frequency, as will the number of plait counts and its articulation. But the length of the thong is the single biggest influence on frequency.

Perhaps the only exception is when a "matched set" of whips is plaited. Most often, the matched set will have the same identical frequency (as close as humanly possible) if plaited correctly.

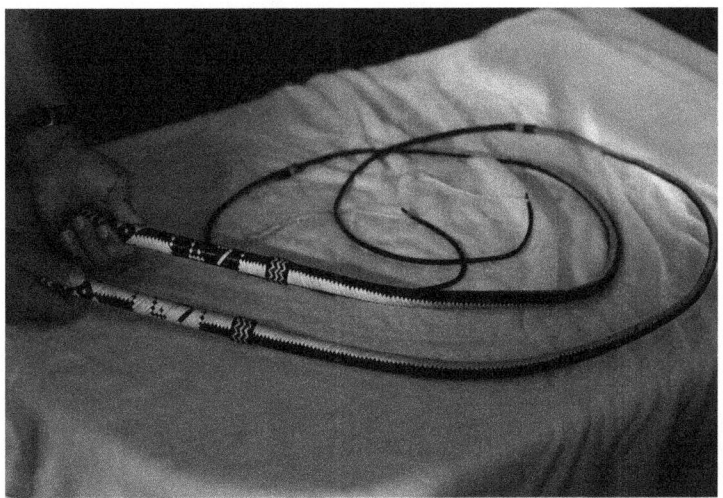

*Photo 22 Matched set of Peter Jack (No. 47) 4'
24 plait white & black target bullwhips*

Chapter 3

Variations in Crackers or Poppers

THE CRACKER (POPPER) one chooses makes a big difference in the sensations for the whip bottom. This might seem obvious, but many whip throwers take the easy approach of leaving the cracker on that the whip maker put on the whip when finishing it. I can only say that if you don't make use of crackers to add variety to your whip scenes, then you are missing out on one of the most important variables.

Aside from the issue of variations, whip throwers who use an original cracker until it wears out are playing with a dirty cracker. Crackers are made out of porous materials, and the fluff can pick up all manner of dirt and contaminants, no matter how clean the play space is. If the whip is played with between bottoms, then there is also a risk of cross-contamination. (WITD 101.27, 101.29) Even when throwing with the same whip catcher, the cracker should be cleaned with alcohol, at least between scenes.

When the original cracker wears out, many whip throwers simply put on one of the spare crackers that most whip makers provide with a new whip. These whip maker crackers are often constructed of black nylon, similar to a carpet thread, or sometimes poly bailing twine. They are durable and great for sport cracking or to learn basic cracking, but they are not designed with dungeon play in mind.

The Traditional Twisted Cracker Finished with an Overhand Knot. The normal twisted cracker is finished with an overhand knot. It begins with twisted thread or twine, like a twisted mason line or twisted Dacron thread.

Think of dungeon play as being on the macro level and the cracker as being on the micro level. At the macro level, the whip thrower wants to be able to throw with finesse, control, and accuracy. The whip thrower wants to be able to feather and then layer sensations from a controlled puff one up to a full-on crisp whip crack.[11]

On the micro level, a cracker begins with twisted nylon or Dacron cord, usually made up of three strands twisted together. This manufacturing process of twisting three strands together to make twisted nylon mason line at the micro level puts potential energy into the mason line.

Because of the twisting during manufacturing, a traditional cracker begins with a three-strand line that already has stored potential energy. Then, a length of the line is folded at the bight, then twisted super tight. There are many YouTube videos on how to make a twisted cracker, and some even use a drill to spin the twist into the mason line. This twisting of two strands of twisted mason lines together further adds even more potential energy to the cracker.

Using a traditional cracker finished with an overhand knot that has, on the micro level, tons of stored potential energy, makes it very difficult to play at or near the speed of sound on the macro level with finesse, control, and accuracy. The twisted cracker often results in

---

11 A controlled puff one is the softest strike you can make with your whip without gravity taking over and causing the whip to drop below the target. Controlled puffs are explained in more detail in Chapter 7. Surface Targeting: Creating Variations in Sensations.

marks where the cracker hits the skin. It is stingier from a bottom's perspective. Now, if this is what has been negotiated, then by all means, use a traditional cracker. But realize traditional crackers have been made with basic whip throwing and sport cracking in mind, and probably not dungeon play.

Photo 23 Black cracker, poly bailing twine cracker, Dacron Desert Minx cracker all finished with an overhand knot.

Crackers for Dungeon Play. For dungeon play on the micro level, crackers need to start "relaxed" with all of the stored potential energy removed. At least two cracker designs achieve this relaxation, which allows control and accuracy in dungeon play.

Tassel Style Cracker. The first type is made with a single or double strand of mason line fitted through an 8 or 9-mm split ring using a ring knot or half hitch at the cracker bight, which will relax as it is thrown. It will unravel and end up essentially a piece of fluff on the end of the whip. I call this a "tassel-style" cracker.[12]

This type of cracker is another useful variable for the whip thrower. In detail, it is made by attaching a split ring to the end of the fall. It

---

[12] Master Robert from the WITD whip practice group shared this style of cracker during a Zoom practice session. Credits to him for this contribution. It is not exclusive to Master Robert. I was at a workshop in Savannah years ago, and Boomer was using this type of cracker for his two-handed whip work.

should be a small split ring, about 8-9 mm. Then, the chosen material (twine, yarn, etc.) is passed through the split ring and tied on using a half hitch or ring knot. The material is allowed to unravel or fluff the entire length. There is no finishing knot. The material can be very soft or have varying degrees of softness all the way up to stingy. Change out is easy because of the split ring. The only caution is that the whip thrower should avoid hitting the whip catcher with the split ring and only play with the fluff of the cracker material.

There are advantages and disadvantages to the tassel cracker. For a beginning whip thrower, this style of cracker will allow dungeon play to be possible much quicker because it establishes a larger margin for error. For a scene that is negotiated for no marks, the fact that this type of cracker has no knots adds another level to achieving the negotiated scene parameters.

For someone exploring two-handed whip throwing, this style of cracker makes that journey so much easier. The precise finesse achieved in single dominant hand throwing is not necessary for two-handed throwing using this style of cracker.

A fun scene variable, the tassel-style cracker also allows a whip catcher to pick their cracker material from a selection and put the crackers on the whips themselves, as the split ring makes attachment easy.

Be aware that the type and amount of material used to make the tassel can make an otherwise balanced whip seem tip-heavy. Too much fluff will give the effect of an air brake on the whip throw's finish, slowing the cracker down as it hits the target.

This type of cracker can be thrown in a controlled puff one through six. It seems to max out around a five or six. It also seems easy to make a "puff," but it is difficult to make it "crack."

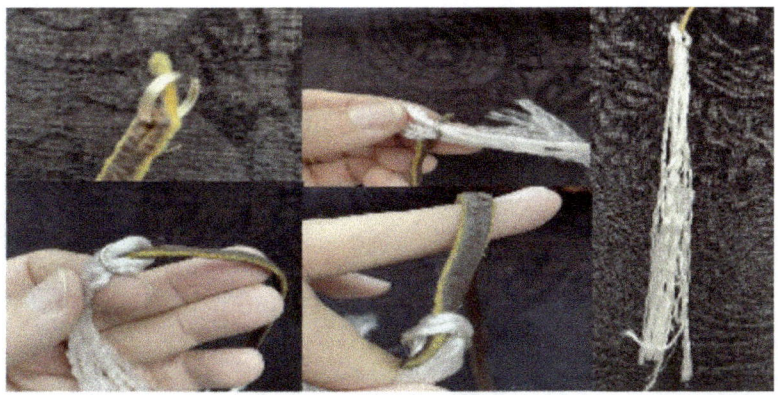

Photo 24 Tassel-style cracker

lady sally-style cracker. The other type of cracker that is great for dungeon play is the lady sally-style cracker. This cracker begins with untwisting and releasing the potential energy in the mason line. I prefer to use twisted mason line for dungeon play. The twisted mason line is three-strand twisted and is deconstructed and then reconstructed using a flat braided ponytail plait. The video will show this better than I can explain it in writing (WITD 101.28), though I will attempt to describe the process in writing here.

Start with a piece of twisted mason line twice as long as the palm of your hand. Take a bight and, with one hand, pinch a small eye, and with your other hand, unwind the mason line. When the mason line is unwound, there will be six strands. Divide them into three pairs of strands. Tightly plait a three-strand braid using the three double strands. Finish it using only one of the six strands in a half hitch. This results in a flat knot that is difficult to mark with. This plaiting does put some potential energy back into the cracker, but it does so in a controlled layered effect.

The lady sally-style cracker performs between a butterfly kiss, controlled puffs one to six, and a full-on clean crack at levels seven or eight. Nice, even angel wings, leaving an even red on the shoulders, are possible with a lady sally-style cracker without leaving lasting marks. This style of cracker can be made with different thicknesses of twisted three-strand mason lines to create different sensations (e.g., No. 15, No. 18, No. 36).

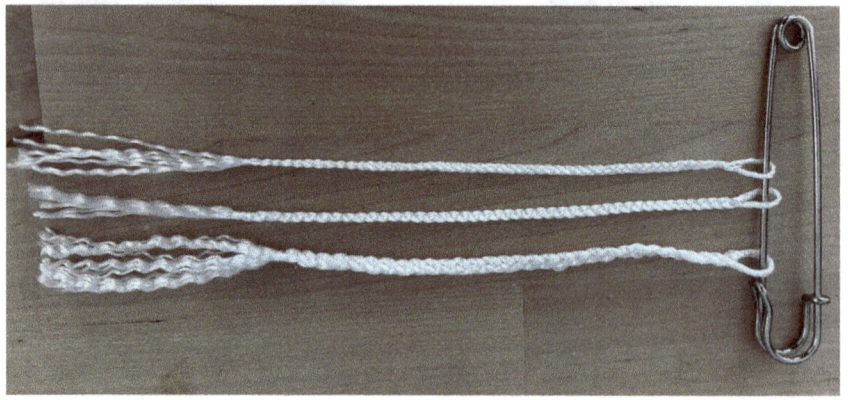

Photo 25 lady sally crackers using No. 15, No. 18, No. 36 3-strand mason line

I have used No. 18 lady sally-style crackers as the mainstay of my dungeon play for over a decade. But realize the size of the mason line used produces its own variations. No. 15 and No. 18 are the sizes I most often use for crackers. A No. 36 size will be twice as thick and thuddy. This is great for breast and genital play when damaging the erotic areas is not the goal, but creating wonderful sensations is the end game. It also allows for longer extended erotic play when compared to a scene with a twisted cracker and overhand knot. The results might appear more dramatic with the twisted cracker, but the scene might be unsatisfying and shorter than desired. Moodstone prefers whip play with the lady-sally cracker. Most of my other whip bottoms also appreciate the difference.

Cracker or Popper Materials. The cracker material and how the cracker is constructed are, in my opinion, the most important variables for the whip catcher and the scene experienced by the whip bottom. The other variables in whip construction discussed up to this point mainly affect the throwing end and are experienced by the whip thrower.

Almost any type of thread or twine can make a cracker (WITD 101.15). This is perhaps the variable with the most options in singletail play, with as many materials that are used to make thread and twine.

Experimentation is encouraged during whip practice to see what materials are durable and create different-sounding cracks and puffs. Changes in tone when doing controlled puffs in practice will give an excellent indication that there will be variations during play for the whip catcher.

Once different cracker materials have been eliminated during whip practice and selected cracker materials have been chosen, transferring that practice to experimentation in play with a whip catcher is essential. Feedback from the whip catcher on different sensations and experiences during play will provide the whip thrower with a growing syllabus of crackers to use on the whip bottom.

The best whip scenes are a blend of two elements: what the whip thrower likes and what the whip catcher likes. Sometimes it is a balance between the loving dominant and pain slut, or the pure sadist and sensualist. Interestingly, when the true sadist and masochist get together with a bullwhip, a third-party referee might be needed (that is a story for another book).

It is with some trepidation that I describe my preferences in cracker materials because, as surely as I say, I do not like cotton twine because it is not durable enough to make cracker material; someone will read this book and email me that they have been using cotton for years and love it.

Therefore, I offer here a smattering of materials and some of the general lessons I have learned from using them as cracker materials. The disclaimer is that all cracker materials should be explored by each whip thrower in practice and then tested to get feedback from the whip catcher who most regularly stands for that whip thrower.

Generally Stingy:

Nylon thread—This thread is like a carpet thread. I have had whip bottoms describe a whip strike using a nylon cracker as feeling like acid.

Dynema—Dynema is normally used to make bowstrings. As one might suspect, it is very stingy and might cut skin.

Dacron—The normal application for Dacron is for bowstrings. Like Dynema, it is very stingy.

Kevlar—This is fire-resistant and can be used as a cracker with fire whips. It is also very stingy.

Horsehair—It is very stingy, and it splinters easily, possibly leaving fragments in the skin.

Silk thread—This thread is very stingy, cuts easily, and makes a very clean, crisp crack.

Fishing line—This material is used for blood play because it is more capable of cutting the skin.

Poly baler twine—This is a common cracker material used for sport cracking. It is very stingy and unforgiving.

Mason line-braided—braided mason line is cheap and easily leaves marks. It is generally less stingy.

Generally less stingy:

Mason line-twisted—Twisted mason line comes in different sizes. The smaller number mason line is thinner and stingier, whereas the larger number is thicker and thuddier.

Cotton twine—It is not very durable, but for arts and crafts and painting with a whip, it holds acrylic paint very well.

Yarn—It is very light, floats, and tends not to be accurate.

Embroidery floss—This is surprisingly durable and stingy but will not cut as easily as silk thread.

Twisted or Braided. Sometimes, the choice to use either twisted or braided crackers is determined by the class of whip it is being used on.

Signal whip crackers are primarily braided crackers plaited into the end of the thong. However, signal whips that have an English eye or signal whips that have been modified allow for the use of a twisted cracker if that is the whip thrower's desired cracker of choice and cracker design. As noted previously, an English eye provides many opportunities for variations in cracker choice and construction. There are many other reasons why a signal whip cracker should be modified (WITD 101.26, 101.29).

The most common cracker is a twisted cracker finished with an overhand knot. This is the preferred cracker type for basic cracking and sport cracking. However, as I stated above, it is not my favorite for dungeon play. I prefer a flat braided cracker finished with a flat knot – the lady sally cracker (WITD pp. 24-28, WITD 101.28).

A lady sally-style cracker is flat braided like one would braid hair, and finished with a half-hitch that results in a flat knot. This flat knot allows a margin of error in throwing because, in most instances, it will not leave a mark. (WITD 101.28).

Other variations emerge from these two general styles of crackers. Generally, a twisted cracker is stingier regardless of the material of the cracker compared to a flat braided cracker. Another variation is the thickness of the cracker. A thicker cracker made with more material is going to be thuddier, and a thinner cracker that uses less cracker material will be stingier regardless of the cracker material used. So even the lady sally-style cracker can vary depending on the material used, the thickness of the thread, and the amount of thread used in a single cracker.

Be aware that there is a difference between a lady sally braided cracker and a braided cracker made by a whip maker. A lady sally braided cracker is a three-strand plaited flat braid, and a braided cracker made by a whip maker is a four-sided braid finished with an overhand knot.

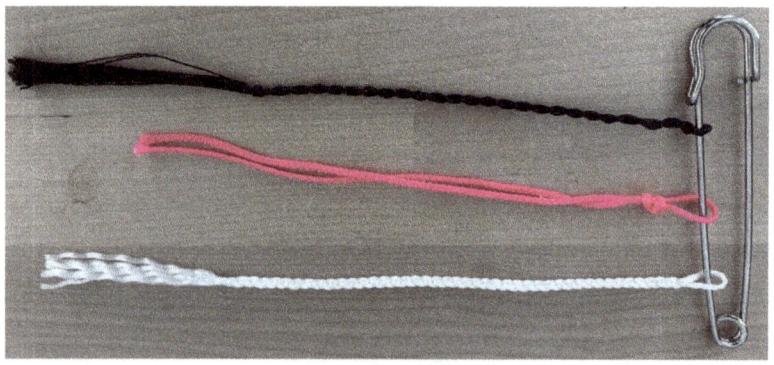

Photo 26 Twisted (stingy), Braided (stingy-marks easily), lady sally style cracker (plaited from twisted mason line)

Overhand Knot vs Flat Knot. The simplest finishing knot is an overhand knot.

A cracker with an overhand knot is more likely to leave marks than a cracker with a flat knot. If the cracker with an overhand knot is all you have and your whip bottom tells you they don't want marks, you will have to throw very carefully.

A flat knot is less likely to leave marks. The lady sally-style flat braided crackers can be finished with a flat knot or an overhand knot. The flat finishing knot on the lady sally-style cracker will give the whip thrower an additional margin of error for making a mistake. In a dimly lit dungeon, this margin of error helps even the experienced whip thrower. This style cracker with the flat finishing knot is also a great variable for the beginning thrower who is still developing their skills with the whip. It allows them to make small mistakes without huge unwanted results on the whip catching end.

Photo 27 Overhand knot vs Flat Knot

Cracker Length. The cracker length is scaled proportionally to the length of the whip. For three to four-foot whips used in indoor play, I generally use the length of my hand from the bottom of my palm to the tip of my middle finger.

A six-foot or longer whip could have a six to eight-inch-long cracker. Attention should be paid so that the longer crackers do not knot themselves as they roll out and finish the crack.

Fluff Length. Fluff length is another variable in whip play. Leaving the fluff too long will result in the cracker fluff becoming tangled or knotting against itself. Long fluff will also act as an air brake, slowing the tip of the whip down as it finishes. I like to measure the length from the last joint of my thumb to the tip as a guide to where to cut the fluff. For whips longer than six feet, I cut the fluff the entire length of my thumb. Longer fluff can also be useful when doing erotic play with nipples or genitals, as the intensity of energy exchange is not so much desired as finesse, control, and light play. The air brake effect can create a cracker stall that is actually desirable for erotic play.

The lady sally Cracker Experiment. This experiment was done by crafting lady sally-style crackers out of No. 15 twisted mason line, No. 18 twisted mason line, and No. 36 twisted mason line. The same bullwhip was used to eliminate a variable, and both of the whip catchers stood for all three different crackers. The whip catchers who stood for this experiment were TrophyWife and nikita54.

Feedback from both whip catchers was, in essence, the same. They reported that the lady sally cracker no. 18 mason line felt good. This was lady sally's standard mason line that she used for many years to make crackers.

The lady sally cracker made from no. 36 mason line is twice as thick and fluffy. At first, nikita54 thought it was made out of a different material. It definitely felt different to both whip bottoms. They both thought it was lighter but also stingy—a more pleasant stingy. Sensations were spread out over a larger area.

The lady sally cracker made from no. 15 mason line results in a thinner cracker than the No. 18. The whip catchers did not need any explanation; this cracker definitely felt stingier to them.

My conclusion is that the No. 18, which was the standard cracker Ladysally made all of those years, gives the best overall experience for the whip bottom. For the whip thrower, it allows the broadest range of possible sensations, from light to stingy up to the crack.

The No. 36 is wider and fluffier, feels lighter to the bottom, and the sensations are more spread out. But, for the whip thrower, it is harder to crack as the fluffy cracker slows the whip down. Again, this cracker is good for beginning whip throwers as it provides a larger margin of error.

For the anxious but curious whip catcher the gentler No. 36 cracker allows them to experience what a whip feels like and get comfortable with the sensations before using a stingier No. 18 cracker in a full-on whip scene. The No. 36 cracker is also better for erotic play with the chest, breasts, nipples, and genitals.

The No. 15 lady sally cracker should be reserved for those who love stingy sensations.

Cracker Resume. Develop a cracker resume. There is a broad spectrum of sensations that can be created with just one single-tail, depending upon the cracker selection. I cannot emphasize this enough - my go-to cracker for pickup play is the lady sally-style No. 18 cracker. Unless someone has negotiated marks and wants a heavier, stingier scene, I use lady sally crackers almost exclusively. But I got there after years of experimentation with different cracker materials and styles of finishing them.

The Great Cracker Experiment. The great cracker experiment consisted of nikita54 standing for a three-and-a-half-foot hybrid signal whip made by Mojave Outliers. The experiment began with a controlled group of throws using a lady sally No. 18 cracker to establish a benchmark. All crackers, regardless of material, were deconstructed and reconstructed using the lady sally technique for making a cracker except the braided mason line. Once a baseline was established, the experimental group began.

Table 1

Order Experienced	Type of Cracker Material	Description of sensations from the whip bottom
1	No. 18 twisted mason line	What I'm used to feeling. Feels good. Like.
2	No. 36 twisted mason line	Heavier, stingy but more spread out.
3	DMC 25 cotton embroidery thread	Stingier, cottony feeling, silky feeling.
4	10 mm silky cord-jewelry cord	Stingy.
5	No. 3 light mercantile cotton yarn	Cottony feeling.
6	No. 3 cotton crochet thread	Nice sting.
7	No. 3 light Bernat cottonish yarn	Soft.
8	Aunt Lydia's crochet thread size 3 100% mercantile cotton	Softer.
9	Crown 100% nylon all purpose twine 2 strand twisted	Bitey, stingy.
10	Braided mason line	Stingiest of all.

Cracker Color. The whip thrower might not recognize the color of a cracker as a variation. It is not directly a variation, as the color will not change the sensation or the way a whip throws. However, the color of the cracker material directly affects the whip thrower's ability to see the cracker all the way into the target zone. This ability to see the cracker directly affects a whip thrower's eye – hand coordination, and finesse in creating surface sensations with a singletail. Therefore, it is an important element to consider.

Environment and lighting greatly affect which color of cracker material is easiest to see. In my opinion, whether indoors under artificial lighting or outdoors in natural light, black is never a good color for cracker material. Ironically, black is the most common cracker material color that whip makers use. This might be because most whip makers are not throwing at a whip catcher. In my experience most whip makers who throw are usually into sport cracking or target cutting. There are, a few lifestyle whip makers who also, unfortunately, use black cracker material.

For outdoor play under natural sunlight, I find fluorescent colors, bright yellow or orange, to be the easiest to see. When the scene moves indoors under artificial lighting, regardless of the lighting color in the play space, white cracker material is the easiest for me to see. Most dungeons are dimly lit, and there is often a variety of colored lighting. A white cracker color will pop under black light. It is also easy to see under dim white lighting.

What is important is not what I have found to be best but what you find to be best for your visual acuity. Do some hands-on research and experiment with different colors.

Crackers and Multiple Whips. Using multiple whips in a scene allows for the use of a variety of cracker types (twisted or plaited) and materials to add an additional layer of variation to the scene.

For a scene in which five different singletails are thrown, there are five different opportunities to vary sensations just by the material and type of cracker chosen and the cracker setup for each whip used in the scene.

As an example, let's say the first singletail planned in the scene is a three-foot snake whip. Selection of a plaited lady sally cracker style cracker with a flat finishing knot (made out of No. 18 white mason line) will allow an even warmup without leaving any marks. If a second snake is chosen with a lady sally cracker made out of horsehair, the second variation in the scene will result in a deepening of the red skin and stingy sensations. Play following with a four-foot bullwhip and a No. 18 mason line lady sally cracker will ramp up the intensity of the energy of the scene and raise the temperature of the skin another notch, but if thrown with care, the whip will still not leave any marks.

If the second bullwhip to be thrown uses a manufactured (as opposed to a lady sally) braided mason line cracker, not only will biting intensity be added to the scene, but the cracker will be painting the whip catcher with marks. Finally, to cool the scene down, the whip catcher could be turned around, and a tassel-style cracker or a No. 36 lady sally cracker could be used for erotic chest play.

The above scenario is just one example of the endless possible variations in play based on the crackers chosen.

Crackers and Two-handed Whip Work. This past year I began my two-handed whip or matched whip journey. I was pleasantly surprised to pick this up fairly quickly.

One of the first things that became apparent was that there is a multiplier effect resulting from throwing matched sets. If I threw matched sets of snake whips and two different sets of bullwhips in a scene (usually I throw two sets of bullwhips - target bullwhips and also the latigo y' dago loaded bullwhips), that would be six crackers per scene. If I throw two scenes in a dungeon session with two new whip bottoms, that equates to 12 new crackers. I quickly realized that I would be using six times as many crackers as before because I like to throw three classes of singletail whips in a scene.

Two-handed whip work requires a matched set of whips. To be a matched set, the crackers must also be matched in that the cracker should be the same length on both whips all the way to the cracker finishing knot, and the extended fluff should also be the same length.

This way, both whips, including crackers, have an identical total length.

However, a matched set of crackers in length does not have to be matched in construction or materials. This provides another set of variables with almost unlimited possibilities. For example, the left-hand whip might be fitted with a lady sally-style cracker made out of No. 18 mason line, and the right-hand whip cracker could be made with a twisted finish with an overhand knot made out of No. 18 mason line. Or both hands are throwing whips with lady sally-style crackers, but the materials they are made of are different, providing different sensations.

Using the cracker materials in our cracker experiment (10 different materials) and different construction methods (currently two methods- (1) twisted with an overhand knot and (2) plaited lady sally-style), the possibilities are too numerous to list.

For most two-handed whip scenes, I do not recommend any variations between the left-hand and right-hand crackers. This variation is just a fun change of pace. Most likely, you will want to stick with the cracker that works best for you and feels the best for the whip catchers who stand for you.

A brief note on safety with crackers. Whip throwers need to be aware of how long their whips are and if the cracker is going to end up touching the ground in the circuit of dynamic throwing. If you know a party is going to be in an industrial-type location, you might want to consider laying a tarp or just using shorter whips.

Chapter 4

Variations in Static Throws

THIS MAY BE the shortest chapter of all because, at this point in advanced play, most whip throwers are no longer using static throws. However, static throws should maintain a place in every BDSM whip thrower's repertoire.

The main advantage of continuing to use static throws is that they can be pulled out of the whip thrower's bag of tricks when needed. A static throw requires no safety circle behind the whip thrower to accomplish the throw. It also does not require any more space than the radius between the whip thrower's point of release and the whip catcher. This makes these techniques ideal for overcrowded dungeons, tight spaces, and house parties everyone hopes they get invited to.

Another advantage to these static throws is that the follow-through, or arc into and exiting the strike zone, is on the vertical plane. The vertical plane gives easy access to one of the most erotic zones, the crotch area.

Bow and Arrow. The bow and arrow technique (sometimes called a slingshot) will typically be thrown overhand. A variation can be made by changing the angle of attack on the throw. Doing so can cause the whip to approach the strike zone from a different direction.

The direction of the strike provides a change in the angle at which energy is entering the body, hence, a different variation than when it is thrown repeatedly overhand. This change in angle can occur by the clockwise rotation or counter-clockwise rotation of the throwing hand. The bow and arrow throw is limited to a single whip technique.

Over the Shoulder. The over the shoulder technique has more variations than the bow and arrow. Alternating shoulders provides a variation as it alternates the forehand side with the backhand side and results in a change in the angle of the strike when caught by the whip catcher. Raising the elbow and sliding the whip off of the upper arm on the backhand side can further alter the strike angle. This technique is not possible on the forehand side.

Another variation of over the shoulder is to throw it with two whips, meaning that there is a whip in each hand. (WITD 201.23). Or, for something really different, the whip thrower can hold a matched set of whips in the same throwing hand and throw both over the same shoulder simultaneously with one hand. This two-whip-one-throwing-hand technique can also be done with a bow and arrow.

Of the two static techniques, I actually prefer the over the shoulder for myself. But for everyone else, it is truly what feels the most natural and comfortable and the technique that gives the whip thrower the most accuracy. I always joke in workshops that the advantage of the over the shoulder is that you get to hit yourself. But actually, if you match the intensity that you hit yourself with the intensity of the throw, then as a top, you have a pretty good idea of how much intensity the bottom is receiving.

Erotic Whip Play. This is a variation in the normal target zone for a whip. It is mentioned under static throws because these techniques are more accurate on the target areas involved in erotic play.

When throwing at the genitals, the whip catcher's legs, pelvic area, and other natural body shapes get in the way of the arcs naturally needed in the horizontal and forward figure eight dynamic techniques. Both the bow and arrow and over the shoulder techniques can approach the body on the vertical plane and can be slightly adjusted. The whip rollout on the vertical plane creates a natural arc, thereby easily accessing the labia, clitoris, or ball sack, whereas a whip thrown in the horizontal plane does not have the same easy access. There will be more on genital play in the vignettes section.

Rhythm and Timing. A variation using static throws can be created using either technique by timing the release of the whip or throw to be rhythmic or non-rhythmic, or in other words, timing the whip throws to be on the beat of the music playing or off the beat of the music playing.

Rhythmic throwing is anticipatory for the whip catcher; non-rhythmic throwing can create suspense for when the strike will occur. If the strikes are erotic and the whip catcher is responding erotically to the energy from the whip, then, of course, complementing the energy can enhance the experience all the way up to edging an orgasm. Reading body language, having a connection with the music and with the whip catcher, and being in symbiosis with the whip make this type of scene possible.

Chapter 5

Variations in Dynamic Throws: Rhythm and Syncopation

DYNAMIC THROWING IS characterized by throwing and recovering, throwing and recovering. This can be done on a single side of the thrower, but it is recommended to alternate sides when throwing and recovering.

Alternating between forehand and backhand ensures both sides of the whip catcher's body receive energy from the whip. When throwing at the heart and root chakras, throwing both forehand and backhand evenly puts energy into both sides of the chakra. It provides balance. It is repetitive and rhythmic, and it can be hypnotic as the energy is transferred rhythmically.

A whip that is thrown in rhythm to the beat of the music that is playing follows the meter of the measure of music at a given point in the song. There are a number of simple ways to create variations in rhythm when throwing a whip.

Throwing by Note. Music consists of notes. The most basic notes are whole notes, half notes, quarter notes, and eighth notes.

If each whip stroke in rhythm to the music represents a quarter note, then 4/4 time would have four quarter notes in each measure. Throwing a forward figure eight representative of quarter notes in 4/4 time would result in one complete forward figure eight being thrown (forehand, recovery on the backhand side, backhand, recovery on the forehand side) to the beat of the music for a measure of music. So either the forehand would be on the first beat of music and the backhand on the third beat of music, or vice versa.

If the whip is only thrown half-time, the whip would be slowed down to match either the first beat of one measure on the forehand or the first beat of the next measure on the backhand. Throwing the whip as a whole note would mean only one throw per every four beats of music, normally thrown on the first or heaviest beat of the measure. In dancing, this is called catching the one. This might be easiest done with static throwing.

If the whip is being thrown in a forward figure eight to represent a quarter note in 4/4 time and recovered and thrown on the beat with the music, then to throw an 8th note, the whip has to be thrown twice as fast. This can be accomplished by throwing a forward volley or the modified arrowhead[13].

Match the Meter. The simplest variation is to match the meter of the music playing in the dungeon. This would be one throw per beat of music regardless of the time signature. The easiest music to throw to has 4/4 timing or some variation of 4/4 timing. Music with 3/4

---

13 An arrowhead is a sport crack that involves a forward cattleman's crack with the whip recovering on the backhand side to do a reverse crack and subsequent cattleman's crack on the backhand side (or cutback) with the whip recovering on the forehand side to do a reverse crack. Reverse cracks are useless in dungeon play, so a modified arrowhead removes the reverse cracks but follows the same whip flow pattern only using the forward cracks.

timing, which is what traditionally forms the structure of waltz music, is difficult because the whip is thrown on alternating sides or in pairs.

Music that has 3/4 timing requires the whip thrower to alternate the accent of the heavy beat between the forehand and backhand. This meter change in time signature requires a new variation from the whip thrower, even when throwing using a simple one-throw-per-beat technique.

Halving the Meter. There are two ways to implement this concept. One is to throw half as fast as the meter in which the music was written. The other way is to look more microscopically at individual notes, and instead of throwing a quarter note on the beat, throw it as you would a half note. Halving the meter works well when the music is very fast and is too fast to throw the whip being used at its natural frequency. Rather than muscling the whip and forcing it to keep up with the tempo of the music, slow it down to half the tempo of the music that is playing.

Doubling the Meter. Sometimes, the tempo of the music is too slow. When that happens, if the whip thrower throws on the beat of the music matching the meter, the whip slows down below its natural stall speed. There are several solutions to that problem.

Throwing a longer whip that has a slower frequency can work. Another possibility is to speed up the whip, doubling the action with the meter or tempo of the music that is playing. Looking at this on the microscopic level of individual notes, instead of being thrown on a quarter note, the whip is instead being thrown on an 8th note. Another way of looking at this is the whip is being thrown twice as fast as the music is playing.

Paradiddles. A paradiddle is one of the basic drumming concepts that use single and double strokes. Typically, in the context of drumming, the para is a single stroke, and the diddle is a double stroke.

They are played in pairs, making a four-stroke grouping. Three simple paradiddles in a paradiddle drumming technique are: (1) left, right, right, left or (2) left, right, left, left, or (3) right, left, right, right. This is easily accomplished if throwing two-whip style as each whip then replaces one drum stick.

If only one whip is being thrown, this paradiddle concept can be accomplished by shifting the paradiddle to the strike zone. Examples of a strike zone paradiddle thrown at the shoulders might be: (1) left shoulder, right shoulder, right shoulder, left shoulder or (2) left shoulder, right shoulder, left shoulder, left shoulder, or (3) right shoulder, left shoulder, right shoulder, right shoulder. The diddle requires modifying the forward figure eight to recover the whip on the same side of the body when the diddle occurs.

Another way to accomplish the diddle is to keep the normal forward figure eight pattern but only strike on the diddle, missing on the opposite side when the diddle occurs. This technique, however, will result in a change of meter similar to a half note for that beat.

Paradiddles can easily be accomplished with two whips using the static over the shoulder technique.

Crashes or, with a Whip, Cracks. A crash in drumming is a hard stroke on the cymbal, causing the frequency of the symbol to crash. This sound can also be made with a stroke of a wind gong. In whip throwing, a crash can be replicated by a clean, loud crack. Loud cracks should be strategically placed to match the music.

If the whip thrower is a type of percussionist who likes playing along with the music, then the whip inserts a crack in the music logically when the drummer crashes a cymbal or when the dynamics of the music scream - crack! Whip cracks might also occur on a heavy kick drum beat; this all is interpretive.

The key is to crack when appropriate for the music that is playing. Do not become obnoxious or disrupt the dungeon with excessive cracking. Rather, enhance the sound energy in the dungeon by complementing the music that is playing.

Accents. An accent in drumming is an emphasis on a particular beat. This is fairly easy to accomplish by the dynamic use of controlled puffs. If the whip is thrown at a controlled puff level three, an accent is created by throwing it at a level four or higher on a beat that needs an accent. Limit the level of the accent to controlled puffs to allow distinguishing an accent from a crash (crack).

Ghost Notes. A ghost note in drumming is perhaps the reverse of an accent. It is a beat played much lighter than the level of beat accompanying it. With a whip, it is almost a brush stroke - what I call a feather or butterfly kiss. The whip is lightly passing over the target area, perhaps not even touching it, but the puff of air is causing a light sensation, thus creating a ghost note.

Syncopation. Think of syncopation as throwing on the "and". One, two, three, four, "*and*". The "and" extends the stall of the whip and allows the whip to be thrown in between beats or on the syncopation of the normal beat. This requires finesse to speed up the whip and to slow it down to play with the rhythms in the music. The whip should be sped up and slowed down without muscling it.

Playing the Drum Kit. (Can be a Vignette!) Our whipper's drum kit will have at least one bass drum, which is usually played with a pedal, a snare drum, at least two tom tom drums, a top hat cymbal played with a pedal, and a crash cymbal or a ride cymbal.

Now, think of the whip catcher as a drum kit. The root chakra forms two bass drums; the shoulders are two tom toms, and the chest area becomes the cymbals. Playing the drum kit in a complete circle around the whip catcher allows the entire whip circle to be used and all of the strike zones to be engaged in play.

Wraps can be incorporated into the rotation around the drum kit. Reversing the direction of rotation from clockwise to counterclockwise adds another variation. Restraining the whip catcher from a single hardpoint allows 360-degree access around a whip circle. Either the horizontal or forward figure eight throws will work with this play setup.

Raising the whip catcher up onto their toes can create a partial suspension dynamic and add another variation to the setup. While this adds a variation, it also greatly increases the difficulty of playing the drum kit, as the whip catcher may be moving at the same time the whip is trying to find its target.

The rhythm of the whip can be thought of as a percussion instrument playing in the dungeon. The whip thrower is getting his groove on, throwing fills and accents. The whip is also an energy implement, rolling energy down its thong and delivering it precisely into the chakras of the whip catcher. This energy flows from the whip thrower to the whip catcher and is transferred by the movement of the whip in rhythm to the energy flowing in the dungeon. This, to me, is the ultimate result in dungeon play.

Chapter 6

Variations in Footwork

Whips in the Dungeon Chapter 10 introduces foot positions by suggesting the thrower relate footwork to activities they already know. I will partially recap it here.

A tennis player should relate their tennis footwork to the motion of throwing a whip. A pool player uses certain footwork when lining up a shot. This is very much like lining up a static throw with a whip. A dart player lines up a shot that reduces parallax error with footwork and body position. A baseball player or softball player can relate the motion of throwing a ball or swinging a bat to throwing a whip and also the associated footwork. A chef standing in front of a stove even has footwork.

Literally every activity that someone does regularly has footwork patterns. The quickest way to good whip footwork is to relate the footwork patterns the whip thrower is already comfortable with to the action of throwing a whip.

WITD Chapter 10 related basic footwork stances to the five common dance foot positions. These foot positions can be found easily online by searching for dance foot positions or looking at WITD Photo 89 (WITD, p. 88). While these dance foot positions are common between styles of dance, there are a few nuances between ballet and ballroom (standard or smooth, and Latin or rhythm).

Most people reading this book will not be trained dancers. So why relate the five foot positions in dance to whip throwing foot positions? I use them because they are common standard foot references that can be related to any activity, whether baseball, bowling, pool shooting, cooking, or many other activities. They give a standard frame of reference and a foot chart to refer to so everyone is on the same page (WITD, p. 88), so to speak.

As you read about footwork, keep thinking of what I call "The Whip Throwers' Mantra:" Small changes on the throwing end result in larger changes on the catching end of a whip.

Foot Positions. For foot position one, in ballroom dancing, smooth, and standard, the feet are together and parallel to each other with toes on both feet pointing straight ahead (WITD, p. 88). For foot position one in ballroom, rhythm, and Latin dance, the toes are pointed out at a 45-degree angle with heels together. In ballet, for foot position one, the toes are pointed outward at an even more severe angle with heels together.

Each of these small foot changes will create variations in the catching end of a whip. Without going through each of the ballroom foot positions, there are slight differences between each foot position in smooth and rhythm dancing.

As a general rule of thumb in Latin or rhythm dance, the toes are pointed out in each position. This slight change allows more hip action and for the figure eight to be done with the hips. In advanced throwing, doing a Latin figure eight with the hips while throwing the forward figure eight with a whip adds another layer of complexity to throwing a whip. Mantra: Small changes on the throwing end result in larger changes on the catching end of a whip.

Shifting Weight. Weight can be concentrated directly over one foot or split between the two feet.

In foot position one, weight can perhaps be split between the two feet to begin with. Then, further into the scene, the weight can be shifted to the left foot. This will result in a variation of sensation on the receiving end of the whip. Weight can then be shifted to the right foot, again resulting in a change of sensation. Weight can be shifted alternating between the left and right foot, creating rhythmic changes in sensation that match the pattern of the forward figure eight and the music that is playing.

This is just one illustration of what happens when applying the Whip Throwers' Mantra.

In first position, the feet are together, with toes pointed forward for smooth and standard dance styles or pointed out at a 45-degree angle for Latin and rhythm dance styles. The weight can be split, shifted back (over the heels), or shifted completely forward over the balls of the feet. Weight can also be shifted over the left foot or completely over the right foot. As the feet are together, this would be accomplished by keeping the weight directly over the feet, then leaning back to shift the weight to the heels, and by leaning to either side to put the weight on only one foot. Each weight shift results in a change of sensation on the receiving end of the whip.

In second position, the feet are shoulder-width apart, with the toes pointing forward. Weight can be split or evenly distributed between feet (WITD, Photo 91, p. 89). Weight can be shifted right or left, centering the weight over either the right or left foot. That shift will result in the whip cracker hitting a contact point and moving to the right or left a few inches.

The result should be that shifting weight from the right to the left foot when throwing the forward figure eight to complement which side of the figure eight the whip is on will result in accurately shifting the cracker contact point between the right and left shoulders or the right and left butt cheeks. Alternating between the right and left shoulders or butt cheeks will be easier in second position, but alternating between the shoulders and butt will be more difficult.

The discussion on fourth position includes tips for alternating between shoulders and butt.

In third position, the heel of the leading foot is locked into the arch of the foot that is behind, forming a T-shape (WITD, Photo 92/93, p. 90). Either foot can be the leading foot in position three. Weight can be split between both feet. If the thrower wants a slightly harder sensation in the target area, the weight can be shifted to be completely on the leading foot. The result will be that the thrower will be slightly closer to the target, resulting in a heavier strike. Conversely, if the thrower wants to lighten the sensation or take something off the throw, shifting weight to the back foot will naturally draw the whip away from the strike zone. Remember, small changes on the throwing end result in larger changes on the catching end (whip thrower's mantra).

In fourth position, feet are about shoulder-width apart, and one foot is a stride ahead of the trailing foot. When the dominant foot is leading, the stance is more like a fencing stance. When the non-dominant foot is leading, it is more like the stride position used when throwing a baseball (WITD, Photo 94/95, p. 91).

Shifting weight in fourth position results in a larger change than shifting weight in third position. In fourth position, shifting weight to the front foot will bring the release point two to five inches closer to the whip catcher than when the weight is shifted to the back foot. This is a technique that can be used in combination with shifting weight from front to back foot in fourth position to achieve shifting the target from shoulders to butt when the whip catcher is on a St. Andrew's Cross.

Most St. Andrew's crosses are built at an angle, so the bottom is leaning into the cross slightly. This angle varies depending upon the construction, but the result for the whip top targeting the whip catcher is that the shoulders are farther away from the toe line than the butt cheeks. This accentuates the normal physical anatomy when someone is standing, where their butt cheeks naturally are closer to the toe line than their shoulders.

Learning to lean forward and center the weight over the leading foot in fourth position when targeting the shoulders and then centering the weight over the back foot when targeting the butt will result in a weight shift that allows both shoulders and butt to be targeted accurately when throwing the whip. This works with all techniques, both static and dynamic.

Fifth position is accomplished by stepping back with either foot and placing the foot just behind the heel of the stationary foot (WITD, Photo 96, p. 92). Weight normally is fully on the back foot when fifth position is first initiated. However, as with any foot position, weight can be shifted to the forward foot or split to cause slightly different targeting and sensations on the receiving end. Because the initial step is back while the whip is traveling forward, some of the energy is taken out of the whip strike. This in itself creates a variation in sensation on the receiving end.

Open Break is an extremely useful foot position. It can only be executed when the feet are in the first or second position. Imagine standing on the toe line in the first position and taking a step back with the dominant foot. This leaves the non-dominant foot on the toe line as a marker, so when the dominant foot is moved back into the first or second position, the thrower is instantly back on their toe line.

An open break comes in handy when the whip catcher's body language indicates they need a break or a breather to process energy. Doing an open break by stepping back with the dominant foot takes the whip off the target while allowing it to continue to be thrown in a dynamic rhythm to the music.

Open break also can be used when the whip thrower needs a break or wants a moment to change their grip or angle of the rollout of the whip without taking a chance on a miss-hit. This foot position allows these changes to be made and then the toe line to be quickly reacquired.

Crossover Break. The crossover break is a common dance step in a number of Latin dances and can be done to either side. A pivot is done on the ball of the foot on the side on which the break is going to occur. Normally, this is done as a 90-degree pivot followed by a crossover step forward in the new direction with the trailing foot (WITD, Photo 98, p. 93). It is a "break" because once the crossover step is completed by the trailing foot, it is returned as a reverse pivot is performed on the pivoting foot.

When using this footwork while throwing a whip, reducing the pivot to 45 degrees or so results in the crossover step following the curve of the whip circle, allowing the whip to be thrown while maintaining its targeting distance.

This is considered advanced footwork when throwing a whip, but an additional variation can be created by delaying the break and not returning the crossover step immediately. Several forward figure eights can be thrown while remaining in this crossover position. Adding a weight shift to the crossover foot and back to the pivot foot adds another variation.

It is difficult to describe all of these variations in writing. The WITD 401.07 Moby Dick video shows crossover breaks going both directions and also the variation where the crossover is held, and the weight is shifted in rhythm with a forward figure eight.

Voltas. The Volta is a Samba step danced as "a one and a two." Adding a Volta to footwork results in a new variation, as the Volta rhythm creates syncopation.

To do a Volta from second position (feet shoulder-width apart), one foot takes a sideways step, and the trailing foot crosses over in front of the leading step.

Multiple Voltas will result in a path that makes an arc, or in the case of whip footwork, that will follow the arc of the whip circle. The lead foot always lands "ball/flat," or in other words, on the ball of the foot first, then fully flat. This happens while the trailing foot crosses over, making a smaller crossing step that is always on the ball of the foot in a checked foot position. Hip rotation and bounce can be added to this advanced step. These add another variation in the sensation felt when throwing a whip.

In my humble opinion, this is quite advanced whip throwing footwork. The best way to learn this step is to watch some basic Samba dance instructional videos. Search for videos using the term Samba Voltas.

Apply this step to throwing both horizontal and forward figure eight dynamic throwing. Voltas performed consecutively will result in traveling the arc of the whip circle. Voltas performed alternating between left and right will result in a stationary Volta that tightens the pattern of the forward figure eight.

Any of the basic footwork (WITD 101.17), intermediate footwork (WITD 201.15), or advanced footwork (WITD 301.07) can have variation added just by shifting weight. Shifting weight to one foot, the other foot, back and forth between feet, or split weight will cause any of the foot positions to vary slightly on the receiving end. Weight can also be shifted over the foot from split weight to the ball of the foot and heel of the foot.

What is the mantra? Say it out loud!

Chapter 7

Surface Targeting: Creating Variations in Sensations

CREATING VARIATIONS IN sensations with surface contact with the whip requires good control of the speed of the whip and accuracy. One key to becoming good with a short whip (the preferred whip for dungeon play) is to learn to slow it down even though it is short, to change speeds, and to maintain accuracy and control.

Think of the energy of a whip as a timeline. For everything up to the point of the crack, energy is increasing, and finally, at the crack, most of that energy is released. On the other side of the crack, the whip has less energy. Play before the whip reaches the crack is subsonic play, and play after the crack is supersonic play. Realize subsonic play can be more intense than supersonic play because, in subsonic play, the energy of the whip is building up to the point of the crack; in supersonic play, the crack has already occurred, and energy is expending. Moving the crack directly onto the skin would be the most intense.

Note that there has been no mention of cracking. The control comes from being able to work with, adjust, and ramp up using controlled puffs. This is playing in a controlled manner just below the sound barrier. The crack is pretty consistently at around 767 mph, depending slightly on the temperature and pressure of the air. Altitude and humidity slightly affect when a whip will actually break the sound barrier. At this speed, we are playing on the edge when we throw a whip in a controlled manner up to and beyond the speed of sound.

One of the ways already discussed for changing sensations is by cracker selection. But once a type and material of cracker has been chosen for use with a whip within a scene, what are additional ways of varying sensations to the skin when playing? This type of variation is going to focus on technique.

Controlled Puffs or Subsonic Play. Controlled puffs are achieved by playing subsonic with the whip. Playing below the crack allows the whip to be thrown with control and finesse. It also increases the energy transmitted by the whip in graduated intensity.

This intensity can be measured by the sound of the puff. This technique can be practiced by throwing at an eight-inch tambourine or inexpensive gong. Throw an overhand at just above the stall speed. The goal is to determine the slowest speed at which the whip will naturally roll out above stall speed and create a light puff while maintaining its accuracy on target.

Once the whip has gently puffed for the whip thrower, replicate the throw. Throw this gentle puff 100 times. This is a level one controlled puff. Then, throw ever so slightly harder where the puff makes a slightly louder or stronger puff – a level two controlled puff. Continue this process until the whip can consistently be thrown on target with controlled puffs, increasing the intensity or sound of the puff from level one through nine. By the time the whip's controlled puffs reach levels seven through nine, most likely, it will be making a crack.

Keep in mind that this controlled puff one through nine intensity level is achieved in practice with a t-shirt or sheepskin target. In a scene, the intensity level of each whip catcher will be different, and the whip-controlled puff scale will have to be adjusted relative to the whip catcher's pain scale from one through 10, with their 10 being red-stop the scene.

Controlled puffs with a whip catcher. Begin by finding your toe line. To find the toe line, start with the singletail thrown at a controlled puff level one. This is the intensity recommended to find the toe line and begin the warmup. Slowly inch forward when the whip catcher feels the puff of air coming off the cracker tip. Ask them to nod their head the instant they feel the puff of air. This is a butterfly kiss. It also marks your toe line.

If the whip catcher's body language is positive, continue on the controlled puff scale to levels two and three. Check in with the whip catcher and ask them where the whip strikes are on a pain scale of one through 10.

Let's say they answer with a one or two. The whip was being thrown within the whip thrower's practice scale of three. Relative to the whip catcher's feedback, the whip thrower's three is the whip catcher's two, so adjust the scale to match the whip catcher's pain scale. Everyone is unique and experiences the whip differently. Even the same whip catcher from one day to the next or one scene to the next may experience this differently.

Subsonic play using ramping up with controlled puffs toward a clean crack can be done in a controlled manner. Consistent subsonic play can easily achieve explicit consent requirements for a scene. Check-ins are frequent, and the whip bottom's pain scale (one through ten) is correlated with the whip thrower's controlled puff scale (one through ten). Most whips will naturally crack around a controlled puff of seven or eight. Most subsonic play is done between controlled puff one and six.

Supersonic Play. Supersonic play is play on the other side of the crack. A crack releases most of the energy in the whip, so logic follows that the follow-through on the other side of the sonic crack will have less energy than the whip had right before and during the crack when that energy was released. How much energy is left in the whip is unknown, but physics and logic tell the whip thrower it has to be less. Logic would say that the closer the crack is to the skin, resulting in the follow-through of the cracker contacting the skin immediately after the crack, the strike will contain more energy than if the crack was placed farther away from the strike zone.

An example might be if the whip thrower places a forehand crack a foot off the right shoulder, and on the follow-through, the cracker barely grazes the shoulder. The energy of the whip was expended a foot away, with most of the energy transferred as sound energy, and very little entered the whip catcher from physical contact. If the thrower moves the crack toward the right shoulder and cracks a couple of inches away from the shoulder, the follow-through will result in more than simply grazing the skin; more energy will be transferred in addition to the sound energy from the crack. How much energy is exchanged in supersonic play is a tricky variable to work with.

Supersonic play is more easily achieved when throwing with an experienced whip catcher and playing more in the realm of implied consent. This should be a whip catcher with whom the whip thrower has played successfully many times. The whip top and bottom should know each other and communicate well with body language, hand, and audible signals. Mistakes in throwing can more easily be made when using supersonic play.

If marks are negotiated and the whip catcher is experienced, this concern is not as critical.

Another consideration in supersonic play is triggers. If the whip catcher has triggers associated with a gunshot, a whip crack often sounds like a gunshot and can be an issue. Some whip catchers love the sound of a clean crack ringing in their ears; others do not. For those who do not, consider using disposable hearing protection or intentionally playing subsonic and not cracking. There will be more about this in the chapter on sensory deprivation.

Intentionally Missing the Primary Target Zones. If a whip is thrown in a rhythm alternating strike zones using a forward figure eight, the whip catcher naturally develops a rhythm with the whip. They can anticipate consistently where the next strike will occur, and if the whip is being thrown with consistency and finesse, they can settle into the level of energy expected from each strike.

Intentionally missing the strike zone on a throw when done in rhythm creates a space or a hole in the energy being transferred. When done with intentionality, it becomes another variable in play. This could be done to change things up and keep the whip catcher guessing a little bit. A whip thrower might not want to be too predictable as the unpredictable adds an element of edginess and mindfuck to a scene.

Perhaps the whip catcher communicated through body language that they needed a moment to breathe and process energy. Intentionally missing the target on one or more throws gives the whip catcher the opportunity to breathe.

Intentionally missing the strike zone does not mean energy is not transferred to the whip catcher. The hole left in the energy transferred by direct contact with the whip catcher is replaced by a different type of energy - sound energy. The whip makes a sound – whoosh - as it travels through the air, followed by a puff or a crack at the end of its travel. This sound energy continues to travel into the whip catcher and the surrounding dungeon.

Variables That Affect Sensation Targeting. The variables mentioned in previous chapters can play a role in varying sensations when surface targeting. Choice of cracker, length of whip, type of whip, style of throwing, variation in footwork, weight shifting, the length of cracker fluff, and the type of finishing knot used on the cracker all create opportunities to vary the sensation when surface targeting.

Continue your whip journey by experimenting, changing things up, and continually getting feedback from the whip catcher.

Chapter 8

Variations in Play Environment

THE PLAY ENVIRONMENT is one of the most important elements in a good whip scene or, for that matter, any scene. It sets the stage for what is to come and, often, what will follow. Not only does it set the stage, but it can also limit what might be possible. Alternatively, it can accommodate the reaches of one's imagination.

Most dungeon play occurs indoors. Even so, indoor dungeon spaces are in no way uniform, as they must conform to the physical limitations of the spaces being used. A cellar or basement dungeon play space is so very different than an attic play space or one set in a bedroom. A hotel atrium set up as a dungeon is completely different than a dungeon set up in one of the hotel's ballrooms or a convention center space. Even the flooring adds a variation. Is it carpet, polished concrete, tile, or hardwood? Is the floor dirty, or has it been cleaned so spotless you could have your submissive eat off of it? What is the temperature like?

Much of the content of this chapter is directly intended for the consideration of event organizers, promoters, and head dungeon monitors.

Advanced whip throwers and catchers also need to consider these variables in a play environment.

Indoor Play. Variables to consider indoors include: the space location, square footage/space between equipment, the layout of the dungeon, flooring, lighting, overhead clearance, hard points, A/C and heating, ventilation, airflow, cleaning stations, hydration stations, first aid, seating or observation areas, aftercare area, social area, kitchen/dining area, specialized play areas, limitations on play in areas, and music - DJ or playlist, live band or streamed music AI assisted like Spotify or Pandora.

The Space Location. A play space located in a basement, cellar, or underground convention space of a large urban hotel is going to feel deep, dark, cool, and sometimes humid. Attics on the converse side tend to be hotter as heat naturally rises, and unless a roof is insulated and the space air-conditioned, play in a naturally ventilated attic house party may be confined to only certain seasons of the year. Sometimes, limiting attic play spaces to late at night is sufficient to allow the space to cool down. Sound in an attic play space travels up and out. Consideration of the distance between neighboring houses and properties is a consideration as a whip crack often sounds like a rifle or gunshot. Unwanted attention by neighbors and passersby is a consideration, especially for house parties in residential neighborhoods.

Sometimes, promoters arrange underground parties in warehouse districts where warehouse space can be rented for a single night. These indoor spaces are often very industrial and dirty, have limited facilities, do not meet fire codes for large gatherings, may not have enough exits, and are not designed for crowded occupancy.

When you enter an indoor play space for the first time, you should walk around the entire space. Look at lighting, ceiling height, and overhead obstructions like chains or nylon straps hanging down to use for hard points. See if there is a logical way the equipment has been arranged to allow for the back swing of impact toys without interfering with people walking around the play spaces or adjacent play areas.

Are there designated "dark" areas of the dungeon for a violet wand or fire play? Is there a designated medical play area or wax play area? These are areas of the dungeon where a whip scene may not be possible. Is there a quiet play area in the dungeon? If so, a whip scene would have to be done erotically and/or subsonic with no cracking.

If the play space is below ground, the humidity in the air, even though it may be air-conditioned, affects how a whip will crack. Temperature and humidity affect the speed at which a whip will break the sound barrier.

Lighting is vital for the whip thrower in a dungeon space. I recommend that you carry your own LED spotlights just in case the lighting in the dungeon space is inadequate. These are made small enough that they can easily fit in a toy bag.

I absolutely love rope lighting around the floor and ceiling perimeters of a dungeon. Rope lighting along the rafters, if there are rafters, is also very nice for mood. Blacklight is a good addition as it makes following a white cracker easy in a dimly lit dungeon. Almost any color of lighting is okay, but subdued or dimmed white lighting is absolutely the best for impact play.

If you have any control over the choice of lighting in a dungeon, DO NOT EVER use red lighting in a dungeon area where impact play is going to occur because changes in skin coloration are often not visible under red light. If someone gets cut or an abrasion begins bleeding, blood does not show up easily under red light. Red lighting should not be used at all or should be limited to aftercare areas.

Also, I recommend not using lighting that interacts with the music or is attached to a computer used to generate the music playlist. It sounds like a cool idea and looks very cool, but in practical reality, it is a dungeon incident waiting to happen. I was at an event that used this type of computerized interactive setup where the lighting interacted with the music playing. Imagine throwing a bullwhip at a whip catcher standing six feet away. Then, imagine the lighting constantly changing colors and patterns. To make matters worse, whenever the music stops, the entire dungeon goes dark, and the lights do not come back on until the next song starts, maybe two or three seconds later. Throwing a whip moving at the speed of sound and, in an instant, going from marginally acceptable lighting to total darkness is just not safe.

Once the lighting in the dungeon is set before play begins, do not change it during a dungeon play set. I was throwing a whip scene on a stage during an event. The only lighting in that area of the dungeon was from the wall sconces. One of the DMs decided that the wall sconces should be turned off. So, in the middle of my scene, I went from having ok lighting to almost no lighting. This was truly the moment in my leather journey where I realized how deeply I go into top space when I'm throwing. At that point, I am hyper-focused and literally tune everything out but the rhythm and movement of the whip and the object of my attention, the whip catcher. That focus was broken with a flick of a light switch, and it was NOT a good experience.

Temperature. Ideally, the temperature should be set so that a whip bottom is comfortable with their skin exposed. It is hard for the whip bottom to fully relax and be in the moment if they are too cold. I've always said if I'm not breaking a sweat as a top throwing an impact scene, then the space is too cold for a bottom to be standing with their clothes off. Ultimately, it directly affects the energy exchange. Some small adjustments can be made by the whip thrower or whip catcher, but often, the play environment is controlled by the promoter, organizer, or dungeon planner. Sometimes, the play environment is even out of the control of the event organizer, and everyone is at the mercy of the owner/manager of the facility being utilized as a dungeon. I have been to BDSM conventions where the hotel kept the conference rooms at meat locker temperatures. These spaces converted for evening dungeon play simply do not work. There might be a reason everyone is playing in their rooms.

Outdoor Play. Outdoor play involves many of the same considerations as indoor play spaces but with the added elements from Mother Nature. Additional variables to consider are sun, shade, allergies, bugs, animals, birds, weather, plants and trees, grass/weeds, mud, and, I am sure, many others that I have forgotten.

Photo 28 Outdoor play.
Moodstone caught trespassing
in a role playing vignette.

Well-manicured grass is fine for kangaroo whips. Be careful of gravel or grass that might hide burrs, thorns, and stickers. You do not want to nick or damage your valuable kangaroo whips. This is when a couple of quality nylon or paracord whips come in handy. The outdoor elements are less of a consideration when throwing with a durable paracord whip.

Long whip play with whips greater than six feet in total length is perfect for outdoors because the limitations of indoor space do not apply. Wraps that cannot be easily done indoors are great for outdoor play. My favorite whip for doing wraps outdoors is an eight-foot black snake whip (12 feet total length). Two-handed whip throwers can throw wraps alternating between left and right hands. This is one technique that can safely be done with stock whips around the torso in outdoor whip play.

Chapter 9

Music - the Greatest Variable of All

OF ALL OF the variables possible in advanced whip play, the most influential variable of all is the music playing in the dungeon on any particular night or for any particular scene. My greatest whip scenes have been when the energy was electric in the dungeon, with multiple scenes going on, with many genres of play, and with the stars aligning with energizing music choices. Those scenes are permanently etched into my mind:

> Moodstone at Spring Fling.
> painboy at the Black Rose convention.
> Gloryus at Thunder in the Mountains.
> Moodstone at Dark Odessey Winterfire.
> painboy inside a drum circle at The Floating World.
> Moodstone with Lady Umbra, & Master Snoflak in a whip
>   flurry at Beyond Leather.
> longstemmedrose at the Capital Ball.
> ladyofdreams at the Thunder in the Mountains after party.

slavelinda at Southeast Leatherfest.

The whip scenes are so memorable that when I close my eyes, my brain can replay the video. One of the reasons the scenes worked so well was not only that all of these whip bottoms were incredible, but they were able to connect with the energy of the whip as it danced with the music playing in the dungeon in every instance.

Moodstone and I disagree on what makes this phenomenon happen. Moodstone is convinced it is the energy level in the dungeon at the time a great scene happens that etches it permanently in the brain's memory. Perhaps she is right, but I'm so connected to the music playing in the dungeon at a particular moment that I feel the music is a key part of that equation. *[Moodstone, in edits, adds these words, "If the energy in the dungeon is in part determined by the music, then we are not in disagreement per se. You might say that you doubt that the energy in the dungeon could be as memorable in the absence of good dungeon music.]*

In most, if not all, of these instances, I can tell you the music playing in the dungeon even 15 to 20 years later. Perhaps the top space or hyper-focus (as I like to call it) required for throwing a whip near or beyond the speed of sound with finesse is another element. But for whatever reason, I can tell you that Jon Bonham's drum solo from Led Zeppelin's Moby Dick (the long play version) was playing when I whipped ladyofdreams at the Thunder after party. Or that the first time I was ever introduced to Rammstein was when I first heard and played to Du Hast at Dark Odessey Winterfire. I had Moodstone restrained and cuffed to the chain link fence cage built around the DJ stand.

Dungeon music has gone through many evolutions. When I entered the leather lifestyle 25 years ago, Enigma was the mainstay of dungeon music. The album Return to Innocence was a part of almost every dungeon's playlist in those days. Considered New Age or World genre music, most of it was instrumental, but some of the songs on the album had vocals, albeit haunting vocals that were sometimes ethereal. At the time, instrumental music was popular as there was a feeling that lyrics would pull a bottom out of subspace by causing their brain to focus on the words of the song and not the energy of the music and energy of the SM scene they were experiencing. I personally do not know the psychology or even physiology of music with words versus instrumental as it relates to turning on or off subspace experiences. But I can attest that 25 years ago, a lot of dungeon music was instrumental.

Following Enigma was a scene-related musician/electronic music composer working on a private project - ButtBoy. In my opinion, ButtBoy was the next step beyond Enigma, and the music actually had sounds or synthesizer effects that sounded like a whip or a flogger playing along to the music. The composer put out perhaps four or five CDs, and to this day, I tell folks not to waste money buying each one. Just buy the Best of ButtBoy album.

Dungeon music evolved again into a phase where electronic and dance music played a role (Delerium is an excellent example). Next, industrial and metal were the mainstays. Nine Inch Nails, Rammstein, Metallica, Disturbed, Korn, Kiss, Twisted Sister, Slayer, Slipknot, Motorhead, and the list could go on. These bands created music with heavy thrashing, a driving beat, and music that screamed crack on almost every beat. Sometimes, the music had distinctive vocals like Five Finger Death Punch, and sometimes, it had unrecognizable lyrics like a Slipknot song (some, not all). But they all had driving penetrable energy.

However, not all dungeon attendees like metal, and those who do may not like metal in the dungeon all the time. Many like classic rock. AC/DC, Van Halen, America, Creedence Clearwater, Orleans, Kansas, Journey, and Styx are all classic rock bands that played driving rhythms and memorable guitar riffs that included soaring vocals. The key to all of this music across genres is that there was a distinct recognizable rhythm, and it repeated itself at some point. Often, there were accent points that welcomed a crack. Of late, EDM or electronic dance music has made inroads, but I believe it is essentially a throwback to the electronic music of yesteryear, only without words.

Sometimes, good whip music is found in unlikely songs and from artists you would not normally associate with dungeon music. An example is Brian Adams' song, the Summer of '69. It is certainly not the typical style of dungeon song, yet it provides a perfect backdrop for a whip scene. And, when it hits the chorus, the music practically screams for a bullwhip crack on every measure's heavy beat. Summer of '69 is one of my favorite bullwhip songs, right beside Rammstein's Du Hast. These two songs have completely different styles, yet they provide a perfect example of the variations possible in advanced bullwhip play created through music selection.

Sometimes, a song or style of song connects with a particular class of whips. Ed Sheeran's Perfect is a good example of this. The song has beauty, grace, and flow that match a short snake whip. It is like a slow dance with a snake whip. I find it difficult to throw a bullwhip to that song as the technique of passive wrist, less arm movement, and stiff handle of the whip simply do not match the flow of the song. Perfect is "perfect" with the flow and grace of a snake whip.

Frequency of the Whip Matched to Speed of the Music. The frequency of a whip is another variable that interacts with the music or beats per minute of the music playing. This is especially true when you are throwing a rhythm-whip style. A five-foot bullwhip will throw at a different frequency than a three-foot bullwhip, just as a four-foot bullwhip throws at a different frequency. A four-foot natural belly bullwhip will throw and feel differently than a four-foot shot-loaded bullwhip or even a bullwhip loaded for martial arts fighting when used in dungeon play. All will have different abilities in the frequency ranges.

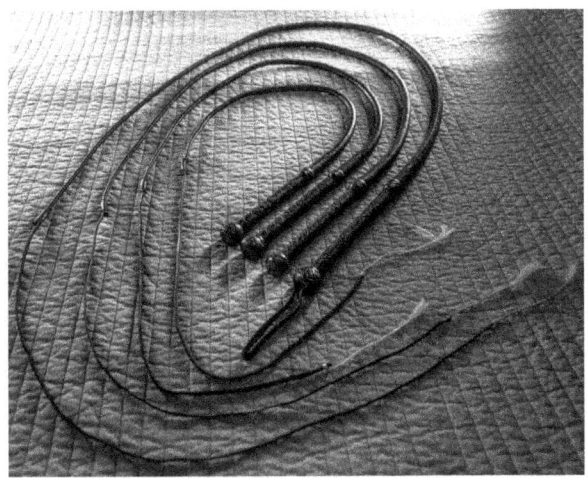

Photo 29 Frequency of a Whip. 6', 5', 4', 3' target bullwhips by Peter Jack.

Different types of dungeon play evoke thoughts of different types of music. When I think of violet wand, fire play, erotic massage, or tactile play scenes, I think of Enya, Secret Garden, or Delerium.

Rhythm-Whips. "Rhythm-whips" is an advanced technique that requires a connection between the rhythm of the whip and the music that is playing in the dungeon. Basically, throwing a rhythm-whip is throwing to the beat of the music playing. Sometimes, the music is slow enough that you are throwing on each beat of the music. Sometimes, you are throwing on every other beat, and sometimes, only on the heavy beat at the beginning of a measure of music.

Cracking in rhythm-whips only occurs when the music "says" to crack. This is regardless of the genre. Sometimes Enya's music, which I normally think of as soft, quiet mood music, will speak to me in the song and say, "crack". Often, an entire song will not have a crack in it and will be thrown to with whip rhythms that are subsonic and along the spectrum of controlled puffs. Secret Garden has some great songs that work in the dungeon but rarely evoke a crack.

I do not like to crack excessively. My philosophy is that a whip thrower should crack when the music is telling you to crack. When the music does not call for a crack, it works better to exchange energy by connecting the rhythm of the whip to the meter of the song that is playing. To crack when the music is not suggesting a crack is a distraction in the dungeon and contributes negative energy to the scene and to the overall dungeon orchestra. It would be analogous to playing in an orchestra and, in the middle of the piece, having the drummer take off into a drum solo that didn't match or complement the song that the orchestra was playing.

Since the whip in the dungeon is playing in harmony with the dungeon music, it is, in fact, a musical instrument itself. The whip is playing along, accompanying the song in a level of percussion while sending energy to the whip catcher. Many times, people sing along to the music playing in the car while driving. They might play drums on the steering wheel or dashboard to keep time with the music, hopefully when stopped at a light. This is no different than what the whip thrower is doing in the dungeon when the whip is connected to the rhythm of the music that is playing.

The same four-foot bullwhip will have a completely different dance feel and energy flow to the whip catcher when thrown to Enigma as compared to that whip being thrown to Rammstein or to Journey. Throwing to modern pop operas such as Il Volo's A Chi Mi Dice will produce a soaring feeling as the whip sails through the air, while the same whip playing to Five Finger Death Punch will finish heavy. The major variable is music. Music expands the whip's repertoire and makes it a primary instrument in the dungeon orchestra.

Playing with a Live DJ. As the music playlist in the dungeon is such an important variable to the scenes taking place, it might be beneficial to adjust the music selections based on the current energy in the dungeon. I have only played one time in a dungeon that had a live DJ. It was an interesting experience because just as a good DJ will read the audience and adjust his playlist to keep folks on the dance floor, a live DJ in the dungeon will watch the scenes in play and adjust his playlist to complement the live play in the dungeon. The music intensifies as the scenes build and slows down after the scenes have peaked.

Suggestions for Dungeon Owners, Event Promoters, and Play Party Organizers. Some people in charge of dungeon music have chosen to rely on an AI algorithm that cannot accurately react to the humans at play in a leather dungeon. I have yet to play to a Spotify playlist that was as good as any dungeon song playlist set by a living, breathing leather person. Pandora and Spotify are made better if you are willing to listen to hours of music and do the thumbs up and thumbs down to "train" the apps to your preferences. But if you are going to spend hours training software to make good choices, why not spend half the time and put together a playlist that you personally selected?[14]

The beauty of being asked to create dungeon playlists is that you can tailor the dungeon music to the tastes of the attendees in the dungeon. I use the same measure that a good DJ hosting a dance party would use. You want to keep the dancers on the floor dancing. In a dungeon, the goal should be to play music that keeps the dungeon goers on the floor playing and all of the equipment being used.

---

14 I've had the good fortune to be one of the people responsible for music for the leather event Weekend of Wickedness for many years.

Chapter 10

Mixing Play Genres to Create New Sensations

WHAT IS A mixed-play genre whip scene?

One might suppose it involves using a broad spectrum of whips and impact toys within a whip scene. Those are all great variations for impact play, but that is not what I consider mixed-genre whip play. Mixed genre whip scening, in my opinion, means using elements of BDSM play not typically expected in a whip scene.

Whip play/knife play mixed genre scenes. A whip thrower always needs a knife either on them or in their toy bag to cut the fluff on crackers and to trim a fall now and then. I carry a small traditional pocket folding knife for this purpose. But there is a whole genre of kinky dungeon play around knives.

Whether the whip thrower uses traditional folders, switchblades, fantasy knives, or hunting knives, using a knife with the whip bottom adds an edge (couldn't help it) to the scene. Just the feel, sound, and look of a knife add to a scene. The snap a switchblade makes when it opens can send chills down the spine of a whip catcher. A hunting knife worn on the belt can create anticipation at the beginning of a whip scene.

Many variations can be done during a whip scene by adding knife play. A good whip scene is about energy exchange and moving energy. Once the warmup is finished and heavier singletail work is done on both sides of the heart and root chakra, energy has been added to both chakras. If the chakras are open often, energy flows freely between the heart and root chakras through the chakra system. But sometimes, a little encouragement is needed to fully open the chakras. Energy can be moved with the knife in a Reiki-type technique or even using a light touch with the blade point or spine. The cold steel of metal on skin that is hot from a whip is not only an interesting and nice sensation, but it is an excellent way to move energy between the heart and root chakra. The knife can be used to move energy around the body and to provide an additional thrill to a whip scene without drawing blood just by using the steel to move energy.

Once the energy is moving freely between the root and heart chakras, the whip scene can continue in earnest with another layer of energy. This can be at the same level of controlled puff, as energy is additive and builds on what is already stored in the chakra system, or it can be taken up a notch or two in intensity and have a ramping effect.[15]

Another fun variation using knife play, if negotiated with your whip bottom, is skin etching using the knife tip. The whip scene could begin with the usual skin warm-up with a flogger, cat or quirt,

---

[15] Ideas for maintaining blades used in a scene—wipe the blade clean with a cloth rag after a scene as body oils, moisture from sweat, and possibly blood have contaminated the blade. When the blade arrives home, clean it with Barbicide or rubbing alcohol, and if the blade is carbon steel, put a light layer of sharpening oil on the blade. Then, put a crystal or two on the blade to remove any stored energy from the scene the blade might be holding. For a traditional folding knife, I normally only use one crystal; for a hunting knife with a longer blade, I will use two crystals, one close to the tip and one near the knife guard. I usually leave the crystals on the knife blade overnight, then place the crystals in direct sunlight from sunup to sunset so they, too, are cleansed and ready to use the next time needed. The blade is now ready for its next scene

and galley whip. Before the scene progresses, the knife etching can be introduced. I use a sharp knife with a pointed tip and lightly draw it across the skin. This will leave a light scratch or etching.

I am the type of dominant who likes to leave his mark on his property. I etched my initial on Moodstone's shoulder prior to one whip scene. As the whip scene progressed, her skin temperature rose, thus making the etching more prominent. Even if the scene is heavy and the shoulders become red, the red in the etching will be redder than the surrounding skin. I can tell you that I did enjoy seeing my mark on Moodstone. In her case, it lasted only for several hours. On other whip bottoms, it might even last for several days.

I offer a word of caution when using knife play in a whip scene. If the scratch is too deep, blood will weep to the surface during the scene. The goal of a good etching is to leave the whip thrower's mark, but not draw blood or turn it into a blood play scene. That type of scene, of course, is easily done given another slight variation to this whip/knife play scenario but adds other factors such as venue, dungeon rules, DM, etc.

Rope/whip play is a mixed genre. There are an infinite number of ways to tie someone in rope and many different aspects of rope play. There are floor ties, harnesses, and suspensions, to name a few. Tying someone and then whipping them can take on a wide variety of mixed-play scenarios and scenes. One may tie the bottom in a rope dress, providing a layer of rope to caress and compress the skin, and then whip over that overlay of rope. This provides a difference in sensation for the whip bottom. When the rope dress is removed, the skin is more sensitive from the compression, providing a different feeling when the top whips over the rope marks.

The whip scene that incorporates the damsel in distress vignette, or the helpless captive rope scene, calls for a higher level of trust from the rope bottom. Obviously, the bottom is not able to lean forward or step out of the way if the whip strikes become too intensive. That is part of the appeal of this type of scene. But if the whip thrower ever wants to play with the person again, they need to be very careful to read the whip bottom and stay within the pre-negotiated limits.

Suspension can be used for another mixed-genre scene involving rope. In this scene, the whip catcher is tied and suspended helplessly, and whip play progresses on acceptable target areas of the suspended whip catcher. The bottom's feeling of giving total control to the rigger and relaxing into the tie changes completely when that same bottom is then whipped. This is another version of the helpless captive scene, so again, extra care must be taken by the whip thrower to ensure a safe, enjoyable scene within everyone's pre-negotiated limits.

Photo 30 Moodstone suspended by Tigrrrr.

It is, in my opinion, somewhat rare to hear of a whip thrower having a consent violation. But when the whip thrower mixes rope play into a whip scene, it becomes especially important to negotiate every aspect of play that the whip thrower envisions. It is important also to never go beyond what was negotiated while the scene is in progress. This means there should be no renegotiating during the scene. The next scene can always include changes in the play negotiations.

Pallet Wrap/Whip Mixed Play. Pallet wrap or Saran wrap (plastic wrap) is sometimes used as a tool in bondage play. It can be used to restrain the limbs, attach someone to a piece of dungeon equipment, or completely encase someone in a mummification type of restraint. Similar to rope scenes, pallet wrap scenes can add a thrilling level to a whip scene.

Pallet wrap provides a layer over the skin that changes the sensation of whip strikes. An intense bullwhip strike is not so intense when shielded with pallet wrap. Because of this, pallet wrap provides variation in play and also serves as a safety measure for the whip thrower who may not be completely comfortable with their own skill level.

A whip bottom who is pallet wrapped to a whipping post in a complete mummified encasement can safely be played with and whipped almost anywhere there is pallet wrap providing a layer between the whip strike and the skin. The head and neck should be avoided, but almost any other part of the body can be played with safely once it is pallet wrapped.

For a more challenging variation, holes can be cut in the pallet wrap, leaving areas of exposed skin that become targets for the whip thrower.

The same cautions apply for pallet wrap scenes as for rope scenes concerning staying within pre-negotiated limits.

Candle and Wax Play/Whip Play. The first and most obvious scene that comes to mind for incorporating wax play into a whip scene is the wax removal scene. The scene will start with wax play, with the wax left to dry on the bottom's skin. Then, the whip thrower has the challenge of removing the wax with the whip. This is not as easy as it may sound, but it provides lots of fun for both the top and bottom.

Wax removal is often a phase in a wax scene where the scene is calming down. The sensation of fresh air hitting the previously waxed skin is cooling and refreshing.

However, we are talking about using a whip for wax removal. A whip scene segmented at the end of a wax scene will probably not be a cooling part of the scene but a way to ramp up or provide a different transition in a wax scene.

Wax scenes always have the potential to be messy, and this is especially true when the wax is whipped off. Be sure to put a large enough drop cloth on the floor surrounding the area where the scene is taking place.

It is unlikely that the top will be able to remove all of the wax from the whip catcher with a whip. Once the whip scene is winding down, tops can use a variety of methods for wax removal. Probably one of the most common is to combine wax play with knife play and use a knife for wax removal. (A credit card works well, too.)

Another scene with wax and whips is to encase the whip catcher's back side from the top of the shoulders to the bottom of the butt cheeks. Then cut out a four-inch square of wax off of each shoulder and butt cheek, thereby exposing the skin on the normal target areas for the whip. This provides an interesting canvas for the whip thrower. When the whip is thrown, it will give contrasting sensations for the whip catcher as the whip either hits the targets or hits the remaining waxed areas. When the scene ends, and the wax is removed, there will be marks only within the four-inch targeted areas – a picture-worthy ending to a different type of whip scene.

Needle/Whip Play Mixed Genre. Needles create a different kind of endorphin rush than impact play. However, needle play can be incorporated into a whip scene with pleasing results.

Once needles are securely in place on the bottom's target areas, they can be covered with saran wrap, pallet wrap, or a Tagederm barrier and then played with using a whip.

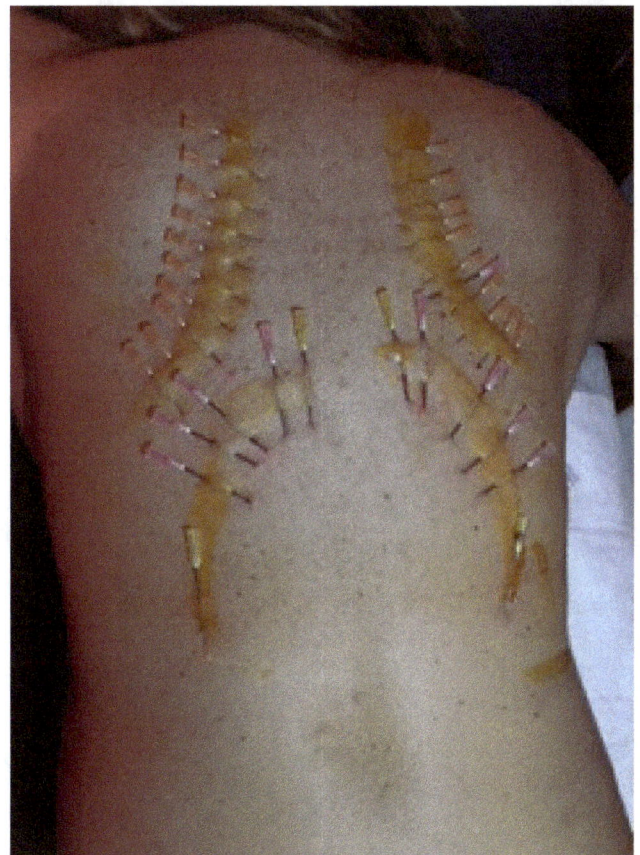

Photo 31 Needle play/Whip mixed genre. Caution cover needles with Tagederm or pallet/plastic wrap before playing

Whips of almost all classes can be used in combination with this type of mixed-genre play. This, of course, is edge play.

Be aware that it is possible to break a needle doing this type of play, and precautions must be taken. A backup plan for needle removal from the skin should be in place just in case an accident happens. This type of planning prevents embarrassing situations where a doctor needs to get involved.

One way to limit the possibility of breaking a needle during impact play with a whip is to use only larger gauge needles. A small gauge needle, such as a 25-gauge needle, might be perfect for many types of needle play, but it is not so great for the hybrid whip/needle scene. I would not use a needle smaller than a 21 or 22-gauge needle as the thicker needle is less likely to break or bend.

If the top uses alcohol to clean the skin before needle play and then uses a sterile barrier such as Tagederm, the chance of infection is less likely. I recommend you take those precautions. I have seen a top who was a piercer do temporary piercings and then use pallet wrap as a barrier, but while the pallet wrap might be clean and provide a quasi-sanitary barrier, it is not a sterile barrier.

There will be more about needle play and whips in the vignettes section.

Chapter 11

Two-handed Whip Work: Twice the Sensations

I BEGAN LEARNING two-handed whip work when I was twenty-four years into my leather journey. I'm about a year and a half into that journey and have much left to learn. But at this moment in time, I actually do have some ideas to share that might help others in their two-handed whip journey. Following the WITD approach to learning singletail and staying true to the focus on contact dungeon play, we continue our leather journey into two-handed whip-throwing.

Practice With Your Non-dominant Hand. One of the practice techniques stressed in WITD is to practice with your non-dominant hand. Every minute you practice with your non-dominant hand will make your dominant hand feel smarter and make the whip feel more comfortable, like an extension of that dominant hand. This technique is a key element in improving your single-hand or dominant-hand whip throwing. But simultaneously, you are building muscle memory and skill in your non-dominant hand and arm.

Hand-Switch Technique. Throw dynamically with your dominant hand (either horizontal or forward figure 8) and after a few cycles transfer the whip to the non-dominant hand and keep the momentum and pattern going. This results in a hand-switch, then switch back. Use this as an intermediate practice routine while saving up for your matched set of whips. Also use it in the dungeon if your dominant arm gets tired and the bottom is wanting more whip. It will add yet another variation to your whip play.

Draw on Adult Learning Theory. Adults learn new skills quicker by applying skills they have already acquired to the new learning task. At this point in our two-handed whip journey, we are not introducing new techniques but working on the techniques we use with a single whip and applying them to throwing with both hands.

All of the practice and play time we have throwing two-handed floggers will speed our two-handed whip journey along. All of the time we've acquired in throwing two-handed cat o' nine tails will speed our journey along. All of the time spent throwing two-handed galley whips will speed the journey along. Even the time spent throwing single-handed floggers, quirts, cats, and dragontails will help, as learning is additive and builds on itself. The part of the brain that has mapped the muscle memory when throwing with your dominant hand now mirrors that mapping to support throwing with the non-dominant hand.

This does not mean non-dominant hand whip throwing will not feel awkward at first. It does not mean your non-dominant hand will be as accurate or achieve the same finesse as your dominant hand. But it means all of these skill points will improve exponentially quicker than when you were originally learning single-handed throwing.

Cost of Two-handed Whip Throwing. Ideally, for two-handed work, you need a matched set of every type of impact implement thrown in dungeon play. Having a matched set (as opposed to an unmatched set) will speed up your learning curve with two-handed whip throwing. This is because unmatched sets thrown two-handed will not throw and feel the same in both hands. It is, therefore, ideal if they are built by the same whip maker side by side and end up as nearly identical as possible.

The following is what one obsessed whip thrower (that would be me) bought on his two-handed whip journey:

> Matched set of traditional handled floggers ($320)
> Matched set of finger floggers ($190)
> Matched set of cat o' nines (hybrid whip-like) ($625)
> Matched set of galley whips ($400)
> Matched set of dragontails ($380)
> Matched set of signal whips (recommend four-foot signal whips) ($480)
> Matched set of three-foot snake whips ($786 [8500 SEK])
> Matched set of four-foot bull whips ($590)
> Matched set of three-foot paracord bullwhips ($240)

These are priced to give you an idea of what I spent on my two-handed journey the year before the writing of this book. Prices will change over time and between whip makers. The point is that a matched set is not quite double the cost of a single whip, as some whip makers give a slight price break when ordering a matched set, but it is pretty close to the cost of two whips.

Minimums, in my opinion, for progressing quickly to two-handed work would be a set of floggers, a set of dragontails, and a set of signal whips. For those who can afford them, a matching set of cats is also an excellent addition. The feel and flow of hybrid cats are very close to the feel and throw of a short singletail (three-foot signal whips), so practicing and playing two-handedly with these cats have accelerated my two-handed whip journey (See Photo 8, cats; Photo 9, galley whips; Photo 14 & 18 Signals).

Photo 32 Traditional handled goat skin floggers by Happy Tails

Photo 33 Finger Floggers by Leather Passion

Photo 34 Matched set of double ended floggers by Abraided Leather

Paracord Whips. A more affordable option in someone's two-handed journey is paracord whips. As a general rule of thumb, a quality paracord whip will be nearly half the cost of a kangaroo whip. For example, I needed a matched set of three-foot bullwhips in my arsenal for those infrequent occasions when I am invited to a house party or have the opportunity to attend a party at a boutique dungeon location. A matched set of kangaroo three-foot bullwhips would be ~$510. A matched set of three-foot paracord bullwhips cost me $240. You can see the logic behind buying paracord for this particular solution in my arsenal.[16]

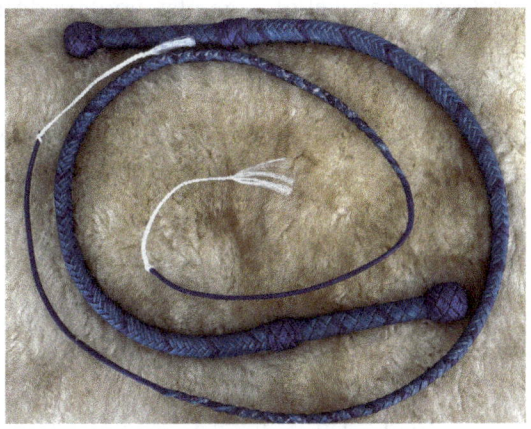

Photo 35 TheSwordGuyBuilds parachord bullwhips

Matched Sets.

In my opinion, it is not as critical for some classes of whips that they be completely identical twins for two-handed whip throwing. Dragontails, to be identical twins, would have to be made from the same grade and weight of leather, from the same skins, and made to be identically the same length. However, for dragontails to be thrown

---

[16] At the time of this writing, the paracord plaiters I recommend are Iris Whips, 21st Century Whips, and The Sword Guy Builds. All have websites, and all are reputable.

accurately in two-handed work, this level of detail is not necessary. Two different weights of leather can be thrown two-handed as long as the two dragontails are exactly the same length (e.g., four-foot tails). I consider these dragontails to be sister whips but not identical twins. For dragontails, quirts, cat o' nine, and galley whips, sister whips of the same length are more than adequate to use for two-handed work.

When it comes to signals, snake whips, and bull whips, it is very important that the sets are more specifically matched. They need to be identical twins primarily because of the whip thrower's mantra that small changes on the throwing end result in large changes on the receiving end and the level of edge play you are doing with these classes of whips. A flogger, cat o' nine, quirt, galley whip, and dragontail are not going to be played with near the sound barrier. Play with all of them is impact play but it is usually not edge play.

With a signal, snake, and bullwhip, all are played with at or near the sound barrier, and that is edge play. But now we are doing two-handed edge play and playing with a singletail with our non-dominant hand at or near the speed of sound. It is important that the feel, build, flow and exact length of both whips be as close to identical as possible. This will eliminate other variables and allow the whip thrower to throw with both hands with confidence that one of the whips will not go awry and land where it wasn't intended.

There are different approaches to plaiting a matched set. Therefore, you should communicate with the whip maker and find out what methods they are using. Below are some methods used by whip makers I buy from.

Fraternal Twin Matched Set. This type of matched set will have each whip made side by side, but one whip finished before the other one. For example, a belly could be plaited for the whip hanging on the left without much attention paid to where strands were dropped. Then the whip hanging on the right would have the same belly plaited with the whip maker trying to match exactly what they did with the whip on the left, often trying to remember or feel where those drops were made. This results in two whips very close to being built the same way but not identical twins.

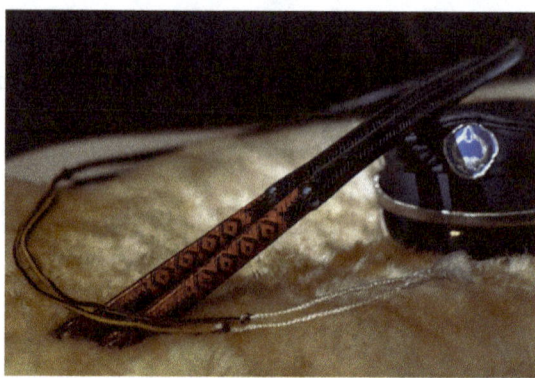

Photo 36 Black king cobra eating a diamond back rattlesnake 4' 16 plait matched set by Smokey Mountain Whips (Blake Gorey)

Identical Twin Matched Set. This type of matched set will also have each whip made side by side. The handles will be cut exactly the same length, and the core built exactly the same way. But when the belly is built for the whip on the left, attention will be paid to the plaiting, and where a dropped strand occurs will be marked. Then, when the belly on the right is created, the strand will be dropped in exactly the same place.

This is also done with the overlay plaiting so that when the whip is finished, both whips side by side look like identical twins. They are a matched set and exactly the same length. The feel and balance between both whips are identical or extremely close to being identical.

Photo 37 Witchcraft Whips 3' matched 16 plait snake whips

Even in real life, identical twins are not completely identical. Nuances will exist, and personality differences. Likewise, with identical, matched whips, personality differences exist. Do not be surprised if your non-dominant hand ends up preferring a particular whip in a matched set over the other whip.

Mirrored Twin Matched Set. A mirrored twin matched set will be plaited exactly the same way an identical twin matched set is plaited up until when the whip maker comes to the overlay. In the case of the overlay, the whip will be plaited like someone is looking in a mirror. The whip on the left will be plaited as if you were looking directly at the whip, and the whip on the right will be plaited in reverse as if you were looking at the whip in a mirror. This results in a fabulous-looking matched set of whips.

Photo 38 handle pattern of Peter Jack No. 47 bullwhips commemorating his 47th year of plaiting whips.

Two-handed Flogger Practice. I recommend that you start your two-handed flogger practice with traditional handled matched floggers. Mine are made out of goat skin. You would do well to start with a matched set made of lightweight leather and leather in the softer spectrum, such as deerskin, lamb, or goat. The softer, lightweight leathers add an additional safety margin when practicing. They will also allow you to transition to actual dungeon play quicker than if you were trying to throw a matched set of heavy, stingy floggers. Because of the softness and added margin of safety, you can afford a miss-hit or mistake without ruining a dungeon scene.

Two-handed flogging provides a nice warmup for your whip scene. You will find warmup goes quicker as you strike the target zone twice as many times by throwing two-handed. This is simple mathematical common sense.

Timing and Rhythm Two-handed. As with one-handed throwing, there are differences in timing and rhythm that can be achieved by throwing two-handed.

You can throw with **together timing** where both floggers are thrown simultaneously and strike the skin simultaneously. You can throw alternating floggers in either a **staggered timing** (syncopated) or a **distributed timing** (opposite each other; when one tail is back, the other tail is forward striking). These can be thrown whirlybird style without crossing the body, or they can be thrown in a four-count or a six-count Florentine pattern (called a three-beat weave by poi spinners).

Throwing two-handed traditional handled floggers relates more closely to throwing a single-handed flogger. Two-handed finger floggers relate closely to the feel and technique of spinning poi. There is more swinging of the tails in two-handed finger floggers than throwing the tails with traditional handles.

All of the time spent throwing two-handed floggers will speed up the journey with two-handed singletails. As I stressed in my first book and continue to stress here, learning for adults is additive, and all of the time spent practicing these techniques, whether with two-handed floggers, two-handed cats, or two-handed dragontails will convert to muscle memory when two-handed singletails are picked up.

Two-handed Cat Practice. My preference for two-handed cat o' nines is to throw with hybrid cats: cats that have a whip-like thong as opposed to cats that have a traditional flogger handle.

Hybrid cats are very time-consuming to make. Many whip makers will not make them and, most likely, prefer not to. As a result, they are pricey (especially a quality hybrid cat o' nine). Still, if you want to become proficient in two-handed whip throwing, the hybrid cats will get you there more quickly.

Hybrid cats have a whip-like thong, which is unlike the thong on a traditional flogger-handled cat. Cats made this way essentially have a whip thong for half their total length, and the second half is finished with nine tails ending in a variety of knots (my favorite being a crown or soap knot) with three or four inches of tassel following the knot.

The stranding width greatly influences how a cat o' nine will "sail" or fly through the air. Most cat makers I have come across use six-mm stranding to make their tails. This applies to any cat, though here I am talking about hybrids. A cat with six-mm stranding will catch more air, experience more drag, finish thuddier, and provide less variation in sensations on the receiving end. A cat o' nine finished with three-mm stranding will fly easier, make it easier to keep the tails together, catch less air, and finish with more precision. A three-mm stranded cat will allow a range of sensations from feathering up to stingy sensations. I own a matched set of tomcats with 3-mm stranding.

I have mentioned that practicing two-handed with hybrid cats is, in my opinion, the most productive way to progress in two-handed whip throwing skills. This is because cats are easier to control in two-handed throwing than are typical singletail whips, yet they provide a closer experience to bull or snake whip throwing than do a set of floggers.

When practicing with the hybrid cats, practice throwing alternating hand, whirlybird, together timing, staggered timing, and distributed timing. Practice alternating over the shoulder, horizontal style, two-handed forward figure eight (four-count Florentine), and six-count Florentine. Learning is additive, and all of the time spent throwing two-handed hybrid cats will get you to singletails quicker.

Photo 39 3mm (by Happy Tails) and 6mm (by Abraided Leather) stranded cat o' nine tails

Dragontail Practice. I own a three-foot dragontail and four four-foot dragontails. Generally, dragontails are matched in length, but the weight of the leather used to make them could vary.

I do not own matching dragons where the weight of the leather is matched. So, I practice with two four-foot dragontails of different weights, sister whips but not identical twins. Since I'm right-handed, I throw the heavier tail with my left hand as I feel the heavier tail sails truer with less effect from gravity. I throw the lighter tail with my dominant hand as I feel that hand more naturally adapts to the impact of gravity on the tail as it sails through the air. You may find this is not a factor, or you might acquire two dragontails of the same weight (a true matched set).

Dragontails are the first two-handed singletails that I practiced with. All of the same patterns I've been practicing apply to dragontails, and I now feel confident enough in my skill to continue six-count Florentine with them.

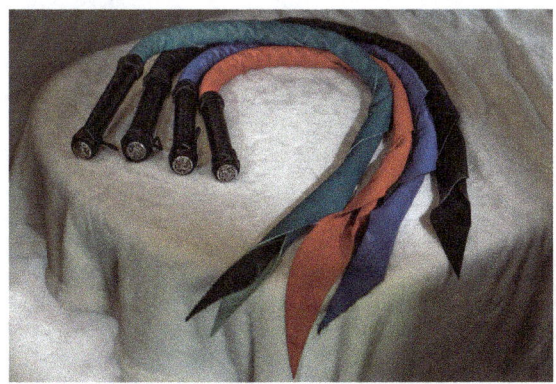

Photo 40 Dragontails side by side.

Signal Whip Practice. I own a matched set of three-foot and four-foot signal whips. As I like to say, everyone should own a three-foot signal whip as it is the one singletail that can almost always be thrown in small dungeons and at house parties. A four-foot signal, however, is a lot more fun to throw. So, for two-handed throwing, a matched set of four-foot signal whips will provide the best satisfaction for the whip thrower and much joy for the whip bottom. Moodstone says they are some of her favorites.

The advantage of throwing signal whips two-handed is that you do not have to manage the fall rollout and don't have to worry about the falls becoming tangled. It is a rarity, even with together timing, for signal whip crackers to become tangled.

All of the WITD practice techniques and patterns apply to three-foot signal whips thrown two-handed, except for the bow and arrow. I personally do not throw six-count Florentine with four-foot signal whips as I feel on the out-and-around part of the pattern, I lose accuracy, and doing it then becomes primarily for show and not for effect on the whip bottom. Perhaps as I become better with throwing two-handed, six-count Florentine will migrate into my two-handed four-foot signal play.

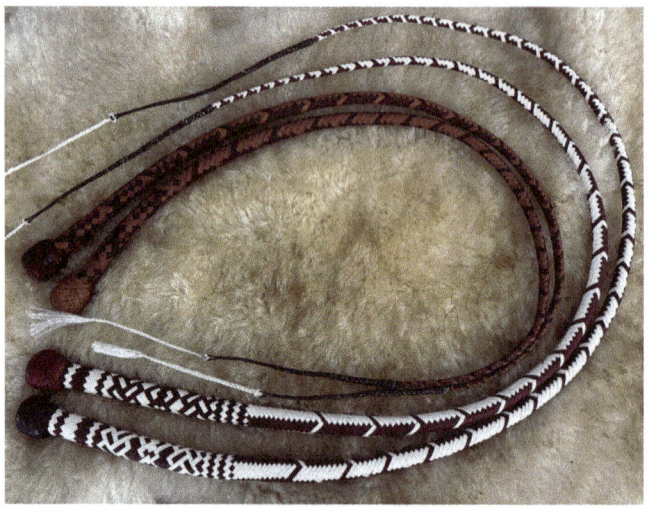

Photo 41 3' & 4' Mojave Outliers signal whips side by side.

Snake Whip Practice. My choice of snakes for two-handed dungeon play is a matched pair of three-foot snake whips. This provides four to four and a half feet total length and a fall to provide fluidity to the motion of the whip and rollout. Snake whips can be thrown using dynamic grounding[17] and distributed timing, and the result is an even strike from feathered to controlled puffs. Stalling each side and flicking will result in distributed to staggered timing with increasing intensity to the level of puff you achieve (Refer to Photo 38). Together timing surprisingly rarely results in tangled crackers. When moving near the speed of sound, one whip will slightly lead the other whip even when thrown together. But, the sound of the crackers will be together to even the discerning ear.[18]

---

[17] Dynamic grounding is when a short whip is allowed to layout in an arc or radius and follow that radius completely laid out in its complete cycle of a forward figure 8. When a long whip is grounded, it is laid out on the ground either in front of or behind the whip thrower. A short whip cannot be grounded because it is too short. So allowing it to layout completely forming a radius on its path of travel while being dynamically thrown is a way to achieve grounding while the whip is in motion.

[18] Together, Staggered and Distributed timing are defined and discussed later in this chapter. Feel free to jump ahead if you are unsure what this means.

Two-handed snake whip throwing can be done using all of the WITD techniques except for bow and arrow and horizontal.

Bullwhip Practice. Two-handed bullwhip practice follows the same patterns described in previous practice descriptions with two exceptions (Refer to Photos 37 & 39). The two exceptions are bow and arrow and horizontal.

As stated before, many dungeons are not large enough to accommodate a four-foot bullwhip, which is about six to six and a half feet in total length, let alone two-handed four-foot bullwhips. You must become familiar with the dungeons and spaces you play in and decide if there is enough room for two-handed, four-foot bullwhips. A three-foot bullwhip will be four and a half feet to five feet in total length and can be used in more dungeons than the longer whips.

If you buy bullwhips too long to throw in your dungeon haunts, then you will be forced to go to the park and sport crack with them. Do not waste your money if your true goal is dungeon play. Buy whips that you can actually throw in the dungeons you frequent.

Two-handed Technique. Static and Dynamic.

Static: Over the shoulder. Two static techniques are taught in *Whips in the Dungeon* – bow and arrow (slingshot) and over the shoulder (sometimes called off the shoulder). Only over the shoulder applies to two-handed throwing. The reason is that bow & arrow requires two hands to throw and, therefore, is exclusively a single whip technique.

Over the shoulder can be done off the same shoulder as the throwing hand or off the opposite shoulder from the throwing hand (cross-handed). Cross-handed is a little tricky, as it is easier for the whips to become tangled. I teach this technique using a thumb push grip, but other grips can be adapted and are fine for over the shoulder. Timing and patterns will be discussed later.

Dynamic: Horizontal or Florentine

Horizontal. Horizontal two-handed throwing is sometimes called over-under. (WITD 201.24) It can be done with an East Coast Swing with both hands moving simultaneously, or it can be done slightly off-timing to create a staggered timing. The hands will release the whip throw opposite each other for distributed timing. Either hand can be on top, but once the whips start flying, they stay in the same position relative to which one is on top and which one is on the bottom. Hands can be switched from top to bottom every once in a while. Just switching one hand from the top to the bottom when throwing horizontally will result in a slight change of sensation felt by the whip catcher.

Photo 42 Horizontal two handed. Over/under style.

Florentine: Four-count and six-count. Six-count Florentine with floggers is fun and impressive to watch when the top can keep the tails together, and it creates flowing and beautiful energy for the top and bottom. When done fluently, it will result in alternating energy from one side of the chakra to the other.

When moving this pattern to singletails, it becomes exponentially more difficult to keep the tail on the target zone with finesse for all six counts. I'm not saying it cannot be done or learned, but it will take many more hours and possibly years of practice before moving this from the sheepskin or t-shirt target practice to live dungeon play (for me).

From an adult learning perspective, all the time spent using this technique will eventually translate to snakes and bullwhips. But for now... I do not practice 6-count Florentine with bullwhips. Having said that, I haven't given up on throwing six-count Florentine. Peter Jack, for my year 48 build, is making me a matched set of 4-foot mini-Zenith bullwhips, which is the scaled-down version of a full-size Zenith bullwhip. The main reason is that I want to play with the added flexibility the tapered box knot adds to the thong and see if it helps with the flow and accuracy of my six-count Florentine in keeping it on target. This is an expensive experiment, but the entire two-whip journey has been expensive.

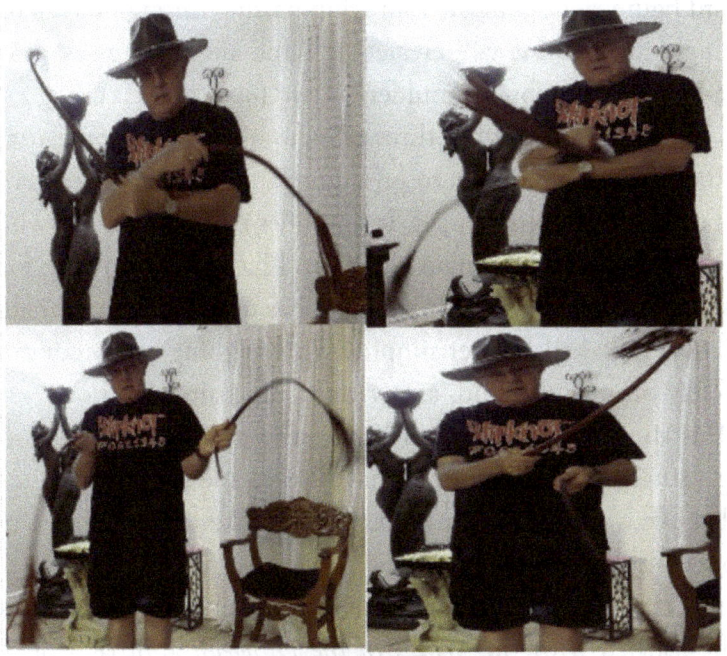

Photo 43 Four count Florentine

Focus Points. I only practice four-count Florentine with either a single or two focus points. Using four focus points would require altering the elevation of the pattern, another variable that would need to be added to the practice. Instead, throw at two focus points and change elevation by flexing and straightening the knees. Use straight knee throwing at the shoulders and flexed knee to lower the consistent two-focus point pattern to the butt. By doing this, you are throwing at two focus points but achieving contact with the four target areas—shoulder-shoulder and butt-butt. I think, eventually, I will be able to make this adjustment with my hand release angle, and it will be much easier on my legs.

Angel wings. If you are trying to achieve "angel wings" on the shoulders, use one focal point. Focus on the middle of the back while throwing a forward figure eight pattern. Your whip passing through its arc toward the single focus point will create the same angel wings as throwing single-handed using both shoulders as two focus points. Using a single focus point allows the whip thrower, who now has to concentrate on what both hands are doing, to give more attention to the pattern and arc of the whips into the target. It simplifies two-handed throwing.

In my case, my dominant right hand has been throwing for 25+ years, and my left non-dominant hand has been throwing for about a year and a half, so I further simplify what is going on by concentrating solely on my left hand, as my right hand already knows what to do. This simplification of focusing on the non-dominant hand and using a single focus target point has allowed me to transition to two-handed live work in the dungeon much quicker than if I were taking a more complex approach.

In short, four-count Florentine can be done with singletails and can be learned with the *Whips in the Dungeon* approach of applying what you already know to your practice. This will result in you quickly bringing your skills into the dungeon.

Six count Florentine, unless the top has had extensive prior practice two-handed with this technique using floggers and cats, will require hours, months, and possibly even years of practice before the singletails can be feathered accurately. This does not mean six-count is not worthy of practice or worthy of incorporating into your dungeon play. It means you should not expect this skill to come quickly but to smile when it finally does.

Three Beat Weave or the Poi-Spinning Approach. Again, if you have experience spinning poi or extensive experience using finger floggers and doing four- and six-count Florentine, then adult learning theory will apply, and you will be building on all of that previous experience. You will get there quicker by taking a poi-spinning approach than by building off of the forward figure eight approach. This might also mean you prefer a different grip on your whips than a traditional handshake grip.

Folks who have cut their teeth on finger floggers might prefer holding the whip between their index and middle fingers. Another grip involves using the thumb and index finger to form a "C" shaped grip and letting the heel knot rotate in the palm of your hand as you throw your whips poi style. There is an entire vocabulary around different techniques and timing using poi. I will not go into it at this time as it is a different direction than my path with leather. I will just say it is equally valid and might be the way to go for different people.

Timing. Together, Staggered, and Distributed.

Together. In together-timing, the whips are thrown at or very near the same time toward the target. Moving at or near the speed of sound, the whips make a controlled puff or crack so close together in timing that it audibly makes one sound, or what sounds like only one sound; because the sounds are so close together, the sound waves overlap, and the human ear hears it as one or close to one sound.

Surprisingly, the whips rarely get tangled when throwing together timing. Even though they are moving near the speed of sound, their timing will be off just enough that the crackers rarely come together and become tangled. The chance of tangling is further reduced if you are targeting one shoulder with one whip and the other shoulder with the other whip. Even when using only one focus point, say the middle of the back, the arc of each whip will travel across each shoulder and make a puff slightly before it gets to the focal point in the middle of the back. The result will be that together-timing can be thrown with confidence and little worry of entanglement.

If the whips get tangled, just untangle them and begin again. Don't let this throw you off. It takes talent to tangle two whips when they are both moving close to the speed of sound! Think of together timing as always throwing on the one or the heavy beat of the music that is playing. Together-timing can be done with both the over the shoulder technique and four-count Florentine. I do not see any way to do together-timing with six-count Florentine.

Photo 44 Together Timing. Closely examine whip rollout shows whips thrown to arrive together.

Staggered. Think of staggered timing as syncopated timing. Or, if you were going to count it, one - and. You will be throwing on the heavy beat or downbeat of the music with the second whip following quickly or close to the original heavy beat on an "and" count.

Audibly, the sounds will be close together but distinctly two sounds, which is so different from together-timing. Some might want to count this as one and two, but it comes quicker than the second beat of music, so better to think of it as one and. I find this rhythm to be the easiest of the three timing patterns. I naturally fall into staggered timing without even thinking about it. I have to focus more when doing together timing and I struggle with distributed timing.

Staggered timing can be achieved using over the shoulder, four-count Florentine and, with some advanced skill, on two of the six beats of six-count Florentine.

Photo 45 Staggered Timing. Whips show arriving one before the other. Syncopated timing.

Distributed. Distributed timing should be the easiest and simplest of the two-handed whip timings to master. However, I have found it to be the most difficult.

To break it down, when one whip is going forward toward the target, the opposing whip is coming back on a recovery stroke or path. Think of the whips as being roughly 180º from each other. In count timing, with perhaps the left hand leading, the left-hand whip would be thrown toward the whip bottom on the one and three beats of the music playing to four beats to a measure. At the same time, the right-hand whip would be thrown on the two and four beats of the music playing. Distributed timing can be thrown in the over the shoulder style and with four- and six-count Florentine.

Photo 46 Distributed Timing. One whip arrives while the other whip is in recovery. Opposite timing.

Connecting to the Music. As with any great whip scene, connecting the energy of the music and the surrounding dungeon scenes to the energy exchange between the whip top and whip bottom is important. Connecting the rhythm and flow of the whips to the rhythm of the music is important and cannot be overemphasized. Mixing throwing techniques and timing patterns to match and interpret the music not only allows connection to the music but also makes the mastery of two-hand work transcend into a virtuoso whip scene.

Introducing Master LeatherRedux. At SouthEast LeatherFest 2023, I met Master LeatherRedux (MLR) for the first time when she attended my three-hour whip intensive. We instantly connected spiritually, as we each had a love of whips and the ability to translate that love of whips into a spiritual connection with the bottom we were playing with in the dungeon.

We shared time and space for two nights in dungeon play, watching each other throw and playing side by side with whip catchers. We did not chat much as we were both there to do one thing - connect with the beloved whip bottoms standing for us and use the energy of the whip to not only drive the energy in the dungeon but to commune with that energy on a different level. When this happens, there is no need to talk, as you can feel the energy and the spirit move from you down the whip to the catcher and out into a shared dungeon space.

Not many whip throwers who simply love to crack can do this type of play, and I would say none of them taking a pure cracking approach to whips will ever achieve a sense of spirituality in their play. The love of leather does not transcend the whip; instead, it is symbiotic, with the whip as a medium for connecting the bottom's chakras with a shared love of leather. We were in the dungeon to commune with leather in a sacred space, and our connection to each other began to grow.

Once the event was over, our long-winded and lengthy messaging back and forth over Fetlife, rarely laconic, sealed the friendship, which quickly blossomed into a leather brother and sister relationship. I'm happy to call MLR a sister and part of my leather family. She is fabulous with Florentine and has graciously agreed to write a section sharing her perspective on two-handed whip work.

Florentine Whips - - The Art of Flow

Sometimes, Florentine, in the kink world, gets a bad rap. Those who can either use two floggers or whips at the same time are often held in awe by others. But that is not always the case. I read a comment on social media that claimed, "Those who do Florentine are arrogant show-offs." Well, I say there is some truth to both perspectives.

Using whips in play is already a small niche. Whether we like to admit it or not, when we are being watched at a play party or event, there is a bit of performance involved. The balance is to find the discipline to put in the time to Florentine well and safely. Theatrics may be inserted, but not at the expense of your connection with your play partner.

For some, whips are used to induce or incite energy, which comes with the euphoria of sub space or the release of orgasm. For me, as a top, Florentine whipping builds a deeper connection and an energetic rush when the vibe is right. Sometimes, it feels like the play has moved to another dimension, creating a meditative, out-of-body experience.

The style of Florentine throwing, historically, relates back to fighters in Renaissance Florence, Italy, who fought with a dagger and a sword or two swords versus the more traditional shield and sword. In modern times, Filipino martial artists are known to use two weapons simultaneously—either two rattan sticks or knives. In some martial arts, a whip and a dagger are used.

But no matter what context, the Florentine style requires an understanding of flow - the energy created to procure various reactions out of a person. Understanding how energy moves from the top's hands and flows through the bottom's body and back out to the top is a deeper level or sense. The energy creates a power circuit between two people in a scene. It is the energy that is sent back and forth in a loop. For both parties, this can be euphoric and sometimes healing.

Photo 47 Master LeatherRedux throwing Florentine

Vet your tops and bottoms if this type of play is something you want to try. Ask A LOT of questions. Ask tops and bottoms about the person in question. Assess their skills as a top or a bottom. Do they have a good aim? Do they communicate with their play partner? Do they do aftercare?

But most importantly, do they flow with the flavor that you are looking for? Make sure you ask and get what you want, no matter what side of the slash you are on.

Here are some helpful hints from a true Florentine artist on how to raise your skill level in Florentine whip throwing.

Pro Tips from Master LeatherRedux

Get the Right Tools

The first thing about learning to Florentine with whips is to get a good matched pair. Whether you purchase a paracord or kangaroo pair, make sure they are made as a set. This will ensure fluid and accurate motion. The conscious knowledge that they are created as a set, will help to rule out any inconsistencies in the workmanship.

Be prepared to spend some money to get a good matched pair.

Can't afford them immediately? Get a matched set of dragon tails or tongues to learn the movement or action of a light and dynamic whip.

Once you get your whips, make sure to condition them. This is a preference among whip enthusiasts. For kangaroo whips, some may say, no need to condition them. Just start throwing them to break them in. I was taught by my mentor ReadnFool to use Pecard's Leather Dressing and apply them on each whip before using them.

Apply the dressing below the area where your hands hold the whip and before you get to the fall or the fall hitch of the whip. The oils from your hands will add moisture to the part [where] you hold whips so no need to add Pecard there. Let the warmth from your hand melt the dressing and get absorbed into the whip. It takes about a day for the dressing to get absorbed. Keep applying for maybe three or four days. Each whip is different. When it stays tacky and won't get absorbed any more, wipe off the excess and start throwing them.

As for paracord whips, some makers will add a wax coating while others do not. Adding wax will change the way it throws and the break in time. It is a preference. I prefer not to have the wax coating since the throw is easier.

Get Throwing! Or Practice Makes Better - - Not Perfect!

Florentine isn't easy and will require practice. Like any new venture, it may not look great at first or even downright ugly. Only practice and time will smooth out the movement and add that flair. So get a hat and some eye protection and start practicing. Make sure you are wearing a long sleeve shirt, jeans and boots.

The throws you can do are the following:

- The 4-beat weave
- The 6-beat weave
- Windmills or twirling them at your side
    - ☐ These can be done on the beat or alternating rhythms

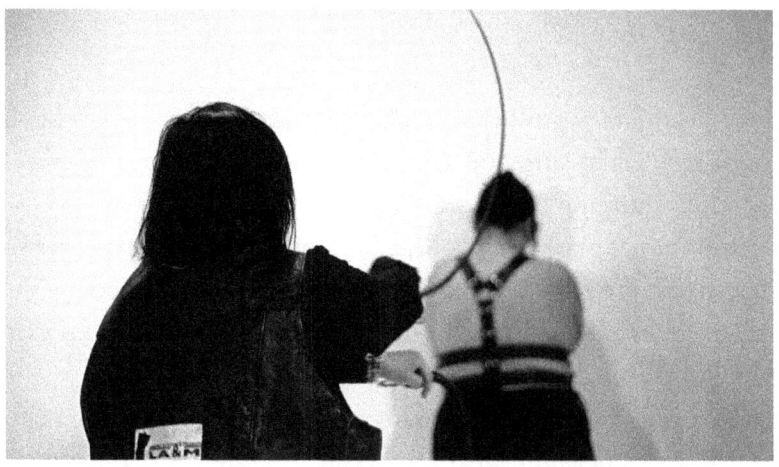

Photo 48 Master LeatherRedux throwing 2 whips

Getting familiar and comfortable with these throws is the beginning of building the muscle memory for doing Florentine.

Once you have the movements down pat, you need to work on your accuracy.

You can get the following items:

- A microfiber blanket
  - Place this at body height to learn where you are hitting
  - Where the popper leaves a mark should help you adjust aim
- Post-its, tissues or handkerchiefs
  - Hang these off a wall [or] off a surface to knock off or touch them consistently
- Bells or cat toys
  - Hang these to see how accurately you can make that object "ding"

Remember to give yourself grace! Don't beat yourself up if it doesn't kick in quickly. You're learning. Don't get discouraged and make sure to get some live instruction. This should come in both a competent top and an experienced bottom. The top can help you with technique, but the bottom will let you know (if they are honest) if you're too high or reaching, which creates inconsistent hits.

X Marks the Spot!

As you negotiate for this type of play, no matter what side of the slash you are on, make sure you have an understanding of marks and a basic understanding of wound care.

The types of marks that come from doing Florentine will vary due to a person's style. When the whip is hitting and connecting accurately, it looks like scratches in the shape of a letter "V". This can be achieved by doing the four-beat weave across the back.

However, with whips breaking the sound barrier, and moving over 767 miles per hour, it is important to know how to handle any cuts or lacerations caused by these kink tools.

Here are some helpful hints to stay sanitary as possible:

- If you cut or lacerate the skin, clean it with soap and water.
- Do not use alcohol pads or hydrogen peroxide as they prevent the healing process. A non-irritating antiseptic is ideal such as Benzalkonium chloride.
- Cover the wound with a sterile dressing of your choice.
- Make sure the wound can breathe or it may trap bacteria.
- Do not use hemorrhoid wipes or baby wipes as these are unsanitary and invite germs.
- Make sure to change the crackers and give them to the bottom or throw them away securely to avoid any blood borne contact with anyone.

Last but not least - - Remember this is for play in the dungeon. Florentine can be used in sport cracking and it looks amazing. But play in the dungeon is amazing for both parties when the top colors and weaves a deep, resonating connection. It does not need to be full of flair or brutality. Instead, it's about enjoying each other and having fun! Also, don't be addicted to crack! (Email from MLR July 13, 2024).

Chapter 12

Advanced Whip Catching: Variations for the Bottom

CONTROL OVER THE scene variations does not lie strictly on the throwing end. On the receiving end, an experienced whip catcher can enhance the scene by making small adjustments. If the whip thrower has a very consistent release point and the whip catcher is feeling a consistent, predictable energy from the whip, then, all of this is possible.

The Whip Catcher's Mantra. Do not stand for a whip, until you have seen the whip thrower throw. This allows the whip catcher to watch and ascertain the whip thrower's skill level, their style of play and gives a clue as to what the whip catcher might have in store if they stand for a scene.

Rhythmic Breathing. I begin each of my whip scenes by forming a connection generated through synchronous breathing with the whip catcher. A savvy whip catcher will continue this rhythmic breathing throughout the whip scene. Breath moves energy through and out of the body. It also provides a rhythmic connection of the body to the rhythm of the whip and the beat of the music playing in the dungeon.

Deep Breathing. Begin standing with your feet shoulder-width apart and with your weight centered over the middle or arch of the feet. If during the scene you feel good energy and want a little bit more, take a deep breath from the diaphragm and fill your chest cavity with air. This will expand the chest and put the backside subtly closer to the whip (assuming the whip thrower has a very consistent release point).

Standing weight shifts. Slightly flex your knees. Do not lock your knees when standing. Locking the knees can result in blood pooling in the legs and potentially lead to fainting. For the times when the whip is providing too much energy, and you need a little bit less, you can shift your weight to the ball of your feet. Stand over the front of your feet, as this will shift your upper body one and a half to two inches away from the whip. This will reduce the impact of the whip and give you a chance to breathe. If you desire a little bit more intensity, shift your weight back to the middle of your foot (your starting point).

If you want more energy and you've already tried the deep breath trick, you can shift your weight back to the heels of your feet. This will move your upper body one-half to two inches closer to the whip. You do not want to step back toward the whip as moving too far might result in the whip wrapping over your shoulder and striking your collarbone or hitting you in the face.

Before your next whip scene, you can try these exercises while free standing: Adjust your body so your weight is centered (starting point). Next, shift your weight to the ball of your feet, which would take you further from the whip strikes. Shift your weight back onto your heels for the position to receive more whip energy.

While doing these exercises, observe how steady your balance is in a free-standing position. If it is not good and solid, then only do this if you have a cross or something else to hold onto to steady yourself.

Dancing in place to the music. Spot dancing and moving to the music is great if you feel the mood and energy. An experienced whip thrower can make adjustments to accommodate the movements of the dancing whip catcher. Whip catchers should expect more marks if you are moving.

It is completely fine and often enhances a scene if the whip catcher expresses feeling through body language and audible sounds. There are also those scenes in which the top and bottom are in a D/s dynamic and/or have negotiated that the bottom cannot move during the whip scene. For me, I find that when a bottom is being stoic and completely expressionless, it makes it more difficult to interpret what the whip is doing to you as a whip catcher. I believe a scene is authentically enhanced with an expressive whip catcher.

Chapter 13

Crafting a Vignette

If all is going well on your whip journey, you should now be comfortable carrying a whip catcher successfully through the slow buildup, crescendo, and cooldown of a whip scene. With the mechanics of the scene taken care of, the imagination truly comes into play. The whip thrower may now start crafting a whip vignette.

A whip vignette begins in the mind's eye with a concept or idea. It invariably involves mixed-genre play, calls for highly advanced whip throwing, and often is visually appealing to the voyeur or dungeon crowd that might be blessed to watch such a vignette.

Concepts. The vignettes described in this book cover very general topics and contain cautions and lessons learned. I am writing not only from the voice of experience but also from the embarrassment of concept failures and lessons learned on the road to final success.

Vignettes should be a continually improving process as there are a lot of moving parts involved in scenes this complex. Sometimes, these are just complex scenes; sometimes, they transition to stage shows or erotic BDSM performance art.

I will begin by saying that what a whip thrower visualizes in their mind almost 100% of the time will not work when that same whip thrower picks up their whip and tries to recreate what they had visualized. At least, it will not work out the exact same way they originally visualized it.

As the vignettes progress in subsequent chapters, I will go through this process of transitioning from the concept in the mind's eye to piloting a vignette, to doing a dress rehearsal, to stage setting based on your location, and to lighting and music selection; it goes on and on as all of the variables that are possible now are at play in crafting a vignette.

Location. The location of the vignette is important, as not all vignettes can be done in all locations. When creating a vignette, one must first identify a space that will accommodate and complement it.

Part of the location consideration is identifying the attendees or groups that will be in the location before you choose it. For example, if you are constructing a whip vignette and the location is hosting a spanking party the night you plan it, the spankos may not appreciate attendees using a whip during their party. I will say, as a general rule, having a well-attended party in a venue of an adequate size for what you have planned is ideal for the added energy in the dungeon. Also, check with the person or group in charge at the venue and make sure that they are cool with what you have planned. Get the green light ahead of time to do the vignette.

Another consideration is the square footage needed to do the whip vignette. Is it single-handed throwing or two-hand work? Are you going to work a whip lane, a whip circle in an arc, or is the whip circle going to be 360 degrees around the whip bottom?

The floor is a consideration: is it polished concrete, carpeted, a dirty old warehouse or converted garage, or outdoors on grass or in a barn dungeon?

Lighting is also a consideration. Lighting goes beyond just having enough light to throw a whip accurately; depending upon the vignette, lighting might be required for safety not only for the whip thrower and whip catcher but also for the safety of the voyeurs and other dungeon attendees.

Materials. Often, a vignette involves a mixed-genre scene or setup. Sometimes, it involves props, costuming, turning vanilla things into pervertibles, and the like. When your visualization of your vignette is challenged to become a reality, you now need to identify materials that will work for what was "dreamed" up. The best example was creating and performing the whip theater for Beyond Leather.

I had visualized putting 100 feathers in Moodstone's back using hypodermic needles/temp piercings, then removing the feathers on stage in a twenty-minute whip theater. The feather quills would not stay in the needle hub all by themselves. Figuring out what material could be used in the needle hub was a puzzle that took several weeks and many pilots to perfect. Just experimenting with different materials, depending on the vignette visualized, can be a time-consuming process. I describe more on this in the Bullwhip Magick vignette chapter.

Safety considerations. There are many safety issues to consider when crafting a vignette. The most obvious consideration is often the only one the venue is concerned with - the safety of the observers and adjacent scenes going on simultaneously to the whip vignette. However, the safety of the whip thrower and whip catcher is also a concern. Once a vignette begins, the whip thrower's total attention must be on the flawless execution of the vignette. Having adequate space and no distractions or interruptions is another layer of safety needed.

Safety overlaps and often becomes integral with materials. For example, finding the right material for the needle hubs in the feather vignette was needed to address the safety concern of keeping the needles in place, but it introduced a new issue. If the material in the needle cup extrudes down the shaft of the needle to the needle bevel, then when the needle is withdrawn following the scene, some of this material might be left under the skin where the temp piercing was done. Safety multipliers apply here. This example of a safety issue with one needle hub is multiplied by 100 when 100 feathers are used for a vignette.

Safety can be an issue on the macro and micro levels when crafting a vignette. It can be multiplied by many times and factors depending on the vignette visualized. Murphy's law is alive and well. If anything can go wrong, it will go wrong.

Scenario. A vignette has a scenario that is a visualized scene. Sometimes, it also has a storyline. Sometimes, the music playlist chosen creates a story or vignette.

A vignette might be tying your whip bottom to an old abandoned RV out in the country, where they become the trespasser caught by the homesteader, and then they are tied up and whipped as punishment for coming onto their land without permission.

It might be turning a whip bottom into a bird by attaching feathers with tape, then "plucking" the bird with a whip. Or, it might be making a dress made out of streamers and cutting the streamers off with a bullwhip to strip the whip catcher as the whip teases them - a true whip strip tease.

Variations and Vignettes | 147

Photo 49 Streamers Vignette at Jax FetFest 3 Jacksonville, FL

Selection of Whips and Cracker Choice. This is integral to the scenario and goal of the vignette but is also limited by the environment, the venue, and the audience. Different whips provide different levels of sound, accuracy, and power. Depending upon the scenario, whether you need to cut an object worn by the whip bottom, need to mark or not mark the whip bottom, and what material the object needed to be cut is made out of . . . all of these things and more point to the type of material the cracker must be made out of and the type of construction for the cracker. Is it twisted with an overhand knot, is it braided mason line, is it plaited like a lady sally cracker?

Lessons Learned. The best lesson is that there will always be lessons learned. You can do the same vignette in two different venues, and it will turn out two different ways. Sometimes, this is a result of a different environment. Sometimes, it is because you have more experience with a particular vignette. Sometimes, it is because a different whip bottom is standing for the same vignette.

From a total quality management standpoint, the conscientious whip thrower is always trying to improve. We are self-critical to a fault, so don't be too hard on yourself as long as you are safe and having fun. Every time you do a vignette, you will learn something new about the vignette and about throwing whips.

My goal is not to have every reader try even one of these vignettes but to stimulate your imagination in crafting your own vignettes. Ultimately, I hope that you will be able to create wonderful new whip vignettes that will captivate not only your imagination but also the wonder of the observers in the venue in which you are throwing.

Chapter 14

Erotic Vignette

MANY PEOPLE THINK of a singletail when they think of erotic play. They are inexplicably drawn toward the contained danger and eroticism of the whip. I have always said that the crack of the whip is the dominant's mating call.

Before thinking about crafting an erotic vignette, first think about all of the erotic variations that can be done with a whip. A singletail is plaited, regardless of whether it is made out of kangaroo or paracord. This plaiting, when drawn across the skin of a bottom, causes a tactile sensation from the friction and drag of the plaits across the skin.

Many rope tops create a similar sensation when tying or untying someone, adding closeness and eroticism to rope play. The same can be done with a whip. In *Whips in the Dungeon*, several techniques were discussed: soft and hard wraps, drag, and draw (WITD, p. 123-126).

Drag is letting the whip drag across the skin using the weight of the whip and gravity to create the sensation. Different sensations will be felt during drag as the thong will feel differently than the fall and the fall differently than the fluffy cracker. Simply dragging the thong of the whip across or around the whip bottom's neck is erotic. Dragging the whip off of the bottom's shoulder can produce erotic chills. (WITD Photo 101, p. 126).

Draw is created by holding the whip between two hands and drawing it across the skin with tension and pressure to create a firmer, more controlled sensation. The whip can be drawn around the waist or between the legs across the genital area. Drawing the whip across the chest and nipples under tension will likewise create erotic sensations. (WITD Photo 102, p. 126).

Underhand Flick. An underhand flick thrown at the genitalia can end in a butterfly kiss or a controlled puff. Variation in the intensity and level of the controlled puff can be done right up to the point the whip naturally cracks. (WITD Photo 103, p. 127).

Bow and Arrow/Over the shoulder. Both of these static throw techniques are ideally suited for erotic play, as the path of the whip in dynamic throwing is impeded by different body parts that limit access for the whip top.

While legs, hips, and pelvis limit access to the crotch when throwing dynamically, these are not limitations when using either of these two static techniques. Static throws are also useful for accuracy when throwing at the chest.[19]

Static techniques give both beginning and intermediate whip throwers fine control of the whip earlier in their journey and allow them to target the chest and breasts/nipples while safely avoiding the whip catcher's neck and face.

---

19 Advanced throwers can control the arc of the whip and the travel the whip makes in recovery and delivery when throwing dynamically and can avoid the face and neck when doing erotic play with the chest and nipples.

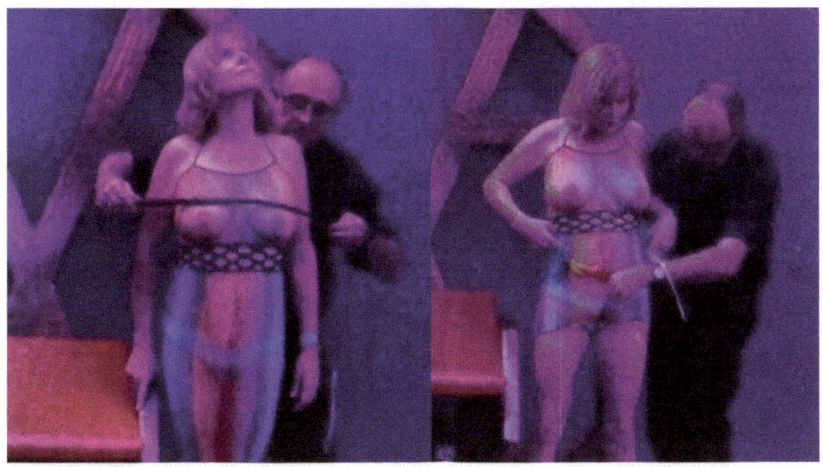

Photo 50 Erotic Whips. Draw Across the Chest & Draw through the Crotch.

Wraps. There are two types of wraps: **soft wraps** and **hard wraps** (or **loud wraps**).

With a **soft wrap,** the whip does not crack but is just thrown beyond the target extremity of the body, and the whip thong and falls gently wrap around the extremity aimed at. The soft wrap and the sensation of the thong going around the extremity is erotic, as is the slow dragging of the whip thong across the skin as the whip is removed from the wrap to recover and throw another.

A hard or **loud wrap** is where the whip is thrown with enough force and energy past the target extremity to achieve a crack. With the crack, most of the energy is released from the whip, and the thong wraps gently around the extremity targeted. Loud wraps, when thrown correctly, are mostly mind fucks. The whip does not hurt, but it sounds like it is going to hurt. The mind fuck is thinking that pain is going to be imminent. Instead, a pleasant erotic sensation is substituted. Mixing soft and loud wraps together in a scene keeps the whip catcher guessing as to what is coming next. Alternating extremities targeted is also another variation.

Photo 51 Wrap with an 8' Black Snake Whip during Beyond Leather Whip Theatre

Body Variations. The texture and sensitivity of the skin in various parts of the body vary. The skin on the stomach has a different texture than the skin on someone's back. The skin between someone's toes differs from the skin around and on the nipple. The skin on the underarms differs from the skin in the genital area (male or female).

Running the plaited thong between someone's toes will create an interesting erotic sensation. Running the same whip between the labia, across the nipples or across the ball sack will also create a sensation that most will find erotic. (Note this will also potentially expose a leather whip's thong to bodily fluids. A confounding result of this type of play for someone who plays with multiple partners is the difficulty of cleaning the leather to prevent the exchange of bodily fluids).

Cracker Stalls. These are fun, but they involve extremely advanced throwing. The whip must be able to achieve a natural rollout through its length to the cracker tip, and the cracker must be fluffy enough and constructed so it creates enough drag when passing through the air to act as an air brake. That air brake stalls the cracker or hovers it above the nipple, and then gravity lets the cracker fluff brush the nipple on its way by (WITD Photo 104, p. 129).

Combination Throws. Butterfly kisses can be combined with cracks in advanced throwing. This is done when the crack is thrown off of the shoulder or butt without touching the skin. On the follow-through, as the whip thrower sets up to recover, the whip completes an arc and gently brushes the skin as it passes by in a butterfly kiss.

There is the mindfuck of the loud crack, with the sound energy released, but the only sensation felt is the butterfly kiss on the follow-through arc. This is supersonic play as you are playing on the other side of the crack (sound barrier).

Photo 52 Whip Crack Just off of Shoulder.

Breath Play. Breath play can be done with the thong or fall of a whip. Many find breath play very erotic. However, several cautions apply when using a part of a whip to do breath play. Care must be taken not to crush or damage the Adam's apple/larynx. Care must also be taken to avoid cutting off blood flow through the carotid artery area. Be sure to do your research before actually engaging in breath play.

Just the placing of the fall around the neck with light pressure will create an erotic sensation and set an emotional tone to the play, even if it is not tight enough to restrict breathing or blood flow.

My preference for this type of play is to use the fall of the whip as a garrote. Using the thong, depending upon how the whip was constructed, how old the whip is, and how well the internal bolsters of the whip were tied, could all factor into whether this type of play using a whip might result in damaging the whip. Whip repair of a bolster is expensive as the whip overlay must be unplaited, and subsequent bellies and bolsters taken apart until eventually the failure is discovered and repaired.

Note this is edge play and not every venue will allow breath play. Be sure you fully negotiate this type of play and are knowledgeable and trained in different types of breath play before you attempt this in a vignette.

Insertable Play. The Turk's head and upper thong can be inserted either anally or vaginally for level-four style play. (Level-three dungeon play does not include penetration sexual play; level-four play has no limitations in sexual play but may apply safe sex approaches). I would NEVER do this unless a condom protects the whip and the condom is well-lubricated.

Concept. A whip is often stereotyped as an implement of pain and for masochists only. The whip is one of the most versatile implements in a dungeon toy bag. Erotic whip play can be done as an ending segment to an impact-style whip scene and used as a segue to level-four dungeon play.

Location. Erotic play can be done in any dungeon location and adapted to any piece of dungeon equipment.

Materials. There are not really any specific materials needed to craft an erotic vignette. However, there are variations of crackers that might be considered.

A big fluffy tassel-style cracker attached with an eight mm split ring to the fall of the whip is one variation. The number 36 twisted mason line provides a much fluffier cracker than the number 18 or 15 mason line. The same is true of a lady sally-style cracker that uses the No. 36 mason line.

Plastic wrap (like Saran Wrap) and Tagederm surgical covering are handy supplies for safety considerations.

Safety Considerations. Paracord whips can be washed with no harm to the whip. However, leather whips cannot be washed. If you are playing with your primary partner, you might not worry about bodily fluids getting on the thong or fall of your singletail. But if you play with multiple partners and plan on using the whip for drags between the labia or butt cheeks, wrapping the whip with plastic wrap will protect it from bodily fluids.

If your leather whip gets bodily fluids on it, wipe it clean with a Clorox disinfectant-style wipe and hang it up to "air" out. Clean, flowing air is a cleaning agent. Most bacteria and viruses thrive in a moist, oxygen-free environment. They do not survive long when exposed to air—certainly not after several days. Hanging a whip or flogger where it is exposed to good air flow for several days will result in germs dying.

Whip bottoms who enjoy genital flogging should own their own soft flogger, and it should be in their bottoming toy bag. Tops should inquire if a bottom owns their own flogger, and the top should use the bottom's flogger rather than their own for genital play.

Piercings can be an issue with whip play. If your cracker gets tangled in a piece of jewelry while traveling at or near the speed of sound, the piercing jewelry can be ripped out. Removing piercing jewelry is the safest approach.

For jewelry that is hard to remove or that you do not want to remove, cover it with Tagederm. The Tagederm will prevent the cracker from becoming entangled but is thin enough to allow the sensations from the whip strike. If I know I'm going to be doing nipple and genital play, I will put a box of Tagederm in my whip bag. Prior preparation prevents pathetically poor performance.

Scenario. For this scenario, envision that a whip scene is negotiated with clear consent by both participants to include sex. As with any type of scene, but especially one that is overtly sexual, both parties must have clear consent to play within established boundaries. Hard limits must be clearly defined and adhered to.

The whip scene takes place in a home dungeon. It begins with the whip bottom cuffed to a St. Andrew's cross. After a good warm-up, using a galley whip, a cat, and double-ended floggers, the top moves to two-handed dragon tails to increase the intensity and get the endorphins flowing.

The whip thrower can use the pommel of the end of a bullwhip to pound and beat the butt cheeks and then very lightly, with fingertips, transfer that energy up toward the heart chakra.

The top then moves the whip catcher from the St. Andrew's cross to an adjacent massage table and lays them face down. Using the bullwhip, the top throws it lightly, creating a controlled puff over the whip bottom's skin. Gravity brings the whip's thong down across the whip catcher's back. The entire length of the thong is slowly dragged across their back.

These drags are continued over different tracks across the body, tracing designs, teasing, and titillating as the whip drags across the skin. The whip is thrown on a horizontal arc above the prone whip catcher, lightly cracking or loudly cracking above the whip catcher. Gravity is utilized as the whip is rolled out to crack and then allowed to fall onto the whip catcher. The whip is recovered with a drag.

Draws are done by the top holding the thong under tension between both hands and drawing it across the skin with tension to create different levels of friction between the skin and the whip. Sensations are varied by adjusting the tension of the draw and also the location chosen for drawing the whip across the whip catcher's body. An intentional soft wrap around an extremity becomes a drag as the whip is slowly removed from the extremity, finishing with this drag technique.

Throws with a crack and recovering with a drag are intermixed with draws. While holding the whip with the fall, the whip thrower will drag the thong with the handle/pommel, providing a weighted end. This end weight will add a deeper sensation to the whip drag than when the whip was held by the handle and dragged across the skin. From there, the scene segues to the bedroom.

Erotic scene play with a whip is limited only by the whip thrower's imagination and the whip catcher's openness to expanding the sensations a whip can create. Hopefully, this vignette can be used to stimulate more interesting whip scenarios as you explore the limits of what a whip can do when used as foreplay in level-four play.

Chapter 15

Quiet Vignette

WHIPS ARE TYPICALLY not quiet, and when we think of a whip, the sound of the crack comes to mind. However, the whip can also be used when playing in a "quiet area" of the venue.

Many years ago, I was at the Black Rose convention with my submissive at the time, and in a huge dungeon with over 120 play stations. There was nowhere to play, and people were waiting at most of the play stations for their turn.

Near the wax play area, there was a separate dungeon room designated for quiet play. In that room, massage was happening, along with fistings, vibrator play, and knife play. There was a massage table open. I crafted a quiet scene with whips on the massage table using many techniques described in the previous chapter. I did not crack the whip once in the hour I played with my submissive.

Believe it or not, there are dungeons in the country where dungeon rules prohibit loud cracking of the whip. In these dungeons, consider playing with the whip using subsonic techniques.

The Pommel. The Turk's head on every class of whip (flogger, quirt, cat o' nine, dragontail, signal whip, snake whip, or bullwhip) can be used as a pommel for impact play. Varying degrees of intensity providing a broad spectrum of impact is possible without damaging the whip. Most well-made whips are counterbalanced in the Turk's head, making this a weighted implement that is quite nice for impact strikes.

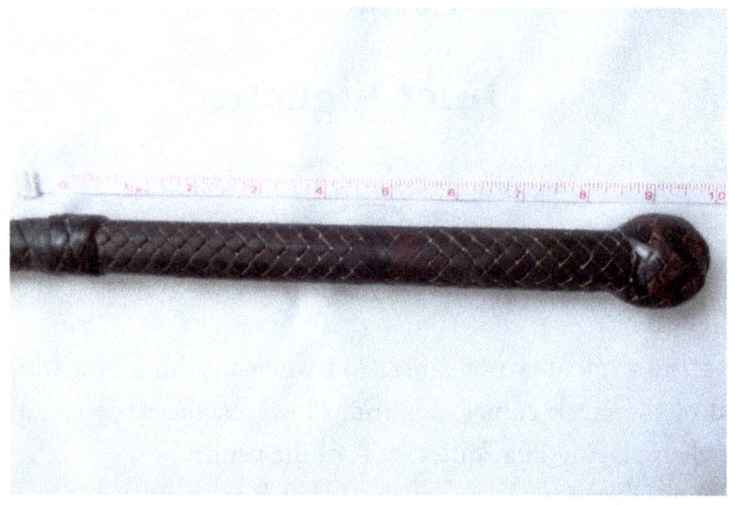

Photo 53 Pommel of a Mike Murphy Bullwhip.

Controlled Puffs. The controlled puff is one of the key elements of the *Whips in the Dungeon* approach to connecting with a whip catcher. It allows the whip thrower to match the intensity of the whip and the energy exchanged with the pain scale of the whip catcher correlated to a Likert scale.

This makes throwing a whip almost scientific on the somatic level of energy exchange. But aside from the technicalities of throwing consistently controlled puffs, the controlled puff is a scaled-finessed way of throwing, which results in throws ending with a "puff" and not a "crack."

As defined earlier in this book, the controlled puff at level one is a throw with a whip that will roll out at the slowest speed above stall speed and maintain its finish on target without gravity adversely affecting its finish. Throwing the whip slower would result in gravity affecting the finish and stall speed, resulting in the whip tip falling and finishing below the target.

To reiterate, this slow controlled rollout, finishing at the slowest possible speed and ending in a light puff on target, is defined as level one. Throwing at level two will result in a clearly and distinctively slightly louder puff. Controlled puffs can be continued below the sound barrier, resulting in controlled puffs one, two, three, four, five, and six. Somewhere around seven or eight, the whip will crack, and at that point, you would not be considered to be doing "quiet play." Dial it back and be satisfied with skilled throwing giving varying sensations by mixing intensities of controlled puffs.

Often, quiet vignettes evolve out of a situation. The dungeon music playlist might be "spa" type music that puts the bottom into a headspace and sets the mood for a more subdued scene. Always try to match your whip rhythms and even the cracks to the music playing in a dungeon setting.

Skill in crafting a quiet scene without cracking provides a challenging opportunity for a whip thrower. Do not let situations where a crowded dungeon or a dungeon with restrictive rules prevent you from throwing your whips. This is the time to demonstrate your finesse and even thoughtfulness in crafting a scene that complements the energy, music, and other scenes in the dungeon. Play along with the other instruments in the orchestra. Be creative and have fun throwing.

Chapter 16

Sensory Deprivation Vignette

PLAYING WITH AND removing one of the whip catcher's senses changes the dynamic of a whip scene. Often times removing one sense enhances or intensifies the other sensory receptors of the body. Sometimes, removing a sense will make the resulting sensations less intense. Sometimes, even our senses are connected with triggers. Knowledge of this and how to adjust for it often allows a scene to be played that would never happen otherwise.

Sensory Deprivation Vignettes. These vignettes involve playing with the senses to enhance whip play. Often, a number of senses are engaged by the bottom during a whip scene. The senses are natural input devices for the body to understand at the somatic level what is happening to it. In the context of SM/BDSM/leather, this frequently involves a combination of pain and pleasure.

Touch, sight, hearing, taste, and smell are the five senses most frequently thought of. In some analyses, balance, and proprioception (body and joint awareness) are added senses. These play into the person being aware of their center of gravity, whether in suspension or not, and the feeling of floating or standing on solid ground with sway or the feeling of being centered.

Knife play, needle play, pallet wrap, and wax play, all previously discussed as mixed play genres with whip play, deal with the sense of touch. In each instance, the skin is being played with, touched, coated, punctured, covered, and/or compressed. In pallet wrap and wax play, the sense of touch is removed or altered and sensory deprived.

Other senses can easily be deprived and are common techniques in SM play. The most intense sense, because it gives such vivid input to the brain, is vision or sight. Blindfolding the whip bottom takes away vision and enhances all of the other senses. It is like the body turns up the volume control on hearing. The reverse is also true. If you use ear plugs or noise canceling headphones (apparently, as I've learned from Moodstone, one of the most important things in a marriage), the color, brightness, contrast, and clarity of vision are enhanced as sight not only provides input for seeing but must do extra duty to provide information on what would normally be heard as well.

Tactile Deprivation Vignette. The skin is the primary tactile sensory receptor affected when receiving a whip lash. Covering the skin can produce a level of tactile deprivation. Depending on the covering used, it can also produce the absence of air on the skin.

Our skin and bodies are used to being surrounded by air. When that is removed, the skin becomes deprived of oxygen, which creates asphyxia at the cellular level. Yes, our skin indeed breathes.

Imagine that the whip catcher is wrapped with pallet wrap in a mummification. The pallet wrap deprives the skin of normal tactile sensations. It also asphyxiates the skin on the cellular level, holds in body heat, restrains the whip bottom in bondage, and creates a protective layer, reducing the impact of the whip strikes during a whip scene.

The pallet wrap increases the sound of the whip strike as the cracker striking plastic wrap will make more noise than striking bare skin. After a nice round of whipping, the pallet wrap is removed. So, what happens?

The skin is instantly refreshed as it can now breathe. The skin temperature drops slightly as now all of the body heat that was being held in by the pallet wrap is released. The skin is now exposed to direct whip strikes, and the sensation of the whip will feel much different than when it was covered with pallet wrap. The sensations after removing the pallet wrap should be enhanced because the sensory tactile receptors were deprived and are now energized into action. The whip top must be careful when bringing the whip bottom back from bondage-restricted mummification to live contact play with a whip. But at the same, the whip thrower can enjoy the different types of responses from the whip catcher.

Hearing Deprivation or Enhancement Vignette. The whip makes a crack that breaks the sound barrier. It is traveling at 767 mph. At the sound barrier energy is released that makes a loud noise and sends a small percussive wave of air expanding out from the tip of the cracker. This whip crack, when thrown at the shoulders, occurs in close proximity to the whip catcher's ears.

Many whip catchers love the sound of the crack. It sends shivers down their spine, and the crack resonates within their psyche. It is the BDSM version of being at a loud rock concert and walking away with your hearing altered for a time. But one result, as with too many rock concerts, is hearing loss. Some whip bottoms enjoy the sound of the crack booming in their ears; other whip bottoms enjoy the intense pain a whip strike can make, but they opt to use ear plugs to protect their hearing. Be sure to check with your whip bottom on their preferences. [20]

---

20 Moodstone always wears hearing protection (earplugs) when she stands for my whips.

Hearing protection can be done for a variety of safety considerations. But ear protection also provides **auditory sensory deprivation** and removes sound energy or dampens sound energy generated by the whip. This, on the one hand, takes an element of whip play away or dampens it, but on the other hand, allows the brain to be more focused on the tactile energy the whip is transferring. The focus is then on the "lash" and not the "crack".

Another consideration is the psychological impact of the whip on certain individuals. A whip crack, to many folks, sounds like a gunshot. For those kinky individuals who have Post Traumatic Stress Disorder (PTSD), a whip crack can easily be a trigger. These triggers can throw someone into a bad head space and have psychological and physiological repercussions.

The whip catcher has an obligation to be upfront and communicate clearly to the whip top if they have this trigger. But that does not mean the whip thrower is not also responsible for preventing the trigger from happening. The possibility of a trigger occurring from the sounds of a whip should be discussed during negotiations. Awareness of the trigger, use of ear plugs or noise-canceling headphones, and a whip thrower skilled enough to play with a whip and restrain the whip in the subsonic play area would result in a successful whip scene with a bottom who might not otherwise be able to enjoy a whip.

If this is still not satisfactory, then work a scene with quiet whip play techniques. Consider crafting a whip vignette using different classes of whips. Floggers and cat o' nines do not make a crack. Dragontails can be cracked, but it is easy to throw them without cracking. Quirts will make a sound, but it would be difficult to get a crack out of them. This is because they end in a viper tongue and not with a cracker.

Blindfolded Whip Catcher Vignette. Humans are very visual creatures. Our primary sensory input for our brain is our eyes. Our vision is, of course, augmented by our other senses. These include touch, hearing, smell, taste, and the lesser-known senses of spatial awareness and balance. Despite having input from other senses, people rely heavily on vision to process the world around them.

Removing sight from the whip catcher will necessarily enhance the remaining senses. The primary senses now available are tactile and auditory. Removing sight from the whip catcher enhances the effect of the whip's kinetic motion and the tactile and auditory energy it is transferring.

Removing sight also eliminates one of the sensory inputs and allows the mind to be more focused on what is happening to the body. One could argue that this allows the mind to slip more easily into subspace, but this varies from whip catcher to whip catcher.

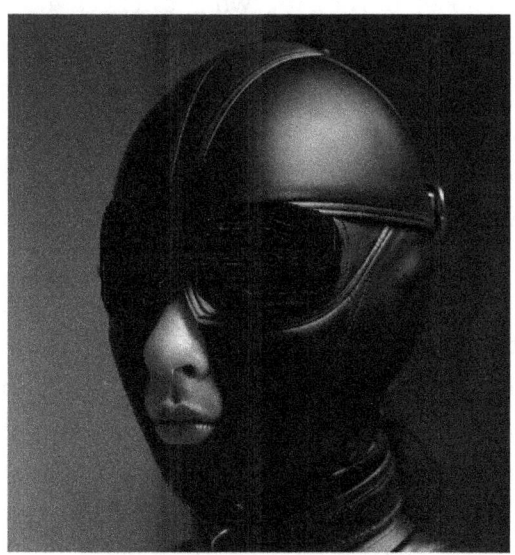

*Photo 54 Hooded Blindfolded Bottom.
Many uses. Sensory Deprivation. Also
adds safety element for fire whips.*

Taste and Smell. Deprivation or Enhancement. Smell and taste are other senses not so commonly played within the dungeon. Smell and taste, in many ways, are connected. Imagine, for example, being able to taste the salt of a piece of bacon but not being able to smell it.

Vick's Vapor Rub under the nose will surprisingly remove most of the taste from the mouth as smell is so closely connected with the taste buds.

The opposite of sensory deprivation is sensory enhancement. Imagine putting leather wrist cuffs on a whip catcher, blindfolding them, and tying the cuffs on a chain wall. On the wall around their head, you thread roses through the chain link. This provides the aroma of roses to the olfactory receptors, providing the pleasant smell of flowers to counterbalance the energy of the whip strikes on the heart chakra.

Chocolate is said to stimulate pleasure sensors in the brain. Most individuals find the taste and smell of chocolate pleasurable. Slip a piece of dark chocolate into the whip catcher's mouth (with consent) during one of the "in-betweens" when you check in with them. Chocolate is a mood booster and possibly a sexual stimulant. Using the sense of taste as a pleasure receptor simultaneously as the tactile sensation receptors are experiencing pain produces a pleasure/pain balance that turns the sadomasochist into a loving dominant. Or can it be possible to be both?

Aftercare with Chocolate. Chocolate or other candy is a tasty way of providing aftercare that uses the senses of taste and smell to provide pleasure following a hard whipping. Whenever food is integrated into play, the top must be aware of any food allergies or other food related medical conditions that need to be considered.

Chapter 17

Blindfolded Whip Thrower Vignette

MANY OF THE vignettes in this book are true stories. This is one of them.

Many years ago, I saw presenter Bob Deegan do this vignette as a demonstration, first at Black Rose and then some years later in Chicago at SINSations in Leather. Deegan would blindfold himself and then throw, tease, and play with his whip bottom with his whip (a four-foot signal whip).

I was always in awe at the finesse and accuracy of this demonstration and wondered how he did it. This is one whip thrower who did not share certain trade secrets. I have some ideas about how he did it, but they are mostly educated guesses. Some of them were confirmed in a phone call with Master Snoflak who used to stand for Deegan. Maybe you have your own ideas as to how it can be done, and as a result of our combined wisdom, you can pull it off for yourself.

First, Deegan was working with a four-foot signal whip that he had thrown for enough years that it was like an extension of his hand. It flew exactly where he wanted it to go. He also had experience working with the same two whip bottoms. I suspect his feel for the finish of the signal whip was very good. When the signal finishes in thin air, it feels different than when it finishes touching skin.

Deegan and the whip bottom would scope out the area where the demo was going to be performed ahead of time. He would find a mark or something distinctive on the floor and identify it as where the whip bottom was supposed to stand; then, he would take his signal and find his toe line or a small box that would be his starting point.

Deegan could not throw without moving, but his movement for this demo was in the form of a two-step one direction and then back the other way. His step movements formed a small box shape. While moving in the box and continuously throwing, he was feeling for the tug at the end of his signal.

Added to that was that he had an experienced whip catcher. They could make subtle movements to lean and find the whip themselves to help the blindfolded whip thrower quickly hit his target.

Being blindfolded enhances someone's sense of hearing and also the feel of the whip's finish. This is how he found his target and played with it.

There is also the showmanship aspect of this type of vignette, where the whip thrower and whip catcher have choreographed and rehearsed the dance so that it looks quite dramatic and impressive.

Teaching a Blind Whip Thrower. Moodstone and I were at Thunder in the Mountains many years ago. We were just finishing a whip scene in the dungeon when I was approached by a blind dominant and his submissive. He wanted to know if I would be willing to teach him how to throw a whip at his submissive.

The couple told me that the submissive loved whips. The dominant owned a four-foot signal whip but had not thrown it with her because he did not want her to have a bad experience with his whip. I told him I had never taught anyone who was blind how to throw a whip but to let me think on it for a day. We agreed to meet the next night in the dungeon. Here's what I came up with.

A four-foot signal whip is four feet from the heel knot to the tip of the cracker. When it is thrown using an over the shoulder or off the shoulder technique, the whip thrower must add the length of their arm and some flex of their thumb to that radius measurement.

After I described how to do it, I had the dominant practice, doing the over the shoulder technique. He repeated this until he became consistent with his throws. Then, I had his whip catcher stand six feet away. I had her very slowly back up a few inches at a time until she could lightly feel the cracker tip on her back. Once she felt the whip on her back, she could make slight adjustments.

I discussed the adjustments with her that I detailed in Chapter 12, Advanced Whip Catching. This couple was just starting out with whips, and the young woman was not an advanced whip catcher, but I taught her these techniques to help speed along the desired result. They did indeed achieve their objective, and they were successfully able to have a good whip scene that night.

Chapter 18

Creating a Canvas Vignette

THIS IS A fun vignette that began many years ago at a convention called The Floating World. I got the idea of taking acrylic paint (the gel paint that comes in big tubes) and using a paracord whip (as you don't want to get paint on your kangaroo or leather whips) with a big fluffy cracker to hold a lot of paint. I brought a white canvas, and I set it up and invited my whip friends, Talan and Domino, to join me in painting the canvas.

So, we were slinging paint at this canvas, and one of Domino's subs came over and exclaimed, "Whipcasso!" Thus, the term Whipcasso was born from the exclamation of an observer who was so excited about what we were doing that she volunteered to stand for us and become "living art".

Domino has adopted the term Whipcasso and, in his whip journey, evolved what was started at The Floating World into a full-blown Whipcasso workshop.

I took the idea and moved in a slightly different direction. I have always liked the idea that evolved out of that Floating World of "living art" being created by throwing paint at the back or chest of a living, breathing whip catcher. Variations to the paint strokes range from feathering to hard strikes to not even hitting the skin but cracking off of the skin and allowing the crack to fling paint onto your canvas.

I will suggest some ideas for vignettes and then encourage everyone to buy some basic acrylics in tubes at your craft store, make up some big fluffy crackers out of cotton twine, take your least favorite paracord whip and make your own fun.

Photo 55 Parachord Whip with Cotton Cracker and Pallet

Painting an Actual Picture on Canvas. This can be done in several ways, and your own creativity can be challenged. Painting with a whip is not an exact process.

One technique is to use a stencil. Tape the stencil on the canvas and then fill it in with paint using your whip. Or tape the stencil on the back of a whip catcher and fill it in! More fun.

Another method is to visualize or sketch your idea and then

analyze it in "layers." Using masking or painter's tape, cover all of the canvas except for the first layer. Paint that first layer, then, when it is dry, tape over any part of the first layer that cannot be covered in the second layer, and so on.

I used this technique when I painted the leather pride flag. On day one, I taped all of the canvas except for the area where the black stripes are in the flag. Then, using my whip, I painted those areas black. I did not fill it in entirely, as I wanted visible whip strokes.

On day two, I covered the black stripes with tape and painted blue using the same technique. On day three, I covered the black and blue stripes with tape and painted the red heart.

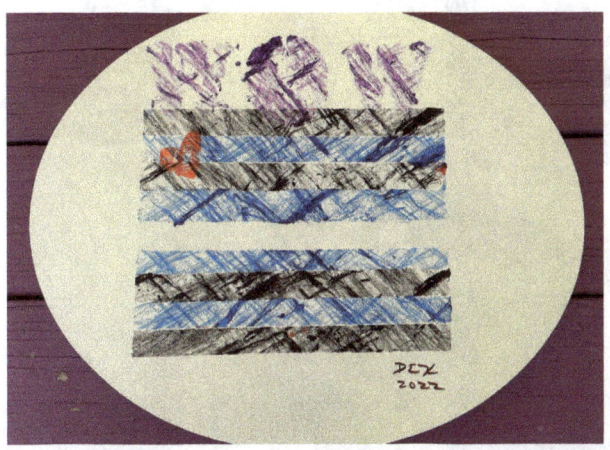

Photo 56 Leather Pride Flag

Painting Living Art. The first consideration when painting your whip catcher with a whip is safety. I recommend the whip catcher wear eye protection. It is best to use clear eye protection so if the whip catcher wants to watch, they can.

After Floating World, the first time that I painted living art, I painted directly on the whip bottom's skin. The back, butt, and chest all provide nice canvases to paint on. However, I noticed the colors of the paint were not showing up very well against the natural skin color of the whip bottom. I recommend taking a three-inch brush and white acrylic and painting the back, chest, or butt—or whatever other body part the whip catcher will present for painting. Acrylic dries fast, so within a few minutes, the white canvas you've painted onto the skin is now dry enough to paint on. With a white background, any color you paint with will show up much better.

Photo 57 Painting with Whips a Collage. Chest or Back

Variations With Other Whip Painters. Whip painting is a great social activity that works best outdoors with other whip throwers and whip bottoms.

You can exchange canvases and paint on someone else's canvas, or the group can organize painting by color. If whip thrower one loads up with blue paint, whip thrower two loads up with red, and whip thrower three loads up with yellow, then each whip thrower can stick with their original color and not have to clean or change crackers. They can round robin between the living canvases, painting their primary color until a change of colors is needed.

It is possible to clean the acrylic off of a cracker using water and to change colors, but it is easier to just change the crackers. When I know I'm going to be painting, I make up a number of cotton twine crackers beforehand. I still use the lady sally construction technique, but I use cotton twine instead of mason line because it holds paint better. It is a thuddier experience for the whip catcher, but we aren't doing a dungeon scene. We are having fun with the paint and our whips.

Water Based Paints. I have not used any other paint besides water-based paints. Surprisingly, the acrylic gel paint that comes in tubes does not spray too much off of the cracker and is not as messy as you might think it would be. I find it excellent for whip painting. If you are looking for a paint that will splatter more or make a wider pattern when being flung off of a whip, then try different liquid water-based craft paints or tempura paint. These will allow you to throw more paint and have less control when trying to brush paint on.

Chapter 19

The Clothespin Vignette

FOR THIS VIGNETTE, clothespins are clipped to the whip bottom in some fashion and then played with and whipped off by the whip thrower. Some may consider that to be advanced target practice. It is really that simple, but as with most of these vignettes, many variations can apply.

As an example, I recently played out a clothespin/whip scene with Moodstone. I put as many medium-sized clothes pins on Moodstone's breasts as I could and flicked them off with my newest whip, a Peter Thorndike four-foot 16-plait bullwhip. It went pretty well, but honestly, it was over too quickly.

Clothespins are fun, but it might not work for some whip bottoms. They require the whip catcher's skin to be loose enough to pinch. Not everyone's skin will do this, and for those whose skin will pinch to hold a clothespin, not every part of their body will hold a clothespin.

Aside from variations in where the clothespins are placed, there are different sizes and different colors of clothespins to consider. Try out different themes, match the current holiday colors, or show your pride with a stylized rainbow encircling your whip bottom's body.

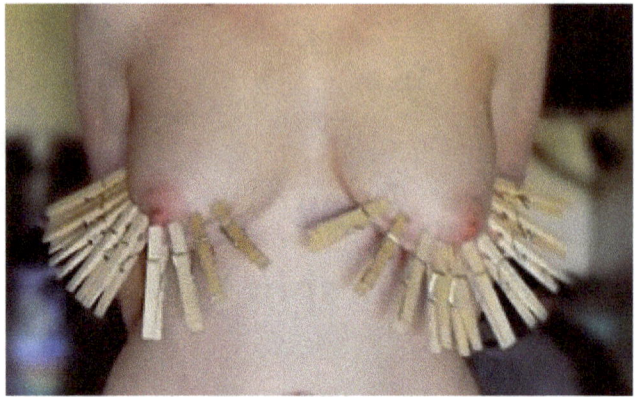

Photo 58 Clothespins on breasts ready for Whip Vignette

Vignette ideas abound, but the one I will share incorporates some bondage, objectification, and clothespins. Suspend your whip bottom on a chain web with their back facing the whip thrower. This can be done with rope, pallet wrap, or with suspension cuffs. Then affix as many clothespins to the skin on the back side of the whip catcher as their skin will allow. This could end up being five or 200, depending on everyone's mood.

Other areas to cover with clothespins, depending on which side is facing the whip thrower, include breasts, chest, underarms, the bottom side of the arms, crotch area, and the inside of thighs. The torso usually is too tight, but again, this varies from person to person. Some bottoms are self-conscious about certain parts of their bodies, so be sure they are okay with your clothespin placement plans in pre-scene negotiations.

As you might guess, the longer a clothespin pinches the skin and restricts the flow of blood to a particular area, the more it will hurt as the clothespin is taken off and blood rushes back into the area that was restricted.

There is no hurry to begin immediately whipping the clothespins off. It's fun to tease them first. Try using a feather to tickle the skin around the clothespin or in areas of the body where the top knows the bottom might be ticklish. Again, all of this must be negotiated prior to the scene. Tickling might be a hard limit for some.

Whip some clothespins off, tease some clothespins with the whip without removing them, and feather some clothespins. Then, in between, using your knife, play with the areas that had been clothes pinned and now have blood rushing back into the skin area. Move energy as the blood returns to an area. Whip some more clothespins off. Do not be in a hurry; enjoy the moment. Kiss and bite the area where some clothespins were removed if this was negotiated. Suck on the skin and pull more blood into that area

Games with Clothespins. The games you can create using clothespins and whips are endless, but here is an idea to stimulate your thinking.

Several whip throwers can participate at once. More than one whip bottom can be in the game, but let's suppose there are two whip throwers and one whip bottom. Clothespins of three different colors have randomly been arranged on the whip catcher. A method for picking a color is used – perhaps using a spinning wheel with three colors, or using a piece of paper with three colors and spinning a bottle on top, or drawing slips of paper out of a cup.

There are many ways to do this. But one whip thrower draws a color, and the other whip thrower has to flick off a clothespin of that color. If they do, they get a point. If they remove a clothespin of a different color, the other whip thrower gets the point. If they miss, the other whip thrower gets to try and remove a clothespin of that color. Again, if they remove a pin of the wrong color, the other whip thrower gets the point. If they miss the try, they return to the original whip thrower.

The game progresses until all the clothespins are removed, and the whip thrower with the most points, wins. Game prizes can be negotiated before the game begins.

Chapter 20

Self-Flagellation Vignette

ALMOST ALL OF these vignettes started as real scenes, either observed or created by me. This was one of those observed scenes.

A whip enthusiast (I say that because she attended the whip workshop at the convention and was very enthusiastic about whips) did a solo scene in the dungeon one night during the convention. She was doing self-wraps and dancing to the dungeon music. It was very erotic and hot, one of those times when it was good to be a voyeur. She was naked and dancing, gyrating to the music. Her wraps were quite hard and were leaving red streaks and welts all over her body. She was using a signal whip and not cracking but letting the full energy of the wrap strike her body. While she was totally into herself and self-induced pain and pleasure, this was quite the sight for the voyeurs in the dungeon.

The horizontal technique is ideal for doing self-flagellation. Throw the whip close to your body on a 90-degree angle from your body and let the whip wrap around on its follow-through with the cracker tip ending on bare skin. Horizontal wraps for intended self-flagellation can be done single-handed or with a two-handed technique.

The over the shoulder technique is one of the basic static throwing techniques. However, the set-up for the throw is to throw the whip over the shoulder towards the back, and it invariably will strike the back or the butt of the whip thrower. Aha! The setup for over the shoulder lets you hit yourself!

If you try to match the intensity of the throw off the shoulder with the setup thrown over the shoulder, the whip thrower can get a pretty good idea of what the whip feels like to the whip catcher. This is a perfect technique for self-flagellation. In this instance, the whip thrower and whip catcher are one and the same person.

Any dungeon whip can be used: floggers, quirts, cat o' nine tails, dragontails, signal whips, snake whips, and bullwhips. Even short stock whips could be used for this type of play as accuracy is not a function of self-flagellation but only doing wraps and self-inflicting pain.

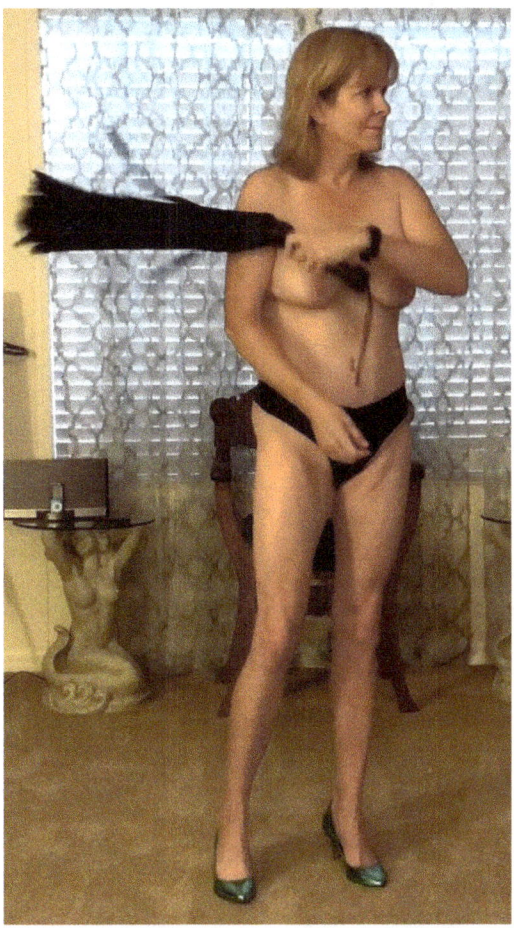

*Photo 59 Self-Flagellation with a Flogger.
Technique can be done with any whip.*

Control. One of the big advantages of self-flagellation with whips is that the person on the throwing end of the whip is also on the receiving end of the whip and is in total control of the scene. You will never hear anyone calling "red" on themselves. Whip catchers with control issues might find this type of scene appealing, as might whip catchers who love the feel of the whip but do not have anyone in the local community who is good enough with a whip to be trusted in a scene.

Chapter 21

Saline Genital Vignette

MANY YEARS AGO, I attended a whip workshop that focused on genital play with a whip. The whip thrower was very skilled and used what I teach as a bow and arrow technique. Some call this a slingshot technique. She demonstrated using a variety of targets, and then, for the whip bottom genital part of the demonstration, her bottom presented his genitals.

His ball sack was about the size of a grapefruit. They had enlarged his balls with a sterile saline solution for the demonstration. The whip thrower proceeded to put blood blisters all over his balls by cracking the whip on his enlarged scrotum. I'm pretty sure she was using a four-foot signal whip, and the cracker, no doubt, was finished with an overhand knot. This knot produced the marks on the whip bottom's scrotum.

How is scrotal infusion done? I am not a medical professional, so this is just a description of a procedure with the caveat that it should not be done without proper instruction. This would preferably be a kinky medical professional who knows how to do it.

The scene that I watched involved injecting a 300-500-milligram sterile saline solution warmed to the human body temperature. The procedure takes about an hour and can be accomplished using syringe injections or an intravenous line. The scrotum will swell to two or three times its normal size. The effects of the injection do not last long afterward. The human body reabsorbs sterile saline solution into its tissues and returns to its pre-inflation size within two to three days.

Any fetish involving a needle is a form of edge play and should be done with extreme care. Sterile saline ball injection carries several dangers. Bacteria can be introduced below the epidermis and result in serious infections.

The general rules of medical play sanitation apply. The saline solution, drip tubes, syringes, and needles must meet hospital-grade sterility standards, and ideally, the entire procedure should be done in a sterile environment. Most dungeon medical play areas are not sterile, but they should be clean and sanitary. Use gloves, be aware of cross-contamination, and clean glove procedures. Do NOT inject sterile saline into the testicles, but only into the scrotum sack.

Labia Fluff or Inflation. This type of play can also be done to the major and minor labia. Sterile saline infusion of the labia is done with syringes. There is no need for large volumes of sterile saline as in using an IV.

There is not a lot of published information as to how much saline to use to fluff the labia. The Fetlife Inflation group focuses mainly on scrotum inflation. One Domme who's done labia inflation said it is different for every woman and it depends on how big you want the labia to be. The common sense approach is to look carefully "before" and to inject the labia in multiple points, one to three cc at a time, until you reach the desired "fluff" you are looking for. Again, this is risky play and should involve consultation and/or participation with a medical professional.

Whip Play on Inflated Genitals. The inflated genitals are going to be more sensitive and possibly register greater sexual stimulation than un-inflated genitals. Whip play can go from very light butterfly kisses to hard cracks, from green to red, and on a spectrum from erotic to masochistic. For those who like whips and also medical play, this is the ultimate vignette.

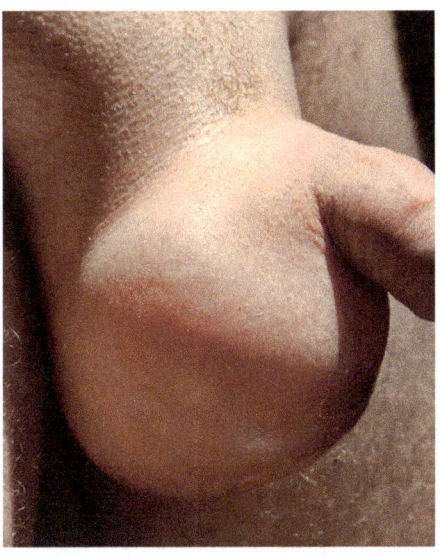

Photo 60 Saline Enlarged Labia or Scrotum.

Chapter 22

The Moby Dick Vignette

As many of these have, this vignette evolved from an actual scene. I was attending Thunder in the Mountains with Moodstone and ladyofdreams (R.I.P.). I had presented workshops on urethral sounds for females and on caning.

On the last night of the event, there were several play parties off-premise. We went to one of the "after parties". It was in a small dungeon, but it had a raised 'stage' area where they had a single St. Andrews cross. The energy was electric in this small dungeon with all of the play stations in use and a line of people in the social area waiting to play.

I had ladyofdreams standing for me at the St. Andrews cross, and suddenly, a drum solo began. I had never heard of a drum solo being used in dungeon music, but what unfolded was Led Zeppelin's Moby Dick. While the radio cut is four minutes and twenty seconds, the live version recorded on an LP is 11 minutes and two seconds. In live performances, Bonham would play the solo for as short as six minutes but was known to drum for as long as 30 minutes, improvising as he went.

To my knowledge, this dungeon set played the 11-minute version when I threw a bullwhip to it; my impression was that it was similar to a long play song, which is usually seven to nine minutes long. This was the most challenging piece of music I've ever thrown a bullwhip to.

It was impossible to keep up with Bonham, arguably one of the world's best rock drummers, playing arguably one of the best drum solos ever composed. But it was not impossible to settle into a rhythm with the bullwhip that complemented and augmented the drum solo; so much so, that ladyofdreams ended the session with several whole-body shudders that told me she had orgasms from the pooled energy of the whip strikes.[21]

So, the idea and concept of a drum solo being the focus of a whip vignette was born. Here is a sampling of great drum solos to try in your own whip drum solo vignettes.

> The Who—Won't Get Fooled Again (Keith Moon)
> Slipknot—The Blister Exists (Jordy Jordison)
> The Surfaris—Wipeout (Ron Wilson)
> Rush---YYZ (Neil Peart)
> Phil Collins---In the Air Tonight (Phil Collins)
> Judas Priest---Painkiller (Scott Travis)
> Foo Fighters---Best of You (Taylor Hawkins)
> Avenged Sevenfold---Beast and the Harlot (James Sullivan)
> The Beatles---The End (Ringo Starr)

This obviously is just a start. Everyone loves different genres of music. Not all music will transcend to the sacred space of the dungeon for play. Some may be relegated to private sessions when it is just you, your favorite whip catcher, and a catchy drum solo that

---

[21] Video WITD 401.07 recreates the Moby Dick vignette so you can see how difficult it is to throw a rhythm whip to this complex a drum solo.

both of you like, that most likely the larger party in a dungeon would not like.

Play for yourselves, groove to the drum beat, and match the rhythm of the whip to the energy and heartbeat of the music. Have fun and crack to the kick drum.

Chapter 23

The Whip Flurry Vignette

ROUND-ROBINS WERE INTRODUCED to me by Master Snoflak. I also call them whip flurries. Many different formats and variations are possible.

As with many of these vignettes, they were discovered at large BDSM conventions. Dark Odessey Winterfyre was the setting for my first introduction to a whip flurry, when Snoflak, _Talan_, and Master Steven did a round robin with Master Steven's slave as the whip bottom. I did not participate but only watched. I was learning and, at that point in my journey, had only done whip scenes where I had a personal direct connection between myself, my whip, and the whip bottom.

A whip flurry is a much different type of whip scene. There are several aspects to it. One aspect is social. Whip throwers are talking, communicating, sharing energy, movement, and the movement of several whips. They may or may not be throwing the same style. They may not even be throwing the same classes of whips. For the bottom, it is a whole-body experience as the whip throwers and whips surround the bottom 360 degrees.

A few months later, at Feel Me Breathe in upstate New York, another whip flurry formed. This time, it started with four whip throwers and a line of bottoms who wanted to experience a round-robin and feel the kiss of multiple whips on their skin as the whip throwers circled.

A hard point in the overhead was used so that the whip bottom could be circled as the flurry progressed.

Parameters were agreed upon. Sno was in charge of the whip throwers and would signal to increase the intensity, slow down, rotate the circle, or stop. The whip bottom communicated nonverbally by raising one foot if they needed a break or to slow down. If they stomped their feet rapidly, it was a signal to stop the whip circle that they had experienced enough.

One of the whip bottoms wanted to be suspended, like a piece of meat. An inverted suspension was done, and a full head hood was placed on her to protect her head from any stray whip. I took the opportunity to play with the bottoms of her feet with the whip while the flurry progressed. This type of sampling continued until all whip bottoms had experienced the whip. As a whip thrower would tire, they would drop out for a break, and another whip thrower would take their place.

The next opportunity for a round-robin at Feel Me Breathe occurred when Robert Dante visited. This round robin was not set up as a whip circle but at a Saint Andrews Cross. Moodstone was blindfolded and Snoflak, Biscuit, Robert Dante, and I participated. Throwers took turns and Moodstone had to guess who was throwing at a particular time. Moodstone knew what Snoflak's whip felt like, but she thought Biscuit was her Master. We both have similar throwing styles. Robert Dante took turns and ended the round-robin by untying and removing Moodstone's blindfold in an exquisite display of finesse and talent with a six-foot bullwhip. Moodstone immediately knew who the whip thrower was because, as she exclaimed, "Only Master Dante would be so bold!"

The following year at Beyond Leather, Snoflak, Biscuit, and I did a whip flurry with two whip bottoms. Moodstone and lady sally stood at the same time. They were hugging each other as the three whip throwers circled. This stance adds a connection between whip catchers as they share energy, breathe together, and experience the whip circle at the same time. They can also share tips when bottoming together.[22]

Safety Considerations. When multiple whip throwers throw, the chances of a whip getting tangled or deflected increase. This is multiplied when the whip throwers throw in different styles. When everyone is throwing horizontally, there is less chance of whips getting tangled, as opposed to when some are throwing overhand and some are throwing horizontally.

Unless there is room for a huge whip circle, then the whip throwers not only have to focus on the target but throw in an opposite rhythm to the whip thrower on either side of them to avoid getting tangled or having a deflection. So, throwing in a small circle requires considerably more skill and working together than if there is adequate room for a large whip circle.

Eye protection is important. Several types of eye protection would be adequate. A pair of safety glasses or safety goggles is best. A leather blindfold would be good too. Fabric or cloth blindfolds will provide some protection but are not as good. A pair of suntan goggles would work in a pinch.

Setup. There are several ways of setting up a round-robin or whip flurry. Possible setups are in the round, single station--single side, or suspended. In any round robin, if more than one whip thrower is

---

[22] Moodstone received a very valuable piece of advice from her friend lady sally that day as they were being whipped together. Moodstone told lady sally that unfortunately, whip throwers tended to lighten their strikes in response to her body language. Moodstone is not a masochist but likes the thrill of enduring pain for a dominant and also for the endorphin rush. Thus, she did not look like she was enjoying her whip scenes when they got intense. The advice, which now sounds obvious, from lady sally, was that she should control her reactions if she wanted the intensity of the whip to continue.

throwing simultaneously, the whip bottom or bottoms should all be wearing eye protection.

In the Round. This would require the whip bottom to be freestanding or secured with a hard point overhead (preferred) if there is enough space for the whip circle. This is probably the most fun for both whip throwers and whip catchers.

From the standing whip catcher, a radius must be drawn to form a 360-degree circle using the longest whip any of the whip throwers will be throwing. Then, taking that same longest whip as a measure, create an outer safety circle. This is why whip flurries in the round style take up so much space.

Impractical for a normal dungeon night, these circles can happen before normal dungeon play begins. Sometimes, it works great as an icebreaker, and sometimes, it can be held very late at night after most of the dungeon play has subsided as a nightcap. They are ideal at outdoor events where a large lawn or mowed pasture can be used.

For safety and to limit deflections, whips getting tangled and striking each other and not the whip bottoms, I recommend no more than four whip throwers at a time participate in an in-the-round whip flurry. This gives each whip thrower in the 360-degree circle one-quarter of the circle to throw in or 90 degrees of the circle.

Three whip throwers are ideal as each gets one-third of the circle, and there is less crowding. Throwing styles are not as critical with three whip throwers. Throwing styles are not a limiting factor with four whip throwers, but they are something to be more aware of as throwing commences.

I suggest similar recommendations for the whip catchers. A single whip catcher experiences a 360-degree total-body experience with the whip. Two whip catchers in embrace will present their backs and sides and, at various points in the flurry, can be instructed to go back-to-back so their front sides are presented. This gives a total-body experience, but not simultaneously as with a single whip catcher.

Three or four whip catchers can be worked similarly to the two-whip catcher flurry. I would not go beyond four whip catchers as the flurry is limited to four whip throwers due to safety and space limitations. For the whip catchers, this will be a sharing, energy exchange experience as they experience the whips together.

Photo 61 Whip Flurry at Weekend of Wickedness with Dex, Love, Lex from Texas and Moodstone standing.

Single Station-Single Side. Single station-single side takes up less space in the dungeon. It can be set up on a Saint Andrew's cross, a whipping post, a chain web, or almost anywhere that the whip catcher can stand against.

The whip flurry can happen in a dungeon layout, provided there is enough space for a single whip thrower to throw the longest whip they will be using. Horizontal style will require a half-moon whip circle and half-circle safety zone. Overhand throwing would be best using a whip lane.

When a mix of styles is thrown, a whip circle is usually more than adequate, as the horizontal style takes more space to throw than the overhand style. In single-station round robins, whip throwers are not limited in number; they take turns throwing as pre-arranged. But whip catchers are limited to one at a time. Another limitation is that it does not allow a simultaneous whole-body experience, but only one side of the body is targeted at one time. The whip catcher can, of course, be rotated and sides and front thrown at, just one side at a time.

For the whip catcher, this is more like a regular scene, with multiple tops participating. For the whip tops, this has a social aspect.

The multiple top scenes can evolve around a game with whips. The whip catcher can be objectified and become one component or piece/part of the game. It can also be interactive, and the game involves the whip catcher and requires them to provide feedback. As occurred at Feel Me Breathe, blindfolding the whip catcher and having them guess which whip top is throwing with them at any moment in the scene is an interesting interaction.

Round robins can be a learning experience. Seasoned whip throwers can provide tips and pointers to newer whip throwers, and the whip bottom can give instant feedback and pointers. They can be competitive as specific targeting exercises can be done between the whip tops to see who is the most "on" on a given night or to see which class of whip or style of throwing is the most accurate.

Suspended. The suspended whip catcher provides an opportunity to add a layer or variation to the round-robin vignette. Just adding suspension adds multiple variables, as there are infinite suspension positions.

I will leave some of this to the whip throwers reading this and the coordination with the rigger (assuming the whip throwers involved are focusing on whip skills and leaving the rope to an experienced, qualified rigger). I will discuss two positions out of an infinite number: horizontal and inverted.

Horizontal. Horizontal has at least two possibilities. Free hanging from a hard point and suspended tied to a piece of dungeon equipment (like a chain web). One of the challenges with horizontal is working with the rigger to position the suspension uplines so that the flying whips won't get tangled in the rope. Positioning the bottom where there is a plane of skin to target with the whips and where rope does not obstruct the arc or path of the whip is tricky at best. I've found suspending on a web chain wall the easiest way to tie a whip catcher horizontally and leave a fully open side to whip in a round robin.

Photo 62 Horizontal Suspension of Moodstone by Apex-S.

Inverted. This is my favorite. Whip throwers can easily set this up using quality suspension ankle cuffs and a proper suspension point. If a rigger wants to participate, why not involve multiple tops?

The whip bottom is suspended by the feet upside down. The whip bottom must be wearing some type of eye protection. Consider a full-head or partial-head hood to protect the head from the follow-through arc of the whips of overhand throwers. Horizontal-style whip throwers do not present as critical a safety consideration as their style complements this particular suspension very well.

Awareness of the length of time suspended is important, as blood will rush to the whip catcher's head, and when they are let down, they will need time to recover their balance.

A whip catcher suspended inverted from a hard point is truly presented as an object to be whipped; objectification at its finest. But it can involve grace and finesse, too. During one round robin, while the rest of the whip circle was wailing away at the inverted whip catcher, I was feathering and teasing the bottom of her feet with my whip cracker fluff. Fortunately, she was ticklish, and her response resulted in a flopping fish on the end of a line result.

Photo 63 Inverted Suspension of Moodstone by Tigrrrr.

Photo 64 Whip flurry from WoW having fun outside.

Communication methods with the whip catcher should be briefed and agreed upon before starting any suspended round-robin. The non-verbal foot signals described in previous whip flurries will not work in suspended round robins. If the whip catcher is always able to be verbal in subspace, then verbal communication is best. If, however, the whip catcher knows their throat chakra tends to close up and they go non-verbal, then some sort of non-verbal signaling should be worked out.

It doesn't matter what system is used as long as all of the whip throwers involved and the whip catchers know what it is. One possible suggestion would be two handkerchiefs, one in each hand. When the whip catcher drops one, it means the same as "yellow" - slow down, ease up, and give them a chance to breathe. Return the handkerchief to their hand when they are ready to continue. If the whip catcher drops both handkerchiefs, it means "red" - they are ready to stop the scene.

Whip flurries are a fun vignette, but it is a rarity to see them as it requires multiple whip throwers with at least intermediate whip skills all at the same venue, the venue having enough space to accommodate the round robin, and the whip throwers all being willing to cooperate together to co-top a whip catcher. Many whip throwers, frankly, tend to have big egos. (I might or might not fall into that group). Reigning in those egos and working together to pull off a round-robin requires coordination and cooperation.

Then, finally, a whip flurry needs a whip catcher who is experienced enough not to be afraid of the total body experience with multiple whips.

When the stars align, these are wonderful scenes and wonderful opportunities for all involved.

Chapter 24

Games with Whips (Kinky of Course)

KINKY GAMES ARE limited only by the imagination of the participants and the willingness of the participants to play and have fun together. To get you started, here are some suggestions for games with whips. Use your own creativity to modify these games or to design your own.

Tic-Tac-Toe. Tic-tac-toe is normally played with Xs and Os, which is easily done in a spanking game with paddles and an evil stick, but it is not so easy to make a zero with a whip strike.

Take a water-based marker (definitely not a Sharpie unless you want to piss off the whip catcher) and draw a tic-tac-toe board on the back of the whip catcher. Draw three-inch or four-inch squares depending upon the size of the back you are creating the game board on. This game completely objectifies the whip catcher.

One whip thrower takes horizontal stripes, and one whip thrower takes vertical stripes (not using Xs & Os with whips or making two stripes/square, but just a single stripe). This game is ideal for a horizontal thrower and an overhand thrower. The horizontal stripe can be done by turning a bow and arrow technique sideways, making it a horizontal release. Or it can be done using the horizontal dynamic technique.

The vertical stripe can be done with a vertical bow and arrow or an over the shoulder static technique, or with an overhand flick. A cattleman's or circus crack could be used to make the vertical mark, but those cracks are hard enough to get to roll to finish on target without cracking two-thirds of the way down the thong.

Then, the cracker material must be considered. I do not recommend a lady sally cracker for this game. Marks are needed. Braided mason line, Dynema, Dacron, or nylon would all be better choices. A single strand of braided mason line, in my opinion, is the best choice. Both whip throwers should use the same cracker material and design to avoid giving one an unfair advantage.

Another approach to making marks would be for each whip thrower to use acrylic paint of different colors. There is no rule that tic-tac-toe always has to be Xs and Os! Be creative.

Remove the Tail from the Donkey. This is a variation of the game Pin the Tail on the Donkey, only instead of pinning the tail on; in this game, the goal is to remove it.

A whip catcher is bent over a spanking bench, and then a tissue streamer is taped to their butt or taped to a butt plug. The whip thrower uses the whip to remove the tissue paper streamer by cutting it. The whip thrower that cuts the streamer into the most pieces wins. The goal is to cut off as little streamer as possible each time. How many tries each gets is a variable to be agreed to before beginning. Again, I recommend a single strand of braided mason line, Dynema, Kevlar, Dacron, or nylon for cracker choice.

Balloon Pop. This is just like the carnival game, but it uses whips instead of darts.

Balloons are surprisingly hard to pop with a whip. I recommend using water balloons blown up with air. Gloryus dips her crackers in tacky glue and then sprinkles with sand. This added abrasive makes popping the balloons easier, but is not recommended for direct skin play. If this game is played outdoors, the water balloons can be filled with water. Duct tape them in place on the whip catcher.

An added layer of complexity for edge play would be to pin the balloons in place with single-use hypodermic needles. If this is done, anchor the needles by covering them with Tagederm. I recommend using braided mason line, Dynema, Kevlar, Dacron, or nylon for cracker material. The whip thrower who pops the most balloons is, of course, the winner. If a whip thrower misses a balloon, the turn will rotate to another whip thrower. Draw straws or pick a number to see who goes first.

Photo 65 Balloon bondage from WoW

Ring the Bell. Suction cups are placed over the whip catcher's nipples, and a bell hangs off each suction cup. The whip catcher should wear eye protection. A timer is set to 60 seconds, and the whip thrower must ring the bells as many times as possible in one minute.

The whip thrower with the most rings will win. Prizes can be given.

Guessing Game. This game was partially described in the Whip Flurry chapter but essentially is a game for the whip catcher to guess which whip thrower is throwing at a given moment.

The whip catcher is blindfolded. Whip throwers take turns throwing for 60 seconds. At the 30-second point, the whip catcher is asked who is throwing the whip. At the 60-second point, without announcing a change of whip throwers, one thrower slips out, and another thrower slips into play. At the 30-second point, the whip catcher is again asked who is throwing, and the game progresses.

It is best if all whip throwers are using the same type of cracker. My preference for this game is a lady sally-style cracker made out of twisted mason line. If all of the whip throwers do not use the same cracker, then this game becomes too easy for the whip catcher.

The Controlled Puff Game. This game is interactive between whip throwers and a whip catcher. It captures the essential elements of the *Variations and Vignettes, Ch. 7,* approach to dungeon whip play.

This game pits the dungeon skills of two whip throwers against each other, utilizing the feedback of the whip catcher participating. The concept of a controlled puff is that a controlled puff "one" is the slowest speed at which a whip can be thrown in any given throwing style and remain on target without adversely being affected by drag and gravity.

A controlled puff "one" must finish on target with a controlled puff just above stall speed. Controlled puff "two" is slightly faster, and the finishing cracker puff is slightly louder. Every whip will display different controlled puff characteristics, just as every whip thrower will analyze this slightly differently. The two whip throwers will have slightly different controlled puffs "ones". But the goal of quality dungeon play, and an essential element for pickup play, is to connect the whip thrower's controlled puff scale (one through eight) and correlate it with the whip catcher's Likert pain scale (One through ten, with ten being Red).

In this game, co-tops take turns throwing with a single whip catcher. They check in and get a feel for the whip catcher's pain scale, warming up at one through three. The whip catcher is blindfolded, and a spotter communicates so the whip catcher does not know which whip thrower is throwing at a given time.

The whip catcher communicates with the spotter that they are ready for pain level four. The spotter calls out four, and the whip thrower throws for 30 seconds, attempting to match their controlled puffs with what they think the whip catcher will evaluate as level four. The spotter asks the whip catcher where they are on check-in and records the response. The second whip catcher joins, attempting to match the whip catcher's level four. This continues, alternating whip throwers, each attempting to match the whip catcher's level four, and the spotter continues recording the results on check-in.

When the whip catcher is ready, the scene moves up to level five, then levels six and seven. I do not recommend going above level seven in a game. The point of the game is to see which whip thrower is able to match the whip catcher's pain scale and correlate the bottom's scale with the thrower's own controlled puff scale. Obviously, the whip thrower who matches their whip throws to the whip catcher's pain scale the most wins.

This game is not so much about winning or losing but improving the dungeon skill of the whip thrower to match the pain/pleasure level of the whip catcher in a finessed and controlled manner.

Chapter 25

Needle Play—Whip Play Combo Vignette

NEEDLES PRODUCE A different type of endorphin rush than does impact play, but a needle scene can be just as mild or intense as a whip scene. What happens when you combine needle play with whip play? With most BDSM play, there are varying levels of intensity, but needles automatically ramp up the endorphins and create a higher threshold to work from with the whip.

Before you do any scene involving needles, be sure to cover all of the safety rules. When you are combining whips and needles, additional safety considerations apply.

Safety. What should not occur during a whip/needle scene is the whip removing a needle and flinging it across the room at close to the speed of sound—that would be very bad. All needles need to be anchored in place. I use a transparent Tagederm surgical film to do that.[23] Tagederm is sticky and will adhere in place. It will provide a protective covering over the needles to prevent any blood spray resulting from the scene. Needle play with whips does not necessarily involve blood play, but if a needle site starts to bleed, the Tagederm helps prevent blood from becoming airborne and atomized.

The hybrid needle/whip scene most likely will begin with needle play. I recommend 21-23-gauge needles for this type of scene. I would not go thinner as the needles might bend or break. Be creative and artistic with the needles and cover them with Tagederm. These can go anywhere you might normally do needle play.

Playing with the needles with a singletail requires finesse. I recommend feathering butterfly kisses on any needles placed outside of the normal whip strike zones of the shoulders, butt cheeks, and chest. The normal strike zones can be played with using the normal controlled puff approach. If the whip catcher is sufficiently enjoying the endorphins, the scene can be ramped up to even the controlled puff seven or eight range, resulting in the whip being cracked.

Take your time with the whip. Putting the needles in place and covering them with Tagederm already got the scene well underway. Warming up the whip catcher into the controlled one-to-three pain level provides a nice introduction to the whip-throwing aspect.

Check in with your whip catcher about their pain level and correlate your whip strikes to match their levels. Read body language and let the whip catcher breathe. It does not require speed but finesse and teasing the needles. Let the needles work for you, and play with them with the whip.

Aftercare. Expect the whip catcher to have an endorphin buzz following the scene. They may be in a different head space or subspace than ever before because most whip catchers have not experienced this vignette before.

---

23 Plastic wrap and pallet wrap could also be used, but I caution against it as they do not meet sanitary standards let alone sterile standards.

Have the normal supplies for needle removal—gauze pads, tissue, and alcohol. Dispose of each needle in a sharps container. Stop any bleeders using gauze or tissue and direct pressure. There should not be any bruising in the areas where only butterfly kisses and light whip play were done. However, in the areas with heavier play, expect bruising. Bruising can be reduced, and healing can be accelerated by using arnica cream unless, of course, your whip catcher likes bruises.

Once the needles are removed, expect some extended aftercare. Hydrate the whip catcher and wrap them in a blanket as the endorphin rush, when it peaks and tails off, may result in shakes and mild shock.

Chapter 26

Bullwhip Magick Vignette: Feathers Everywhere

I NEVER HAD a desire to do performance art until someone invited me to put a showcase together. I agreed initially as a favor and to support the efforts of a leather event, Beyond Leather. What I did not expect was how much fun I had doing it and the energy that the show created in the room and between my whip catcher and myself. As soon as I had finished, I wanted to fix the lessons learned, put together another showcase, and do it again, better than the first time. I was hooked.

This vignette took months to plan, with several pilots and many hurdles, but it was a once-in-a-lifetime experience. Hopefully, every advanced whip thrower will have an opportunity to demonstrate their creativity with a bullwhip and create magick.

About four months before Beyond Leather, Master Oakman contacted me and said that on the first night of Beyond Leather, the theater would be a Whip It Good Theater. (Every evening, for those who have never been to Beyond Leather, there are kinky theaters--burlesque, drag, demonstration scenes, mud or oil wrestling). They sell tickets and donate proceeds to a worthy leather cause. There were to be two 20-minute acts in the Whip Theater, and Master Oakman asked if Moodstone and I would be willing to do the first act. I said yes, even before I had visualized what I would do.

Visualization of the 20-minute Whip Theater, Act 1, by Dex. For the requested whip theater act, I visualized a beautiful peacock, Vegas-style showgirl. I would remove all of her feathers using my bullwhip. It sounded simple, but how were the feathers going to be held in place so that my whip would remove them?

I came up with the idea of using needles and placing the feathers in the needle cups to hold them in place. I ordered bright blue ostrich feathers of different sizes from Amazon.

Moodstone researched thongs, headdresses, and hand fans. She found a glitzy thong made by Victoria's Secret that was a color match. It had rhinestones for the g-string portion and was NOT cheap. The headpiece off of Amazon was a headband that was stretchy and could hold feathers to form a peacock feather hat. The hand fans were so she could have something to do with her hands during the whip theater act.

When I received the feathers, we did a practice session at home. I put some needles in her back and inserted the quill from a feather into the needle cup. What I discovered was that the feathers' quills were all different sizes and that none of them fit snugly into the needle cups. They would all fall out.

I thought perhaps Play-Doh rolled up into a tiny ball and put into the needle cup would provide a tiny filler that would grip the feather quill enough to hold it in place, yet not so tightly that the whip could not remove the feather on a whip strike. The Play-Doh was a movement in the right direction to solve the problem, but it was too flexible and not stiff enough to hold the feathers in place.

The next attempt to resolve this solution was to try various types of modeling clay. Sculpy modeling clay did the trick. It was stiff enough to hold the feather quills in place, but in a pilot test, I was able to remove the feathers with my whip. However, Sculpy dries out and becomes hard. Fresh, unopened supplies were needed for each practice and also for the performance theater at the venue.

To turn Moodstone into a Vegas showgirl using feathers held in place with needles was going to require some prep time before the Whip Theater. But how much prep time, how many needles, and what gauge needles? More research.

I ordered a couple of boxes of 25, 23, and 21-gauge single-use hypodermic needles. Without being a medical professional, ordering that many needles wasn't easy, as not all vendors would sell them to me. It took some time and research to find a source.

I discovered on testing that the 25-gauge was too thin and flexible. They were not sturdy enough to hold the bigger feathers. They also would bend when hit with a whip strike. I did not want to risk having a needle breaking and being embedded under the skin and then having to dig it out with some advanced medical play. 23 and 21-gauge needles seemed sturdy enough, and both worked. I settled on the 21-gauge for the whip theater.

The placement of the feathers and how long it would take to place them and prep them had to be worked out. I experimented at home with placement and how they looked and fanned after set in place. Then, I figured out how many were needed. We practiced each Saturday for a month leading up to the whip theater performance to figure out where and what pattern would give the best coverage to turn Moodstone into a peacock.

I settled on 100 needles. Unwrapping 100 individually wrapped and sealed single-use hypos takes time. Add to that the time needed to roll small balls of Sculpy to go into the needle cups, place the Sculpy in the needle cup, insert the needle in the correct pattern to provide full peacock coverage, and then place the correct size feather in each cup. We piloted this prep process on a Saturday, which took me an hour and a half. I was happy with the results, but several important aspects became evident.

Making the tiny clay balls out of Sculpy was a critical element. They had to be the right size to hold the feather in place, but not so large that when the quill was inserted it displaced clay down the needle shaft and extruded it out the needle tip. To do so would have chanced embedding or leaving remnants of model clay beneath the skin upon removal of the needles. This was a safety concern, and it took hours to figure out the right amount needed.

The other safety concern evident after the pilot was that most of the needles stayed in, but a few, depending upon the angle of the needle, came out. We couldn't be in a theater with 400 people and be throwing used hypodermic needles around the stage or into the audience. I needed to figure out a way to firmly anchor them in place.

My first idea was to cork the tip with small corks. But this would take a lot of time, and there would be a chance of small cork fibers being embedded in the skin upon needle removal. After some thought, Tagederm seemed to be the best solution. It came in four by six-inch rectangles and could be placed over a six-inch row of needles anchoring them in place. It just had to be positioned so the needle cups were exposed and the feathers could be inserted. That sounds simple but Tagederm transparent surgical dressing is sticky and tricky to get cleanly in place, exactly where you want it. I ordered two boxes of Tagederm off of Amazon.

Adding Tagederm to the prep process added time beyond the one and a half hours it took to do the prep for the pilot. However, one of the things that was evident after the pilot was that I could NOT do all of this by myself without help. I called on my dear friend Master Snoflak and asked if she would be willing to help us with this performance scene/whip theater. Snoflak is excellent with needle play, and she is also a great whip thrower. In her slave days, she was part of the Bob Deegan workshop ensemble and was trained by Deegan to throw whips. I consider her one of the best horizontal singletail whip throwers in the country. I sent her photos and diagrams of the pilot needle play placement. We had several conversations on the phone and by email.

Now that I had the process of turning Moodstone into a Vegas show girl, the SM version, figured out, I had to decide what to do during the 20 minutes of the performance scene. I did not want it to be me just throwing a bullwhip for 20 min. I carefully picked music and edited it so it was exactly 20 min long and burned it to a DVD for the theater's music assistant. The playlist consisted of Viva! (Orion Mix) by Bond, Perfect by Ed Sheeran, Love Runs Out by One Republic, and Sound of Silence by Disturbed.

I planned to begin our performance by grounding an eight-foot black snake whip diagonally across the stage. Then, I planned to position Moodstone in the middle of the stage, straddling the black snake whip. The performance scene would start with me picking up the snake whip and making a reverse crack, with the whip passing between her legs and cracking off my right hip. I would then do soft wraps with the snake around her waist.

I would continue with hard wraps, with the snake cracking loudly behind her, then gently wrapping around her waist. Next, using rhythm whip techniques to complement the song, I would throw a three-foot snake whip for one song, put it down, and throw a four-foot target bullwhip for one song, then a four-foot latigo y dago bullwhip for one song. After three songs, I would invite Master Snoflak to join me for a whip flurry to end the performance art scene. My goal was to play with the feathers and remove a few along the way but to leave most of the feather removal for the flurry portion of the scene. So, preliminary planning for the whip theater was complete. Now, we just had to pull it off.

We arrived at Beyond Leather on Thursday and settled in. There was dungeon play that evening, and I observed a whip scene—Lady Umbra was playing with her slave. I'm a pretty good judge of whip skills, and it did not take me long to realize that this young woman throwing horizontal style was very good. She had great finesse and control of her whip at all times. I complimented her on the scene once it was over.

I decided that if she was willing to participate in the Whip Theater, it would be nice to call her out of the audience to join the whip flurry at the end of the performance scene and help us remove feathers. The following day, I approached Lady Umbra with the idea, and she graciously agreed to help.

The convention head producer was in charge of the theaters for the event. I briefed the convention producer on the Whip Theater act and our plans. I asked if perhaps I could access the stage that afternoon briefly and check my whip circle. I needed to ensure there was room to throw the eight-foot snake whip (12 feet total length). This is a long whip to throw indoors, and I had no idea how big the stage was. He said no, that the stage was being used all afternoon, and we would have to just go for it at showtime. He said there wasn't an area beside the stage where we could do needle prep.

The convention head producer also told me that immediately before the Whip Theater was The Opening Ceremony. He said that for opening ceremonies, the room divider would be closed on the theater, sectioning off the back third of the room. This was where all of the dungeon equipment was staged to set up the dungeon for play following the Whip Theater later that evening.

This back third of the convention hall was jammed with dungeon equipment, except for the medical play area, which was in the back corner, with the floor tarped and the equipment set exactly as it would be for dungeon play later. The producer said this was a perfect area to do the needle prep and also an appropriate area to do it in. When showtime came, all we had to do was walk Moodstone out of the medical area into the hall and walk about 100 feet to the side curtains leading up the stairs, and we were on the stage.

That afternoon, I was at the bootblack stand getting my leathers blacked in preparation for the evening whip theater. I had my whip bag with me, and the stand was just down from the convention hall where the whip theater would take place. One of the side doors was open to the convention hall, and I peeked in. The other whip act that followed us was on stage rehearsing their performance. I noticed a person in the hall working with them on lighting.

During a lull, I approached him, introduced myself, and asked if, when they were done practicing, it would be possible for me to jump onstage and check my whip lengths and mark a couple of spots with masking tape. He said he also handled the music for the performances, and I gave him my DVD with music on it. He asked me what type of lighting I wanted, and I said dimmed white light. Nothing fancy. Dimmed white light is the best lighting for whip play, anyway.

I was able to check my snake whip length prior, and I knew the opening crack was going to work. I also marked all the spots where Moodstone would have to stand with masking tape. She had three spots to stand on the stage during the performance: center at the beginning, moving to the back corner on a diagonal for the next three whips, and then back to the center for the whip flurry.

The Skulpy tiny balls would have to be created an hour before the needle prep began. I had a plastic tray from the Dollar Store and a chuck to stage them onto. I gloved up and began making 100 tiny Skulpy balls two and a half hours before the Whip Theater was supposed to begin. Once these were made, the tray was covered with plastic wrap to keep them from drying out and to keep them sanitary. They were carried down to the medical play area behind, where the Opening Ceremonies would take place.

One and a half hours before show time, we began needle prep as planned. We were the only ones in the medical play area and were uninterrupted as we started needle prep. I would unwrap each needle, place a tiny ball of Skulpy in the needle cup, and hand it to Master Snoflak to insert into Moodstone's back and place in the predetermined pattern. Both of us were gloved. Things were proceeding as planned.

For those crafting a vignette as complex as this performance scene, it is advisable that all involved in the associated preparation area be informed as to what is going to happen—the DMs, Head DM, Head of Event Security, and Convention Co-Producer—all need to know what is going down. Informing these people on the fly, during preparation, happened one at a time until everyone was satisfied and happy that this was an authorized activity in preparation for one of the whip performances.

When it was showtime, we walked Moodstone down the hallway and into a curtained waiting area to go on stage. Someone said they were ready for us, so we went on stage.

The music started, and I began with a thunderous crack of that eight-foot snake whip between Moodstone's legs. Then, I did two soft and two hard wraps around her waist with cracks. Care had to be taken to wrap exactly around her waist, as if I had wrapped too high, I would have disturbed some of her feathers.

Photo 66 Setup for opening crack of performance scenes at Beyond Leather & Weekend of Wickedness. Reverse crack between the legs finishing off of the right hip of the thrower with an 8' snake whip.

The snake and two bullwhip songs went well. It was a thrilling challenge to use three different whips of different lengths, throw them in rhythm to the music that was playing, use footwork while throwing that complemented the whip rhythm and appeared as dancing with a whip, and at the same time remove feathers from six feet away without removing the hypodermic needles and sending them flying around the convention hall. I was hyper-focused and pumped up on adrenaline.

In hindsight, I removed too many feathers and should have left more on for the whip flurry ending. For those up close to the stage, I'm sure they were aware of what I was doing and how difficult it was. Anyone beyond the first few rows likely had no appreciation for what they were watching. After three songs, I called Master Snoflak and Lady Umbra up to the stage. We circled Moodstone, removing the remaining feathers without removing any needles.

As the whip act ended, the music/lighting manager realized that many in the audience didn't understand what they had just witnessed. He prompted me to say a few words about the scene. Ideally, this would have been better in the beginning, but it was done in the end.

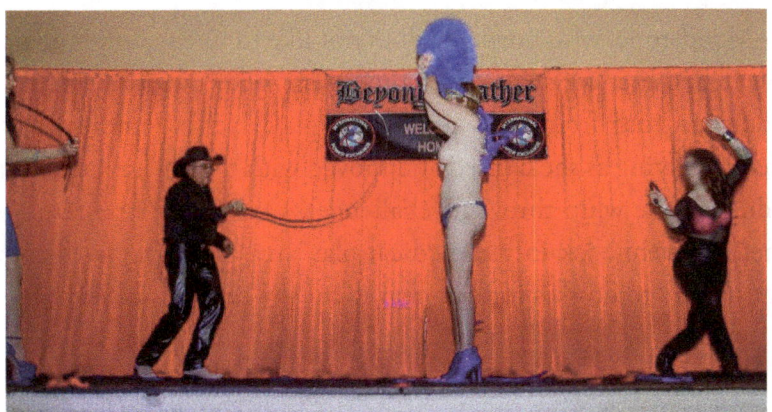

Photo 67 Whip flurry with Master Snoflak, Lady Umbra and Dex at Beyond Leather.

For 20 minutes on the stage of Beyond Leather, Bullwhip Magick was happening. This was the biggest adrenaline rush I've ever had while throwing a whip. Even with all of the distractions, once I stepped on stage, top space kicked in, along with the hyper-focus it takes to throw a whip in the dungeon. The world stopped, time stood still, and with 300-plus people watching, I had the best time of my life. It was a once-in-a-lifetime opportunity to throw my bullwhip at Moodstone with the leather world watching - a peak moment for any whip-throwing exhibitionist.

Photo 68 Rotating the Whip Flurry at Beyond Leather.

Moodstone, who normally does not like to be the center of attention, felt the energy and adrenaline rush mixed with an incredible endorphin rush from the whip/needle play. Her blue peacock hand fans were flying as she danced and moved with the music (incidentally adding to the whip throwers' challenge). One of her first responses, when we were back in the medical play area removing needles, was that we *had* to do this for our next event - Weekend of Wickedness.

Photo 69 Weekend of Wickedness feathers performance scene.

With all of the months of prep and lessons learned, it was a memorable experience, and I was more than ready to do it all over again in a smaller venue, taking the lessons learned and making the second dance of bullwhip magick even better.

Photo 70 Master Snoflak and Dex Circling a Round Robin during the WoW performance scene.

Chapter 27

Roses Roses: The Flower Vase Vignette

THE CONCEPT FOR this vignette began when I attended Master Dale's knife-play class at the Weekend of Wickedness event in upstate New York.

Master Dale began his presentation by pallet wrapping a dozen very mature, long-stemmed red roses to the demo bottom. I'm unsure where he got these roses, but the thorns had been left on the stems. As he placed the roses around the demo bottom, he compressed the rose blossoms and very tightly wrapped the demo bottom until they were fully mummified in pallet wrap.

Then, he taught knife play, and as he taught, he carefully cut the pallet wrap over each individual rose, until the rose blossom exploded out of the hole he cut in the wrap. It seemed as if the rose blossom burst open, springing forth in all of its glory. When Master Dale was done, he had created a living flower vase and a full, beautiful arrangement of roses. I thought this would make a great whip performance scene as I visualized whipping off all of the rose petals during a 20-minute whip presentation.

I decided to pilot the Roses Roses vignette before attempting it in front of an audience. This turned out to be another instance where the scene I visualized turned out differently when it was performed live. I learned that this was a very layered, complex scene. While the layers added context, texture, and aesthetic appeal, there are trade-offs that I will discuss here.

Roses Roses Vignette

The goal was to turn Moodstone into a living flower vase. I envisioned using two dozen roses - one dozen red and one dozen white. I could not find white, so I had to substitute yellow.

I bought the roses two days ahead of time, which ended up being one of the problems with the pilot. I bought the roses on Thursday and put them in water with no food; by Saturday night, they were still too fresh. I learned that I needed roses that were fully opened at the time of the event and "ready" to drop their petals. I needed to buy them about a week earlier than the day that I needed them.

I wanted long-stemmed roses with the thorns left on them. It turned out they were hard to find, as the florists I visited had stripped the thorns off of their roses. I was actually not able to source long-stemmed roses with the thorns left on the stems, even with an extensive Google search. I probably should have asked Master Dale.

My first pilot vignette took place at The Woodshed Orlando. I began by taping a drop cloth to the floor where the scene would occur. I then put Moodstone in a rope dress with a simple diamond pattern on the front and the back. I chose a hard point with 360-degree access around it. I put her wrists into partial suspension cuffs and attached her to the hard point. Then proceeded to lift the winch until her arms were above her head.

I cut the rose stems short, about six inches long, and put a rose in each of the Vs of the rope dress, 360 degrees around her body, with extra roses in her chest cleavage and around the butt. Then, I pallet-wrapped her, compressing the rose blooms as I wrapped her down to her knees. This is why there is a need for a hard point. At this point, she was essentially a mummy, free-standing. If she falls over, she might be injured, so the hard point is a safety thing.

Then, I indulged in a little bit of knife play. I cut the pallet wrap so just the bloom of the rose blossomed and opened. Once all of the roses were opened, I had a living flower vase with petals ready to drop.

Obviously, they needed to be whipped off. For the next part of the pilot, I threw a snake and a bullwhip, and that is when I discovered that the roses were too fresh. While I made a royal mess on the floor, the roses would not give up their petals, even under the lash of a bullwhip.

The next part of the plan was to cut the pallet wrap off. I used a Gerber Zip Knife for this, and it worked really well. Then, I continued to whip the roses held on by the rope dress but without the pallet wrap. At one point, about an hour into this, I realized I was not going to get all of the petals off of those fresh roses. That was when I ended the scene.

In debrief, Moodstone said she could hardly feel the whip through the pallet wrap. From the audience's perspective, there is a living flower vase: the pallet wrap creates the visual of a living flower vase with roses blooming through it. From the whip bottom perspective, it creates a layer that eliminates most of the sensation for her. On the whip-throwing end, the pallet wrap creates a loud noise when hit with a bullwhip but doesn't add a lot to the vignette from a technical accuracy perspective.

We were scheduled to perform this vignette for Jax Kinkfest that fall, so I decided to do another pilot scene. I planned to forego using pallet wrap. I decided to use spring flowers instead of roses, which were less expensive and would drop the blooms easier without having to season them for a week.

I still used a rope dress to hold the flowers, along with a drop cloth, as that made cleanup so much easier. Without pallet wrap, the hard point requirement went away, and the setup location became much more flexible.

As with any pilot, feedback and reflection will improve the vignette the next time it is done.

Thus, the vignette evolved. My next attempt again took place at The Woodshed Orlando. I began with a simple rope chest harness. My bottom's arms were not restrained. I had enough rope left to make a simple V from chest to crotch front and back.

I spaced medium-sized clothespins around the rope above the breasts and across the back on the upper and lower chest harness horizontal ropes. I used the V front and back and spaced clothespins down the V to the top of the pubic mound and to the top of the butt crack.

Next, I used the chest harness to hold six spring flowers in place, arranged like a bouquet, with a flower on either side of the breast, one between the breast, and three across the back harness. Last, I clothes pinned the breasts. My bullwhip targets were ready.

I was surprised at how easy it was to whip off the flowers. They were the most fun to play with. The clothespins, however, were very challenging to remove, depending on the location of the rope. The plus side was that the rope provided a secure enough anchor for the clothespin that the whip bottom was actually taking pretty heavy whip strikes with my attempts to remove them.

The clothespins directly on the breast were easily removed with no real challenge other than the longer they remained on, the better the response from the whip catcher when they were removed. A couple of clothespins on the side of the body were just not going to come off because of the body's physical shape and the direction the whip had to travel.

Magically, the clothespins all fell off by my walking up to the whip catcher to check in on her during one of the in-betweens between dungeon songs. When we were done playing, the dungeon smelled like a florist's cutting room; if I had chosen to use roses, the aroma would have been overwhelming.

Losing the pallet wrap made this vignette less complex and easier to accomplish. The whip skills required stayed pretty much the same, and without the pallet wrap, my beloved whip bottom actually got to enjoy the whip.

With two pilots using slight variations, I was ready to do Jax Kinkfest. I chose to do a diamond pattern rope dress and place spring flowers 360 degrees over Moodstone's body, recreating the living flower arrangement. I had a 20-minute play set of energetic dungeon music, and I whipped the flowers off during the music set. A drop cloth made cleanup easy.

The music playlist for this performance art session was Dance With Me Tonight (Olly Murs), Strange Days (The Strutts & Robbie Williams), Love Runs Out (One Republic), Separate Ways (Journey), and Show Me The Way (Styx).

Photo 71 Flowers Vignette from Jax FetFest

Chapter 28

Streamer Whip Strip Tease Vignette

THE FLOWERS VIGNETTE at Jax FetFest in October was such a hit that Kat, the event's organizer, asked us to return to Jacksonville in the spring and do another whip demonstration and workshop. I didn't want to do the same performance scene twice in the same year, so I had to come up with something else equally fun to watch but easy to prep and set up.

Years earlier, I had been at a Wild West arts convention competing in their whip cracking and whip targeting competition. I finished the competition tied for first place, and the tiebreaker was cutting a streamer attached to a tennis ball fitted with a cord. The judge swung the cord with the tennis ball around his head. The streamer was trailing behind the tennis ball, and the goal was to see how many times you could cut the streamer as it came by. This vanilla experience gave me an idea for a new kinky whip vignette.

What if I somehow fashioned a top and skirt out of streamer material for Moodstone and then used my whip to cut the streamers off one or a few at a time?

I first tried using rolls of crepe party streamers. What I discovered was that the crepe streamer had elastic embedded in it and that it was not easy to cut, regardless of the type of cracker material I was using. I wanted something easily cut with a single strand of braided mason line cracker. (This cracker is normally more intense and stingier than what Moodstone likes in a scene, but in a performance scene in front of a large crowd, adrenaline, anxiety, and stage fright provide an adequate cocktail to take her mind off of that, which made this cracker an excellent choice.)

It was off to Walmart to buy colored tissue paper. I took a yardstick and cut 18-inch strips of colored tissue paper. As a rule of thumb, one packet of tissue paper cut up will be sufficient for a top and another for a skirt. The variable here is the circumference of the whip bottom you are working with for the performance art session.

The top and bottom streamers were cut one and a half inches wide and 18 inches long and were held in place by a modified TK[24] rope harness on top and a simple waist rope harness for the skirt. The modified TK framed the breasts but left the arms free. This way, a whip bottom can move and dance during the whip performance scene.

Tension of the TK should be such that the breasts are well enhanced and framed but not so tight as to make it difficult to slip the tissue under the top rope line of the TK to secure and fashion the top 360 degrees around. The waist harness is a simple rope belt. Passing it through the crotch area is okay, but it is not necessary to create a rope belt around the waist. Again, it should not be so tight that you cannot slip tissue 360 degrees around the waist to form a tissue skirt. When the whip bottom spins around, the tissue whirls up and shows more skin. This is nice for the audience and adds to the difficulty of removing tissue with the whip.

The color of the tissue paper gives this vignette a lot of variation

---

24 A traditional TK restrains the arms behind the back. A modified TK is tied the same way but leaves the arms free.

with little difficulty. It can be music theme-driven or occasion-driven. So have fun with the outfit and make the colors fit an occasion.

Photo 72 Streamers Outfit from Jax FetFest ready for the Showcase Whip Scene.

The song music set for the Jacksonville Screaming Streamers Strip Tease was We Will Rock You (Queen), Flowers (Miley Cyrus), Dance Monkey (Tones and I), Ordinary World (Adam Lambert), and Love of My Life (Queen). It was a great success and a big hit.

We re-did this particular vignette for Weekend of Wickedness that summer, and it was not as big a success. Jacksonville's venue has more of a club, party-style vibe, which worked for this type of vignette. WoW has a more spiritual type of vibe, and while the performance session was equally as good, the satisfied feeling you have when a sweet moment is over was not there. Knowing the audience, the venue, and the vibe expected goes a long way toward selecting the perfect vignette for a particular situation.

Chapter 29

Bloody Mess Vignette: Blood Play with a Bullwhip

IN MY 25 years of throwing whips, I've been approached a few times by people who fantasize about being cut by a bullwhip. I do not do this type of whip scene, but I wanted to include a bit about it in my book as there are people who do want this and tops who enjoy playing this way. Crafting a vignette that involves blood play with a bullwhip involves many considerations.

Well-informed consent is required for participation on both sides of the whip. I recommend having a spotter who has some first aid and medical background. You will need an appropriate venue at which to conduct the scene, as there will be airborne and atomized blood flying around. An appropriate music choice, to me, is critical.

The physiological and psychological makeup of the whip bottom is important as the goal of a vignette like this isn't to mentally damage the whip bottom. For some, a scene such as this may have a healing effect. For many, blood play is a spiritual experience as blood symbolizes the life force that flows and provides life. I refer you to the scene described in WITD with Master Malik and slave linda WITD, pp. 131-7).

The most important variable in this type of play is cracker material selection to provide the desired cut of the skin to cause bleeding. My beloved lady sally-style cracker is not a good choice. The single braided mason line leaves marks and abrasions, but I doubt it would cut easily.

Cracker options that cut:

- mono-filament fishing line
- twisted cracker made of silk thread
- thin Dynema cording
- braided mason line (but probably not my first choice as it marks easily but is not easy to cut skin with)
- Kevlar (would be in the same class as braided mason line, in my opinion)

Cautions against considering this type of scene: Many states classify this as assault, even if consent was involved. Finding a venue that would allow this type of scene because of liability issues that might evolve in the afterglow might be tricky. Realize up front that while many fantasize about this type of scene if they do not have prior experience bottoming for heavy scenes, fantasy and reality often are two different things. Retrospectively, they may have regrets. I would recommend extensive negotiations and very clear written consent.

This type of scene, to me, is very dark. I much prefer a different type of energy and positive vibes.

Chapter 30

Consent, Communication, and Safety

CONSENT, COMMUNICATION, AND safety are key variables in any type of whip play. This topic was covered in Chapter 11 of *Whips in the Dungeon* (2019), but it is so vital to all BDSM play, and whip play especially, that it is worth going over again.

Regardless of whether you only throw with a primary partner or if you, as I do, throw with anyone who's willing and negotiates a whip scene, HOW do you negotiate, communicate, and establish consent before and during a whip scene?

Negotiations. There are several approaches to negotiations. The **checklist** has been around for decades. Checklists are a great way to negotiate, assuming you have a well-constructed checklist that covers a broad spectrum of play, sexual preferences, triggers, and hard and soft limits.

Checklists are a good approach if you think that there might be a possibility of a relationship developing out of your play date. They are a time investment and should be completed by both top and bottom, as someone's hard limit might not be a hard limit for someone else. Then, if a relationship does develop out of negotiated play, the checklist should be revisited every six months or so to see if any hard limits have softened, to note if any new curiosities exist, and to touch base with how a relationship has grown through dungeon play and D/s.

DITSA. Desire, Injuries, Triggers, Safety, and Aftercare. Acronyms are memory devices that help us remember important things when else we might forget. You will not see this acronym anywhere else in the lifestyle other than in my previous book. I made it up years ago to remind me of things I wanted to cover while negotiating pickup play with someone I was playing with for the first time. You could easily craft your own acronym, but you need something that covers the bases. This one has held me in good stead for 25 years.

Desire. Primarily, this is about the desires of the whip catcher. Certainly, my first book described it as such.

Perhaps you are playing with a newbie who's not only never experienced a whip but has not even experienced a flogger. This scene might turn into an exploratorium of every impact tool you have in your toy bag on a particular night. Each impact toy introduced is part of the bottom's desire to experience and explore, to discover what they like and don't like.

Or it might be an experienced whip bottom who has been whipped many times and enjoyed it but only recently relocated and moved to the area. They are trying to find a new whip top they can trust.

Some might have had a previous whip scene with you, an introductory scene, and they are back for a second dance. Perhaps you only introduced them to a signal whip or a snake whip, and they want to experience a bullwhip. They might want to go deeper. Before, your scene remained within their pain levels of four to six, but this time, they are interested in playing at their six to eight levels. You might have only worked their back and butt last time, and this time they are curious about what it feels like on the chest.

Desires have many aspects. Perhaps the whip bottom has a medical appointment on Monday and cannot afford to have marks. Other reasons a whip bottom may not want marks include family, children, vanilla relationships, or even medical reasons. Someone might have a beloved tattoo on their back and fear the whip scarring or defacing it. (In my experience, tattoos are safe from any damage a whip might do).

The desire not to have marks is important and also relates to intentionality in play, as this desire might play heavily into your cracker choice for your whips as well as the style, level, and intensity you play with. A lot of desire is the perception and wishes of the whip catcher. They are to be respected and their wishes honored.

For many years, I only considered the whip catcher's desires. I focused on what they wanted, their goals, and on giving them a good experience. But then I met Moodstone, and she desired to please me and make me happy. Her desire was that I would fulfill my desires.

I had never before thought about what I wanted to get out of a whip scene. It is safe to say at the advanced level, especially as whip throwers get many miles on their whips and throwing arms, that they should be focused on what they are looking for in a whip scene, as well as the whip catcher's desires.

Injuries. This sounds like a simple topic, but sometimes, people don't like to talk about previous injuries or medical issues. Both parties in a whip scene need to be honest with each other if the whip scene is to be fun and successful.

Someone might not be able to stand for more than 10 minutes. This is valuable information at the negotiation stage because perhaps the whip catcher could sit straddling the back of a chair for the scene, or use another piece of dungeon equipment other than a St. Andrew's cross.

Other medical issues include possible low blood sugar with diabetes, sensitive surgery areas, or medical devices to avoid on the body. Consideration of any injury or medical issue that might be affected during play should be discussed. Whip throwers are not mind readers.

The whip thrower should also share any injuries or limitations. As a personal example, I have a 35% rotator cuff tear in my right shoulder and popped my long bicep in that arm about 10 years ago. It does not affect my throwing at the beginning of an evening, but sometimes, as the night wears on, my right shoulder will drop, and I notice on the forehand side my whip strikes start to drift down off the targeted areas. This is a sign to me that the scene needs to wind down and stop. I've had whip catchers think they did something wrong when I abruptly stopped a scene and then had to explain why. It is much better if this is all explained upfront.

Triggers. Sometimes, a situation or other variable can trigger an adverse psychological response as a person is reminded of bad past experiences. This could be connected to something that happened in vanilla life that is not directly related to kink, but an association can be triggered by something the top does during a scene. This inadvertent trigger can most likely be avoided by being upfront about it, discussing it, and coming up with a viable plan to avoid it, adjust for it, or adapt around it.

As discussed previously in this book, some people react badly to the crack of the whip due to PTSD. In negotiations, the top and bottom might agree to doing a subsonic whip scene or using hearing protection. Or if the whip bottom has had several successful whip scenes with you using subsonic or hearing protection, you might try a workaround and do the warmup and intermediate work subsonically, and then during an in-between, check-in and tell the whip catcher that, if acceptable to them, you are going to start cracking and that it is a bullwhip. By clearly stating and giving a heads up that a whip is going to be cracking, you give the whip catcher with the trigger clear notice, and they have the opportunity to say, "Yes, I'm ok, let's try it" OR "NO". This workaround should be discussed beforehand as part of ongoing negotiations.

But the bottom line is, if someone has a trigger, it is important during negotiations to identify it and discuss how to proceed so both the whip thrower and whip catcher are on the same page.

Safety. Injuries and triggers are related to safety, but safety covers all aspects of whip play.

A beginning whip thrower who has a willing bottom for target practice in catching their whip, for safety, might put a neck pillow on their whip catcher's neck.

A whip catcher might consider wearing eye protection during a whip scene. Definitely, during a whip flurry vignette, the whip catcher should be wearing eye protection.

The whip catcher should remove all jewelry from the ears, neck, and chest. Do not bottom for a whip if you are wearing nipple jewelry, as a cracker can catch it and rip the piercing out. If nipple jewelry or genital jewelry are closely fitted and Tagederm or another similar covering is used to cover them, then whip play can be done with risk acknowledged and agreed to. The simplest solution is to remove the jewelry or not play near it.

Then, there is safety for the whip thrower. A beginning whip thrower would be advised to wear a stiff-brimmed hat, eye protection, and long sleeves. Even as a thrower who's thrown for 25 years, when I'm doing dueling whips or two-handed work, I wear a stiff-brimmed hat.

In a dungeon, Dungeon Monitors are usually there to ensure everyone playing is safe. Some dungeons do not have whip areas, and any area or piece of equipment can be used for a whip scene as long as there is sufficient room and, when needed, a spotter. This isn't just to keep dungeon voyeurs or spectators safe. The spotters also ensure that someone doesn't walk into a whip and disrupt the scene that is in progress.

Safety considerations when setting up a whip lane. Sometimes, there are dungeons that set up a whip area or whip lane, and the DMs setting this up may not be whip throwers and might not know what size the area needs to be. When the whip lane is so small that the fall catches (on the recovery swing of a figure eight) on the boundary tape the throw finishes off target. This creates an unsafe setting for the whip bottom.

A Call To Action. Whips belong in every dungeon. A three-foot signal, a two-foot snake, and a two-foot bullwhip all throw like a child's toy and are no longer than a flogger. There should be no restrictions on throwing these whips anywhere a flogger can be thrown in any dungeon. For a four-foot signal whip, which is the most common whip found in a dungeon, a whip lane should be a minimum of ten feet wide and eight feet deep. A station to accommodate a four-foot bullwhip needs to be eight feet wide and ten feet deep.

I recommend using a ten-foot by ten-foot area to build a single station to accommodate both four-foot signals and four-foot bullwhips. It actually takes less area to throw a four-foot bullwhip overhand than to throw a four-foot signal whip horizontally.

Aftercare. Aftercare for a whip bottom takes many forms, but it is meant to ensure that the whip bottom comes down safely from their whip experience and endorphin drop. Often, experienced whip catchers do not need any more aftercare than a bottle of water and a hug.

But everyone experiences the whip differently. After some heavy scenes, when the endorphin drop begins, the whip bottom may have shock-like symptoms. Mild chills, shakes, and body temperature drops are possible. It is good to have a throw blanket on hand if that happens.

Do not let a whip catcher walk alone on shaky legs without assisting them to a safe aftercare area. The whip top must pay attention to the effects of the scene on the whip bottom and respond accordingly.

As part of negotiations, I discuss aftercare. If the whip catcher needs extended aftercare, I make sure they have someone available to provide what they need. I will give them a hug, with permission, and a bottle of water and help them to the aftercare area to be with their chosen aftercare person.

Remember that aftercare is not just for the whip bottoms. Be sure to stay hydrated and take breaks as needed between scenes[25].

Consent. Explicit Consent. This is pretty straightforward. There really should not be all of the consent issues floating around these days that I constantly hear about, but there are. Perhaps it is because when I began 25 years ago, it was in the infancy of the Internet. Email flew at 14.5 bps, and it took two minutes for a web page to build. I emailed the webmistress of the local munch group, and it took three emails just to squeak out from her the location of the local munch group. I had attended three munches and had gotten to know maybe a dozen people before the leader of the munch group even hinted or let on that they had a private listserv, and that was how the group communicated between munches. He warned me that it was moderated and that if I didn't want to get kicked off, I needed to be a gentleman. Then it was another month before I was invited to an educational presentation at someone's home garage dungeon. After a few months of attending educational events, I was invited to a house play party. What does all of that have to do with explicit consent? Nothing directly, BUT:

In today's world, with Fetlife and ample social networking resources, anyone who is interested in kink can sign up for a BDSM

---

25 Moodstone for years has given me a foot rub after many of our scenes. I cannot tell you, as a whip top, how wonderful this feels after standing for several hours on a polished concrete dungeon floor.

event, sign a waiver, show up, and, the first evening, be in a leather dungeon in full play, clearly not knowing anything about what they are watching or doing. They can do this without having any leather educational experiences or even without having attended a munch. Regardless of your experience or lack of it, my advice to avoid inadvertent consent violations is to closely follow the DITSA guidelines first of all.

Once you are ready to play with someone, establish a connection with them with permission. Breathe together, in and out, get in rhythm with your breathing, connect with the music in the dungeon, and feel the energy. With permission, hold each other's hands or place each of your hands on each other's chest and feel each of you breathe the life breath that makes us humans.

Begin slowly, lightly, and warm up the skin. Use the dungeon music as your guide. Warm up for a song and check in on the in-betweens. An in-between is the pause between one song and the next in a dungeon music playlist. The in-between check-in is what will ensure explicit consent. The in-between is perhaps one of the most important variables in a whip scene[26].

Each and every time you check in with the whip catcher and ask them, on a Likert pain scale of one to ten, where they are, they tell you, and you get explicit consent to continue. Do this at every check-in. During DITSA and negotiations, perhaps you agreed on a warmup of one to four and play at four to six. Correlate your controlled puff one to eight, that you've been practicing for so long just waiting for this scene, with the Likert scale answer the whip catcher gave you. This tells you exactly where you are at with someone. Each time, gain explicit consent to continue. Don't go above the agreed-upon pain level you negotiated.

---

[26] The in-betweens work best if there is a pause between songs. As a top, you use it not only for check-ins with your bottom but also to change implements; it might be migrating from a warmup flogger to a cat o' nine or from a snake whip to a bullwhip.

I tell everyone the first time I play with them, especially experienced whip catchers, that this first scene may be boring for them. It is an introduction for me as I am getting to know someone new - perhaps not new to whips, but new to me. It takes me four to six whip scenes with someone before I know them well enough—we've had enough mileage together with the whip and slowly ramped up endorphins over several scenes or dances—to take that next leap with the whip.

So, most of my whip play evolves from an explicit consent approach, checking in frequently and re-establishing consent as the scene progresses. But this is not optimum whip play from several perspectives. It is safe whip play, and it yields good results. The whip catcher enjoys it, and it does not violate anyone's consent. But it breaks the headspace or subspace of the whip catcher on every in-between. However, it is what I consider necessary until I have an established whip relationship with the bottom.

Other forms of communication break the headspace less and still can be used to establish explicit consent. You could mutually agree on hand signals: the whip catcher raising one to five fingers or fingers on both hands when the pain scale exceeds six. Raising one foot when the whip catcher needs time to process (sort of like a yellow). Placing the foot down signals the whip catcher is ready to continue and gives explicit consent to do so. Stamping the feet rapidly or dropping a handkerchief could mean "stop the scene". Non-verbal forms of communication could be less intrusive into headspace

Implied Consent. Implied consent is possible when two people have played with each other so much they can read each other's body language, they know what each other likes and dislikes, and they can play within each other's limits without explicit communication. Implied consent does not mean that communication, checking in, and continuously reaffirming consent throughout a scene is not happening. It is happening through body language, hand signals, and other forms of communication developed by a whip thrower and catcher who are familiar with each other and scene regularly.

I usually say this takes five or six whip scenes. Implied consent is a natural approach for people who are in an established relationship. The D/s relationship dynamic, being regular play partners, perhaps having done a checklist together, and having familiarity with each other allows play where constant check-in isn't necessary. Trust is developed over time and space, with multiple scenes that allow the whip catcher to settle into subspace and the whip top to play within the known constraints they have learned regarding the whip catcher. This, to me, is optimum whip play for a top who loves to throw the whip—to throw unconstrained within my own limitations is exhilarating and a great focused head rush.

How do I get there? I don't have a strict formula but here is one possible scenario I could use. I start with explicit consent, as previously discussed. My first scene with anyone is usually nothing more than butterfly kisses and warmup levels one to three. In fact, the flogger and cat o' nine may be more intense than the actual singletail.

In the second scene with someone, I warm up at levels one to three and play at the four to six level, all with a snake whip. The third time I play with someone, I will introduce the bullwhip and follow the same formula as the previous one: warmup one to three, snake whip four to six, and bullwhip six to eight. Depending upon how a whip catcher reacts to the bullwhip and how they handle pain levels six to eight will determine whether I continue approaching future scenes with explicit consent and playing at levels four to six with a snake and six to eight with a bullwhip. I may vary this formula based on the situation, but it is generally the way I play.

There may come a point when the whip catcher has successfully played at the six to eight level and wants to go farther, or they tell me they could take more, or they were right on the "edge," and I stopped. Those are signals that the whip catcher is ready for play using implied consent.

Now, the whip catcher might have been very experienced and ready to play at that level in the first scene. What I'm describing is as much my own approach and my own limitations as a whip thrower as it is about anything to do with the whip catcher. I get it. What I'm sharing is what has worked for me and evolved over 25 years of throwing.

As someone who loves to throw the bullwhip in the dungeon almost more than they love breathing, I have been very blessed to have known and have been trusted by even tops that love the energy of the whip; so many wonderful whip bottoms that have stood for the bullwhip. Not all of these whip catchers I've mentioned, I would say, are pure masochists, but the ones who set the stage for an unbridled whip scene that literally allows the thrower to focus completely on the movement of the whip, the dungeon music, and energy flow. When the entire focus of the scene can be on energy flow, then magickal things happen.

Epilogue

Qi Gong—
Moving Energy with Your Mind

Hard Physics and Woo. When I started throwing 25 years ago, I was all about hard physics: the dynamics of Newton's three laws of motion, the effect of gravity on a whip thrown horizontally, aerodynamic concepts of stall speed and drag, Bernoulli's principle of lift, and anything physics-related that might even remotely affect throwing a whip. I was actually a disbeliever in Woo.

But somewhere along my journey, I observed phenomena in the dungeon that I could not logically explain with physics or even chemistry (yes, endorphins involve chemistry and electrical impulses transferred through the body to the brain.) I saw whip bottoms release energy out of the palms of their hands. I saw whip bottoms so hypnotized by the rhythm and energy of the whip that they could not stand, fell asleep, and would have fallen to the floor if not restrained on a cross.

I cannot imagine a whip bottom catching a whip traveling at or near the speed of sound, absorbing that energy, traveling into subspace, trusting the whip and the whip thrower so much that they become so relaxed and hypnotized that they fall asleep. Yet I have witnessed it. I've seen whip bottoms focus energy down the chakra to the root chakra and orgasm from it. Such pleasures, all from a bullwhip strike!

The only way I could make sense of some of this was to begin viewing the body on a somatic level. I surmised that all the energy systems we learn about in physics exist on the somatic level within the human body. But there needed to be some sort of system to connect things all together and make some sense. The system of chakras provided that for me.

The simple guide to utilizing the chakras in whip throwing is to recognize that the whip naturally focuses energy between two chakras: the heart and the root chakra. Applying progressively more energy in equal amounts to both sides of the chakra, the focus of the forehand and backhand throws of the whip sets up an opportunity for energy flow through the chakra system. This can be aided in the in-betweens by using the hands, Reiki style, or moving energy with a knife or other implement. Ramping this energy up, maintaining this, and cooling this back down takes the whip catcher into subspace and on a journey.

Everyone reacts differently; even the same whip catcher on two different days will respond differently. This is why throwing a singletail never gets old. Sometimes, this energy system opens up, and magical things happen: bullwhip magick. Sometimes, the energy closes the throat chakra, and alternate means of communication have to flow into place. But in it all, I have become aware of the unseen Woo.

Last year, I attended an event with my now leather sister, Master LeatherRedux. We had never met before; she did not know me, nor did I know her. But that changed quickly. She watched me throw for two nights in the dungeon. She said to me, "Throwing the whip is a spiritual experience for you." It wasn't a question. It was a statement, a positive conclusion that she had drawn from watching me throw a whip in the dungeon two nights in a row. I believe she recognized this about me because, for her, it is the same experience - a spiritual journey.

There are so many examples of whip bottoms giving their heart and soul to the kiss of the whip. Every time I pick up that sacred piece of plaited leather, it is a spiritual experience. The art of the whip is a journey, and for a moment in time, it is just the whip, the music, and the whip bottom standing before me - in time.

The headspace, top space, hyper-focus, and spiritual connection the whip provides to the top are only matched by the responsiveness of the whip bottom during a scene. Building energy in the heart and root chakra creates an energy flow that can only be described through a spiritual connection with woo between the whip top and bottom. There is no other way to describe it.

The whip, moving near or beyond the speed of sound, slows down time; time stands still, and moments slip away as the whip carries both whip thrower and whip catcher to a new plane of existence. Theoretically, if one could be there infinitely, one might live forever, but alas, at some point, there is aftercare.

So eventually, when the whips are broken in, I need to be able to trust them to finish where I point them; when this happens, they are more than just an extension of my arm; they are an extension of my mind. Beyond that, I am able to move into qi gong mode; athletes would say they are in the zone. Time slows down, and I hyperfocus or go into top space. I'm able to move energy with my mind and with a thought, and the whip is simply a tool to allow me to do this.

Qi Gong[27]. I've begun to learn about the qi gong theory. Traditional qi gong theory says that we can focus on a feeling, emotion, part of the body, or goal and that our qi, or energy, goes where our mind sends it. Qi gong, in my understanding, is a subset of the chi triad.

---

[27] Master LeatherRedux introduced qi gong by teaching breathing exercises during monthly whip practice.

Tai chi relates to fluid movement and flow. Qi gong is often referred to as the 'internal' portion of tai chi.

I've always described the flow of Peter Jack's whips as a ripple on a quiet pond, yet the whips finish on target where I point them. Imagine that ripple of energy beginning in your core with your qi and rippling out to finish where your mind sends it, perhaps into the heart or root chakra of your whip catcher.

Picture the whip moving at or near the speed of sound, and the whip top is playing with the last one-half to one inch of fluff and exchanging energy. Actually, a lot of energy is exchanged from a whip moving at this speed with a very brave soul standing on the receiving end. On one level, this takes a lot of eye-hand coordination, and at another level, a consistent release point.

If you've seen me throw as I've just described, you know that I'm moving and doing footwork while the whip is staying in rhythm to the music that is playing in the dungeon. I say it is the definition of edge play. Certainly, there is muscle memory involved, but I am not thinking about all of the things that are going on at any one point in time, and given my repetition rate of throwing, I am not consciously processing all of the things that are going on at any given point in time. I cannot see the cracker speeding into the target, and its finish. It is moving too fast. If qi gong can send energy and move energy with the mind, then that is where I believe I'm at. I look, I point, my mind sends energy, and the whip finishes.

The Connection. We stand facing each other. Visualize energy flowing out of the earth and up each of our legs into our torso, pooling in our torso. We then connect by each placing our right hands on each other's chest, with the left hands on top of each other's right hands. Visualize the energy moving from each of our torsos through our arms and our hands and into the other's chest. We breathe deeply, synchronously, and with each breath, push energy into the other person. Meditative breathing is the meditative moving of energy.

Visualize it, and put it into your mind. Move energy with your mind as you breathe synchronously with your scene partner and the music playing in the dungeon.

Qi is the energy that makes us feel alive. Qi gong or chi gong allows one to focus on a feeling, an emotion, or a part of the body, and that qi goes where our mind sends it. In this instance, my qi gong is focused on the heart and root chakra of the whip bottom. The qi or energy from the earth through our core travels down the whip at or near the speed of sound and goes where our mind sends it.

When I throw, I visualize sharing that energy through the movement of the whip and transferring energy into the heart and root chakras of the whip bottom. I hyperfocus, send my whip, and my whip and energy go where my mind sends it.

For the whip bottom, it is essential to continue that meditative breathing as energy is flowing into the chakras from the whip. Visualize and focus on the whip and in your mind, accept the energy that it brings to your soul.

Reconnection. At the end, we reconnect and synchronously, meditatively breathe together. Take that shared energy and calm it down. A hug completes the cycle.

I have always begun each session with a connection with my whip catcher, and we breathe synchronously together. I was doing this for years before I ever began reading about tai chi and qi gong. I think, look, and the whip finishes where I am looking. I feel the whip bottom respond with about how much energy, how hard or how soft the finish is and my mind points energy to the chakras, and it happens.

I've struggled with different ways to describe it. I've called it a hyperfocus or top space. But I am throwing the whip with my mind. My body isn't capable of doing what my mind can do at those speeds and complexities. Time slows down, and the whip thrower has entered a sacred space. A short whip that is supposed to be quick, move faster, and be harder to control has now psychically slowed down, and it finishes where your mind sends it.

Yes, the extension of the hand, as you know, is an existential state. The extension of the mind is beyond an existential state—it is a state of being one with the whip. This is the art of the whip. If a whip is a type of rhythm instrument that can transfer energy percussively to a beat, then the art of the whip is to master the instrument to the level of virtuoso.

Conclusion

The Art of the Whip

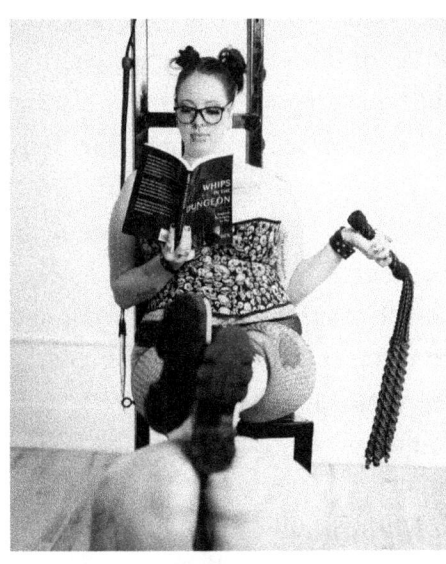

Photo 73 Female Top reading Whips in the Dungeon with a living foot-stool.

MY HOPE IS that this book has been read as a close companion to *Whips in the Dungeon: Singletail Techniques for Play*. This book builds on the basic and advanced techniques previously set forth in my first book and should have brought you further into what you can do with your whip skills.

My ultimate intent in writing this book is to get the creative, kinky mind juices flowing - to help you visualize new ideas and think creatively about how they can be actualized when throwing a whip.

Over time, with mileage with their whips and awareness of possible variations, each top will develop nuances in how they craft a scene that is unique to them. Much as each piece created by an artist is distinct from another, each scene crafted by the whip top will be a unique piece of living artwork.

What do I expect to see, now that you are an intermediate to advanced whip thrower, when I watch one of your scenes? I expect to see that you are comfortable with all classes of dungeon whips. You will be able to use them naturally as an extension of your hand and arm.

You should also have confidence in your throwing ability, in that you can throw accurately, with finesse and control to the level of creating controlled puffs with the cracker of a singletail that can be correlated to the Likert pain scale of the whip catcher you are throwing with. When your skill can be matched with the pleasure/pain level of your whip bottom, optimization of a scene is achieved.

You should have developed an understanding of woo and the energy flow between chakras, whether or not you use the same terminology. You should be able to read body language and tailor a scene to favor the heart or root chakra based on feedback from the body language of the whip catcher.

Footwork is important at this advanced level. Even if you do not move around and change your footwork much when throwing, you should now recognize that small changes in the throwing end of a singletail can result in large changes on the receiving end of the whip. Controlling and varying these changes slightly with footwork is another variation that should now be readily available to the advanced whip thrower.

I hope that at this point, you will naturally allow yourself to be in the moment, in symbiosis with the music, translating that energy into the energy of the whip and delivering it to a willing whip bottom. This type of whip play is a spiritual experience where the energy exchange comes alive, and there is nothing in the world but the movement of the whip and the responses of the whip bottom.

Not every whip bottom who likes whips will ultimately be able to achieve the peak energy levels a whip can produce. Perhaps only the true masochist who also loves the sting of the whip will achieve these levels. The trust in the whip thrower takes time. Not all whip bottoms complete the journey to that magic level. It isn't a necessity for them to do it. What is necessary is that the advanced whip master takes them safely where they can go and that both enjoy the experience.

I have always realized that there are no givens in life, even more so at this stage of my life. Every day I do not pick up a whip is a day I do not get back for the rest of my life. Also, a day I do not get optimum enjoyment out of my throwing is a day not lost but not optimized.

As a seasoned whip thrower, what do I like in an advanced whip scene? The laconic answer is that I enjoy play that progresses through implied consent. When I play with an experienced whip catcher I have played with many times, trust has been developed, and I can read their body language. This allows for play to progress unimpeded.

Throwing a whip when the energy is right in the dungeon is a spiritual experience. Being able to play with an experienced whip bottom and simply focus on the music and the dance of the whip is, for a moment, experiencing whip heaven. This is ideal for me. This is what I hope that you, as an advanced whip thrower, get to experience as you continue your journey with the whip.

Appendix A

Care of a Kangaroo Whip

Storage. Kangaroo, as with any leather, has to be cared for and loved. Ideally, you should store kangaroo whips hanging up in a temperature-controlled environment with moderate humidity.

Store your short kangaroo whips by hanging them completely unrolled and hanging straight. My arsenal is located in an inside closet that has one-inch by two-inch pine strips screwed to the three inside walls of the closet six feet from the floor. To these strips, I've attached cup hooks three inches apart all the way around. I use the cup hooks to hang the whips for storage. That way, my whips can be hung straight when not in use or not being transported to or from a venue for play.

Why is an inside closet important? Outside walls often are subject to temperature and humidity changes, and your whips can develop mold. Even if the wall is insulated, it will experience temperature changes that result in moisture and humidity that will affect the leather and conditioner being used.

If the whip has a wrist loop, hang it by the wrist loop. If there isn't a wrist loop, take a scrap of leather or kangaroo strand and make a loop to hang the whip by.

If the whips develop mold, it is usually present around where the roo stranding skives overlap as the whip is plaited with the plaiter's soap. If this happens, wipe the mold off with a clean cotton rag. Clean the whip with the plaiter's soap and then apply a thin layer of conditioner.

A whip that has developed a tendency to mold will need to be cleaned and reconditioned regularly, as the procedure I described may not get 100% of the mold off, and it can come back. It will take several cleanings and reconditioning sessions to overcome this tendency. Also, revisit where you have the whip stored and change its environment to somewhere more temperature-controlled.

Conditioning the whips. I'm not a fan of lacquered finishes on whips. It gives it a shiny look, but it blocks the dressing from getting into the leather. Condition the whips with a paste-type leather conditioner. Do not use a spray, oil, or lotion-type conditioner. Many whip makers brew their own concoction and include a tub with every new whip sale.

Pecard or Fiebring makes a paste-type conditioner, which is good. Pecard has petroleum jelly as one of its ingredients, and there is a discussion in the whip world about conditioners with petroleum products that, over time, break down the leather. For many years, I have used the conditioner that Peter Jack sent me with a whip order, but from time to time, I have used Pecard, and I have not seen any difference. I condition my whips about every six months or if they feel dry on my hands. After conditioning, wipe off any excess with a lint-free rag.

The handle portion of the whip and Turk's head do not need conditioner as your hand oil naturally conditions these areas every time you throw. I condition the fall of a snake or bullwhip every time before I throw. The fall is made of a different type of leather (red hide, white hide, latigo, water buffalo, cowhide) than the kangaroo whip, and it will appreciate frequent conditioning.

Many whip throwers claim that conditioning the fall makes it tacky, so they condition their falls the day before they throw. This allows the conditioner to soak and absorb into the leather, and the fall is not tacky. I have not found this to be a problem and prefer to condition my falls right before I'm going to throw them.

One of my dungeon routines is to sit down with my whip, inspect each whip, and condition the fall as a prelude to beginning play. If I'm throwing with a new whip bottom or with someone I've never played with, I will sit with them and introduce and talk about each whip as I go through this conditioning ritual.

Water and Kangaroo Whips. Water and kangaroo don't mix well. If you will be throwing outdoors in inclement weather, then acquire some paracord whips. I have a paracord for throwing in inclement weather and for doing acrylic art painting. Paracord is recommended for beginning whip throwers as an inexpensive way to get into whips, but it has applications well beyond the beginner level. Another advantage of paracord whips is that they can be cleaned with soap and water.

What should you do if you accidentally get your kangaroo whips wet? Hang them up right away to dry, and begin the drying process by soaking up as much water as you can with a cotton rag or towel. Turn a fan on in the room where they are hanging to create airflow. Then, as soon as they are dry, condition them with a paste-type leather conditioner and throw them. Continue conditioning and throwing daily until they seem like their old selves again. Then make a note to yourself never to get them wet again.

Appendix B

Carrying Cases for Whips

IF YOU ARE going to go to a dungeon, house play party, or anywhere with your whips, you need something to carry them in on the way to the venue.

Over the years, I've seen many different bag styles, and I've found my preferences, which I will share here. In my opinion, it should be a "vanilla" bag that will not attract any undue attention in public. You don't want someone who "sees something and says something" causing you any troubles or delays when you are simply transporting your short whips to a venue to throw them consensually.

In my travels, I haven't found any toy bags specifically designed to carry whips, with the exception that in Australia, there is a bag that has been developed to carry stock whips. Mike Murphy used to sell this bag in his online shop, and while we do not throw stock whips in the dungeon, this style bag is handy for carrying short canes, floggers, cats, etc. I have not found it ideal for bullwhips, snakes, or signal whips, as it is too long and not the shape you need.

Over the years, I've seen instrument gig bags of different types used, and they work quite nicely. I personally think a guitar bag is too large for whips, but I have seen it used to carry dungeon toys. If you are just carrying bullwhips, you might try a guitar gig bag.

I have used a bag made by Duluth Trading Company for many years. It was originally designed to carry a pneumatic wrench. The handle of the whip goes where the handle of the bag design accommodates the pneumatic wrench handle, and the thong of the whip coils in the area where the body of the wrench would have gone. Snakes and signals coil where the body of the wrench goes, and cats fit nicely along the bottom of the length of the bag. Unfortunately, this bag is no longer made, but other manufacturers may have canvas cases to transport your pneumatic wrenches. Recently, one of my whip workshop attendees brought their whips to class in a Christmas wreath storage holder that had a handle. It seemed to work well for them. Maybe there is some other vanilla carrying case out there that is even better. Your search for the ideal whip bag is now commissioned.

A lariat bag from a tack shop makes a great bag to carry long whips in. Of course, you can carry shorter whips in it, too. But as it is designed for a large coil of stiff lariat rope, it is ideal for a long whip coiled in a circumference.

Two-handed whips create a new transport problem. There are two of everything to transport. I am not consistent in my transportation philosophy. Sort of notional in my old age. For my single-hand whips, I have for years coiled them and secured them by wrapping the fall around the coil to keep it from uncoiling. Some whip throwers feel like this would damage the whip. I have found that just transporting the whips to a venue and then back home to be rehung in the arsenal has not created any issues with my whips.

For throwing two-handed, I want the matched sets to remain as close to each other as possible in the way they are thrown and transported, so I don't like coiling them but like transporting them loosely arranged in a larger coil and not secured with the fall. To do this, my bag of choice is a large portfolio case from Staples. It has three sections. In one section, I put a matched set of four-foot signal whips; in another section, a matched set of four-foot bullwhips; and in the middle section at the bottom, I put a matched set of cat o' nines, and on top of them a matched set of four-foot dragon tails. The only variation would be to exchange the four-foot signal whips for a matched set of three-foot snake whips.

Traveling with whips. This is common sense, but I will share it with everyone anyway. Do not, if you can help it, transport your whips in a car trunk or non-temperature-controlled truck bed. I carry my whips in the back seat or floorboard in a more temperature-controlled environment. I have a crossover-style vehicle (some would call it a small SUV), and I transport them in what I call the "way back," but since it is connected to the front space of the car, it is temperature-controlled. Do not leave your whip bags in the car overnight, even if the car is locked. Keep them with you in your hotel room or where you are staying. There is no need to encourage a thief to break into your car.

I have flown with my whips, but prefer not to. Do not attempt to take whips and toys in carry-on luggage! Whips and any other BDSM toys should be in checked baggage. I make an inventory list and put it on top of my stuff in my luggage. I also individually wrap each whip and toy in an oversized zip-lock bag (one or two and a half gallons are big enough). Then, cross your fingers that everything will safely reach your destination.

If you can insure your luggage, do so. I prefer to drive to an event, even if it is across the country, and will take several days, mainly because I do not want to lose control of where my whips are at any moment.

Whips are irreplaceable in that they are handmade. No two are exactly alike; even a matched set will be like a human twin and will have nuances and differences. Then, too, there's the mileage you've put into breaking them in, making them your own, traveling safely into play in the dungeon, and the wonderful memories each has brought to you and your whip catchers. They are valuable in themselves, but to you, they are irreplaceable.

Travel with a soft rag, a small tub of conditioner, and your whip repair kit. Your whip repair kit should have snack bags, a permanent marker, small band-aids, a small tube of triple antibiotic ointment, a small fid, small scissors or small folding knife, new crackers, and crackers in labeled snack baggies for any whip bottom you've previously played with that is on your dance card for another scene.

Appendix C

Top Space and Top Drop

FOR MANY YEARS, I did not realize there was even such a thing as top space or top drop. I began to be more self-aware of top drop when an incident happened at a leather event. I was in the dungeon throwing a four-foot bullwhip (six-foot total length) in marginal lighting. My eyes had adjusted, and I was on, in the zone, and having a great time. The DM decided to change the lighting and turned off the wall sconces around the room. Given where I was throwing, this essentially put my scene entirely in the dark. If I was doing violet wand, I would have loved it, but since I was throwing a bullwhip and now could not see where the whip was going, the result pulled me out of top space.

This was my first recognition of top space, not because of the head space I was in while throwing, but because of the drop I experienced almost immediately. I have since learned more about top space and will pass on my experiences in hopes it helps other tops.

I realized that when throwing a whip, I hyper-focus as the whip and cracker move toward the whip's bottom. I'm not only focused on the whip but also on the bottom and reading the bottom. Body language, nuances, the color of the skin, and painting with the cracker a certain area of the body are all elements of achieving the hyper-focus that creates a top space.

In top space, time slows down. Even though the whip is moving close to or above the speed of sound, it seems like it is moving in slow motion. Everything slows down. The focus is so intense that even though you are aware of other scenes around you, of observers, voyeurs, and sometimes a DM, everything is blocked except the movement of the whip and your whip bottom.

Top space is as calm and beautiful as a well broken-in whip, conditioned to your hand, moves toward its target. I've often said my breathing becomes rhythmic, and my blood pressure becomes lower. If I could be in a dungeon throwing a whip, I could live forever. At least it is the way I feel when I'm in the zone and throwing.

There is also a downside to top space. In my experience, when I'm throwing in top space and something or someone breaks my focus, it is very hard to get it back. Most of the time, I am not able to do so. Years ago, I would try to begin again after the issue was resolved. But in reflecting back on these scenes, I have never been able to achieve the same space after restarting the scene. So, as I've gained more experience not only throwing a whip but also knowing myself, I will most likely not continue a scene once my top space has been broken.

If it turns out it was an issue with a venue or the way an event was being run, then I will probably not attend that event again. Life is short, and if you love throwing a whip, why would you attempt to throw it in a space where optimum top space could not be achieved?

Achieving this top space also means that when the scene is over, or if you are lucky enough to throw multiple whip scenes in one evening, later that night, or the following morning, expect a drop. This is called top drop, and many types of play and scenes can cause it.

But what is the top to do? Be conscientious; check in the following day with the whip bottom or bottoms you played with. Checking in and talking about about your mutual experiences will help with the drop. Eat and drink a healthy meal the morning after.

Take your whips out of the toy bag, examine them, feel the leather, and reflect on the previous evening's play. Take them and throw them for a few minutes at one of your practice targets. As you are throwing, relive and reflect on the memories of the evening before. Then, put away your cherished whips and begin planning for the next play or dungeon event.

Appendix D

Bottom Space and Bottom Drop

EVERYONE EXPERIENCES AND processes a whip strike differently. Just as no two strikes are exactly alike, no two whip bottoms will experience receiving a whip the same way. Everyone processes energy and endorphins differently.

Bottom space or subspace will also be experienced differently, and one of the huge variables beyond the somatic differences between whip catchers is the amount of energy that occurs and the resulting endorphin rush. The larger the endorphin rush, the higher the chance of a deeper subspace experience. When this occurs, the top has to be prepared for various reactions the whip bottom might have from the experience.

Hypnotic Experience. Whip bottoms may become hypnotized by the rhythm of the whip, and energy entering the body in a rhythmic pattern will result in a whip bottom relaxing and falling into a deep subspace. Sometimes, it is almost trance-like.

Sometimes, whip bottoms lose their legs and cannot stand any longer. If you know a whip bottom tends to lose their legs during an endorphin rush experience, then restraining them with cuffs or rope before you begin is advised. When they are not able to stand, at least they won't fall. You can then remove the restraints and have them sit down. Having a chair close at hand in those situations is recommended.

Whip bottoms who fall into a trance-like state can even fall asleep when being whipped (definitely restrain these types). Or, during aftercare, when they begin their "drop," they might fall asleep. After a reasonable repose, gently bringing them back to reality and waking them up continues their recovery from the scene.

I am not a real cuddly Dom with anyone who is not collared to me or in a close personal relationship with me. I will offer and accept hugs, but that is about it. I do a lot of pickup play. If the whip bottoms need aftercare, I provide a bottle of water, and I make sure they have a significant other or someone else available to do the cuddly type of care. When you are in a 24/7 collared relationship, the best aftercare is simply transitioning to sex following a whip scene and cuddling in bed together. Waking the morning after, having breakfast, and talking about the previous night can stave off or lessen the effects of most top and sub drops.

Two Types of Sub Drop. The first type has already been touched on. This occurs almost immediately following a whip scene or any type of scene that has produced an endorphin rush. It occurs as the endorphins ramp down and the body feels a drop. Sometimes, this is like the body going into a mild shock, and a blanket, water, and a hug are recommended.

The second type of drop occurs the day after or sometimes several days after a scene or large play event. This is more of an emotional drop as the body misses and craves the endorphin high but is now experiencing a drop that can result in an emotional drop. For frequent BDSM convention goers, this type of drop has a name—Condrop.

Hundreds of attendees added energy. Several days of endorphin highs for the bottoms and several days of layered top space for the Dominants results in a drop that is deeper and more lasting than what is usually experienced after a typical, good dungeon session. Often, during these types of drops, it is important to have someone to talk to or someone available to reach out to. Talking about your feelings and what you are experiencing is important in swinging the drop.

A good top will contact the whip bottom the day after a scene and check in on them, sometimes even for several days. This is conscientious and caring for the whip bottom that obligingly stood for your whip. It is connecting with someone you shared a dungeon experience with and making sure they are ok.

Cleaning your play area. Dungeon etiquette has long established that equipment used in a scene is cleaned with some sort of sanitary process (Clorox wipes, alcohol and a rag, Cavicide are examples).

However, often, when a scene is over, the whip bottom is deep in subspace, and the top is also sometimes loopy from being in a hyperfocus for an hour or so of intense play. If this is something you know can happen with you and your whip bottom, you should find a friend willing to clean the equipment for you after your scene.

I've always maintained that the normal dungeon protocol is backward. When I walk up to a piece of equipment to play on it, I might not know if it was cleaned adequately or at all after the last scene that took place on that equipment. The best way to ensure the equipment is properly cleaned is to clean it and, if necessary, the play area before a scene begins. It is the ideal time to do any cleaning that needs to be done.

However, you will find that this is not the norm in dungeon spaces. If you don't have someone to help with this, you or your whip bottom will have to be prepared to clean your equipment after your scene.

Appendix E

Signs That a Venue Is Not Whip Friendly

IF YOU TRULY love whips, you will do your due diligence and research any event or venue before you arrive to determine whether they are whip-friendly. If they are not, do not waste your time; look and go somewhere else because they don't get it, and chances are, even if you invested your time in trying to educate them about whips, they still would not get it. Some people are only interested in their forms of kink and aren't willing to accommodate your kink.

This appendix shares some actual experiences and lessons learned and provides some suggestions so you don't make some of the same mistakes I've made in traveling my journey.

You might walk into a huge convention dungeon space, and there are rows and rows of equipment side by side, each other laid out almost like a classroom. But there is no place with more than four feet between two pieces of equipment. The only place that might accommodate a whip is on the stage, but the stage is off-limits. Here's your sign that the venue is not whip-friendly.

Another dungeon may have ample room, but everywhere that there is a space with enough room to throw your whip, the overhead is obstructed with a hardpoint and nylon webbing hanging down for rigging. Here's your sign.

On the dungeon wall of a different venue, there is a sign that says "No Bullwhips," but there's no mention of snakes, signal whips, or singletails. Whoever is in charge is obviously not knowledgeable about whips. Here is your sign.

You go to the bathroom of a public dungeon, and the dungeon rules are posted on the wall. The first rule is no excessive cracking. While you are waiting in the social area to play, the DM interrupts a scene in the dungeon to tell the participants to quiet down or use a gag as they are disturbing the social area. Meanwhile, the adjacent social area is full of people laughing and conversing out loud. Here's your sign.

On the dungeon wall is a sign that says no whips longer than four feet long are allowed. This is a real issue because a four-foot bullwhip is six to six and a half feet in total length. Are they ok with a four-foot bullwhip, or do they mean the total length of the whip? Most likely, the DM won't know.

Then, you have different throwing styles. A four-foot signal whip, which is four feet in total length when thrown horizontal style, needs ten plus feet wide for a throwing circle, then more if the whip thrower is going to move any when they throw, plus some amount of safety circle behind them. A bullwhip thrower throwing a four-foot bullwhip in a forward figure eight needs six feet of space in front of them and a six-foot wide lane with two to three feet of safety space behind them. A four-foot bullwhip actually takes up about the same space as a four-foot signal whip, just shaped a little differently, maybe even a little bit less. But to have this conversation with a head DM after you've traveled hundreds of miles and spent several hundred dollars in registering for an event, not to mention hotel and food, is

NOT the kind of conversation you want. Because most times, they are going to say NO.

Usually, if there's a dungeon sign on the wall that includes anything about whips, most likely, it is not a whip-friendly dungeon.

You attend an event that allows whips, but when you get there, you find the whip area is on a different floor of the hotel from the dungeon, in a room with no music, one St. Andrew's cross, no heat, no dungeon lighting just the overhead hotel lighting. Here's your sign.

At an event in a dungeon, the DM says you can't throw there because they don't want to be responsible for you putting someone's eye out. Note to self, promoters, DMs, and all dungeon attendees: everyone signs an event and dungeon liability waiver. This is a leather/BDSM event: there might be whips flying.

One of the local dungeons had no restrictions on using whips, but the space was laid out where there wasn't an adequate whip lane anywhere without moving a piece of dungeon equipment for the length of the whip scene and then moving it right back. No, none of the equipment can be moved (even though it was designed to be portable). Here's your sign.

Appendix F

Breaking in a New Kangaroo Whip

THERE ARE SOME tips for breaking in a new whip, whether paracord or kangaroo.

Don't leave a whip in its shipping box. When it arrives, take it out right away. Smooth it out with your hands, and if it is a kangaroo, give it a bit of conditioner.

For kangaroos, condition the thong every day before you throw during the break-in period. Remember to wipe off the excess with a lint-free rag. Once the whip is broken in, only condition the whip when it feels really dried out, or at least twice a year, about every six months. Condition the leather fall regularly. I condition my fall every time before I throw.

Don't manually manipulate the whip to break it in. Break it in by throwing it. Throw using the techniques and style in which you normally throw. Try to throw your new whip every day. It is important to get mileage on the whip and begin targeting targets that have meaning for dungeon play. This mileage provides muscle memory to the leather as it breaks in around your personal style of throwing and also allows the whip to grow as an extension of your hand and arm.

My favorite targets are a t-shirt free hanging off of a wire hanger and a sheepskin. However, of late, I've also been using an eight-inch tambourine a lot as the size of the tambourine is close to the target size when throwing at a whip catcher, and the tambourine produces a sound that gives you feedback as you break a whip in as to the consistency of the strikes. A small wind gong (six to eight inches) also makes a nice target, as you can tell the strike's intensity by the sound the gong makes.

As the whip breaks in, it will develop some memory as to the way you, in particular, throw. It will become an extension of your arm and hand. You will develop some mileage with this whip and begin getting to know it and to trust it to do what you want it to. The goal is to break the whip in, have it finish on target, and be able to finesse it in consistent controlled puffs. By the time the whip is able to do that, the whip thrower will have the ultimate confidence in the whip to be able to play in a dark or dimly lit dungeon with skill and finesse.

Here is a whip construction note: If you examine the plaiting on a whip's thong, you will notice that there are four plaited sides as you turn the whip around its circumference.

One-Dimensional Break-in: A plaited whip thong normally has a belly and a spine. The whip most naturally rolls out with the belly. Some whip throwers only throw with the natural rollout of the belly.

On the forehand side of the forward figure eight, they throw with the belly and can throw and recover only on the forehand side. Or if they are going to throw a backhand, they can turn their hand over, palm toward the target, and the whip will have turned and be ready to throw with the natural belly even on the backhand side. It is possible to throw forehand and also backhand with the belly, if the hand is turned over when a backhand is going to be thrown. This results in the whip only being thrown in one dimension. Hence, the break-in for this style of throwing should only be one-dimensional.

Two-Dimensional Break-in: The whip naturally wants to roll out with the belly, but the whip can also be thrown against the spine. It won't roll out naturally (at least not at first) but should arc in a straight line. Many whip throwers swear that a whip will crack louder and easier against the spine than when thrown with the belly.

For example, in my style of throwing a forward figure eight, I throw with the belly on the forehand side, and conversely, on the backhand side, I throw against the spine. Most of the time, the whip only moves in those two dimensions. For my single whip throwing style, I break in the whip in two dimensions. As the whip breaks in, the spine will slowly begin to achieve a good natural rollout. The spine will never have the ease and flow in rollout that the belly has, but it will become flexible enough that it no longer simply arcs.

Four-Dimensional Break-in: Some whip throwers want their whip to be broken in on all four-dimensional planes. (Master Robert, a regular at the monthly Zoom whip practices, is one whip thrower who espouses this approach). They throw the whip with the belly, then turn the whip one-quarter, turn and throw again, turn one-quarter, turn and throw again, turn one-quarter, turn and throw again. They do this over and over until, finally, the whip is broken in on all four sides and does not favor one more than the other.

This takes time and patience, but the end result is the whip thrower can pick up their whip in a dark dungeon, and it does not matter which side of the whip they are throwing with, as there is no longer a distinct belly and spine. This whip, when broken in on all four dimensions, will hang perfectly straight and not favor one side over the other when thrown.

Now that I have begun my two-whip journey, if you are throwing a four-count Florentine, either a two-dimensional or four-dimensional break-in is advised. If you plan on or are throwing a six-count Florentine, then a four-dimensional break-in is definitely the way to go.

I am approaching my four-dimensional break-in differently than the quarter turn and throw method. My four-dimensional break-in is done by throwing the four-count and six-count Florentine in the way I throw it. So, the whips over time will break into my style of throwing and with the flow I develop when throwing these patterns and weaves with the whips.

Regardless of which dimensional approach you take to breaking in your whip, if you just throw it using your normal style at targets that give feedback similar to the feedback needed in dungeon play, you can not only break in your whip but fine-tune it to be ready to use in the dungeon. In short, break in your whips by throwing them using the style you throw in the dungeon. Throw them personally, and let the whips get to know you and your style as you put mileage on the whips.

Appendix G

Singletail Sheet Music

I DO NOT use single-tail sheet music, but I want to discuss and let you consider this topic for advanced play. The whip thrower can actually write their own singletail sheet music and map out details of scenes before they occur in the dungeon.

Just like practicing for a concert performance, singletail scenes can be mapped out and practiced with music, mastering the patterns, techniques, and rhythms in play while capturing the footwork to complete the music set. This type of dungeon whip practice and scene preparation is not for everyone. Some prefer the spontaneity of throwing in a live setting with an unknown playlist. Others prefer well-planned sheet music and a known music set. Just as some play the guitar by ear, others play an instrument with sheet music and sight read. Some musicians play by ear. They can just hear the melodies and chords in a song and play them. Other musicians prefer to sight-read. Some great musicians cannot play by ear but learn to play by reading notes and notation written for their chosen instrument.

Different instruments use different types of notations. Guitar notation is not the same as drum notation, for example. Some musicians play by improvisation, or the modes and tonality of the music emerge and are even different on different nights of a gig. Many great musicians who improvise and play solos do not even play those solos precisely the same on two given nights.

Some of the considerations for throwing a whip in rhythm to music are similar to those a musician must consider.

I prefer to throw a whip to music. I let the music mode, tone, and genre influence the whip during a song or set of songs in dungeon play. The music even influences the whip choice and footwork I use during a song. I feel the music and modality as I am throwing. This allows me to create a symbiotic partnership with the music and my whip to connect that rhythm and energy with the whip catcher and surrounding dungeon play. I would classify my throwing as playing by ear, improvisational.

Putting notes to sheet or rhythm to score establishes documentation of what might be possible for future generations of players of all types of instruments, even the whip thrown in a dungeon.

To my knowledge, no one has attempted to notate the movement of a whip thrown to music in a dungeon. There is no textbook on how to do this; everyone reading this book can add to or take away from what I am suggesting by creatively adding their own shorthand to the notations suggested. The notation suggested in this chapter is limited by the fact that most musical notation has specific software and characters developed to represent specific techniques when playing an instrument. Whip notation is unique and has never been done before. A whip is easily associated with being a type of rhythm and percussion instrument. For singletail sheet music, I am going to adapt standard drum notation.

As an aside, the music I am using to illustrate singletail sheet music was written before 1926. That is because that music is out of copyright and, therefore, free for anyone to use. It is not representative of modern dungeon music. I cannot get my head around throwing a whip to Ragtime-style music in the dungeon.

Forgive this appendix and my writing, but singletail sheet music will use a Sousa march as an example of what might be done and the notation that might be written for singletail sheet music.[28]

Simplified Whip (Hand) Notation. This description is for those interested in mapping out their throwing to a dungeon-appropriate song with lyrics. First, find the lyrics online, copy and paste them into a word processing document, and double-space the text of the lyrics. This will create a blank space below each line where the whip movement can be hand-notated in a simplified format.

If using a forward figure eight, throwing both forehand and backhand, use a slash to designate the whip being thrown on a beat. If throwing with controlled puffs, a number at the beginning of a measure or line can indicate the intensity or level of the puff. Use an X to designate a crack.

Here is an example of simplified whip hand notation in a line of a song:

/ Forward throw
\ Backhand throw
X Crack

---

[28] However, if outside-of-the-box thinking is applied, and consideration of music before 1926 was not amplified or electrically or electronically enhanced, then the marches of John Philip Sousa might be considered the heavy metal music of that generation. They had a rhythm. They were popular in their day and got people's hands clapping, feet tapping, and everyone excited. Sounds like heavy metal and industrial music to me. Sousa composed 136 marches in his career, a considerable body of work, and wrote the individual band and orchestral part for each march. Sousa's marches ended with a pronounced heavy note. If the note was a low note, this was called a button; if it was a higher note, it was called a stinger. "Oh my" sounds so much like a clean crack to end a song with. Sousa's only flaw was he did not write a part for whips!

1-8 Controlled puffs indicate the intensity or loudness of the throw.

Let Me Call You Sweetheart by Beth Slater Whitson and Leo Friedman (1910).

Let me call you Sweetheart
4/ \ / \
I'm in love with you
4/ \ / \
Let me hear you whisper
2/ \ / \
That you love me too
5/ \ / \
Keep the love light glowing
6/ \ / \
In your eyes so blue
6/ \ / \
Let me call you Sweetheart
7/ \ 8X \
I'm in love with you
8/ \ / 8X

Of course, advanced notation could be more complex and draw from variations of drum notation. The example evolves from the percussion clef and modifies existing drum notation to adapt it for throwing a whip.

A notation with a note shape indicates whip throw using a controlled puff technique. If the stem is on the left side of the note and pointing down it indicates a throw from the left side of the thrower. Thrown two-handed, this would be a left-hand throw. Thrown single-handed, this would be a backhand throw for a right-handed thrower or a forehand for a left-handed thrower.

A notated note shape with the stem on the right side pointing up would indicate a throw from the right side of the whip thrower. For a right-handed thrower, this would be a forehand throw, and for a left-handed thrower, this would be a backhand throw.

Simply put, the stem coming off of the note indicates the side of the thrower from which the whip is thrown. Additional notation might be a number directly below the note indicating the level of controlled puff to be thrown (one through eight). Increasing the intensity of the controlled puff might be likened to a music crescendo, and decreasing or descending the intensity of the controlled puff would be like a decrescendo. A butterfly kiss with a whip might be noted like a ghost note in drum notation.

An x with a stem coming off of it indicates a crash in drum notation from a type of cymbal. This easily translates to a whip crack. Whip cracks usually occur at the controlled puff levels greater than eight. The location of the crack can be indicated similarly to drum notation. For example, if the x is just above the staff, this indicates a crash on the ride cymbal. A ride cymbal is usually larger and lower in tone than a crash cymbal. This would translate in whip notation to indicate a crack on the butt or root chakra of the whip catcher.

A whip-crack noted using drum notation as a crash cymbal would likewise notate a crack to the whip catcher's shoulder or heart chakra. The crack (x) with a stem on the left side would indicate a crack on either the left butt or the left shoulder. The crack (x) with a stem on the right side would indicate a crack on either the right butt or the right shoulder.

Footwork can also be notated using the ballroom dance foot positions (one through five) that WITD whip throwers already know. This notation can be written below the staff at the beginning of a measure and annotated below subsequent measures of the foot position changes or shifts.

Hand notation. Singletail whip notation would most often be done by hand as a quick, easy way to document and indicate the whip thrower's intention in throwing a whip to a particular piece of music. Since sheet music is copyrighted unless the song was written before 1926, most likely, the music a whip thrower would be interested in throwing to during a scene or in the dungeon is copyrighted. The easiest way to notate modern music is to purchase a copy of the sheet music, then hand notate it with whip notation documenting the type of throws, intensity, and footwork planned for a scene.

If this is the way you learn best, then you should build on these suggestions and devise your own notation or shorthand for annotating music to indicate your whip and foot movements. This ultimately is analogous to sheet music but has an element of choreography in it. I do not take this approach but want to mention it in this advanced book. Just as with an instrument, many sight read and play with sheet music, and many play by ear and improvise with the feeling of the music.

Playing by Ear. My approach would be likened to playing by ear. When your whip skills get practiced enough that muscle memory takes over, and your whip is an extension of your hand, then you no longer have to focus solely on throwing the whip to completion into its target. This allows you to hear and feel the music and to throw in rhythm to it. You play to the energy in the music and play subsonic or crack when the music influences the crack.

It also allows the opposite, which is, in my opinion, where my throwing is at. I can hyper-focus on the target and zone in. Time and space stand still, and it is only the movement of the cracker into the target area that I focus on. This allows me literally to dance with the music, have multiple footwork positions and hand positions, and even change the type of crack and style of throw to match the rhythm and energy in the music without changing the accuracy of the whip tip on delivery as my hyper-focus has remained in singularity.

When I'm throwing butt-butt/shoulder-shoulder, I have four focus points. When I'm throwing only shoulder-shoulder to create angel wings, I'm throwing with two focus points. When I'm throwing two-handed, I'm throwing with only one focus point. As I gain more muscle memory, I will be able to throw two-handedly, with two focus points, and so on.

Appendix H

Extemporaneous Thoughts of a Seasoned Whip Thrower

THE SCENARIOS I described have thousands of variations and even a few more vignettes, but the point of all of them is to get you thinking and to inspire you to imagine your own versions and create your own scenarios.

The first whip I ever bought was a snake whip and a matching tomcat from Happy Tails. There was no one in my local Hampton Roads BDSM community at the time who was throwing a whip.

I asked Stan Sherman in a phone call, one of the owners of Happy Tails, how I should throw it. He said to learn to throw the cat o' nine like I would a flogger and to keep all nine tails together. Then, throw the snake whip the same way. In a small apartment, I had precisely three feet between the bedroom wall and the foot of the bed. I tucked a balloon into the footboard and practiced flicking the knot on the balloon without touching the balloon. This was the start of an incredible journey (25 years to date) with the singletail.

I had been throwing for a year and had developed my own style.

By the time I made it to my first BDSM convention, Black Rose, and attended a whip workshop by Bob Deegan, I had gotten pretty good with my snake whip, throwing a forward figure eight. Deegan threw a horizontal style, which, during the time he was popular and teaching up and down the East Coast, was called Deegan style. Later, this term evolved into East Coast Swing. Which, in simple terms, is just a horizontal technique.

East Coast Swing is an easy technique to learn and very accurate with a signal whip. Most of the techniques taught in that first workshop didn't help me because I had already taken the path toward overhand throwing with a snake and later a bullwhip.

The first bullwhip I bought on my journey was at the Boston Fetish Flea in 2001. Midnight Blue (from the Houston, TX area) was vending at that event, and he had a four-foot Mike Murphy 16-plait shot-loaded bullwhip. It was unusual for a Murphy because he was known for his natural two-belly build and usually had shellac finished his whips. This whip was left natural and had a red hide fall. It became my main dungeon whip for the first decade of my journey.

When Murphy stopped making whips, I retired this one to the armory. Recently, I passed this trusted piece of leather on to a younger, passionate whip thrower in Idaho so it could once again continue its journey.

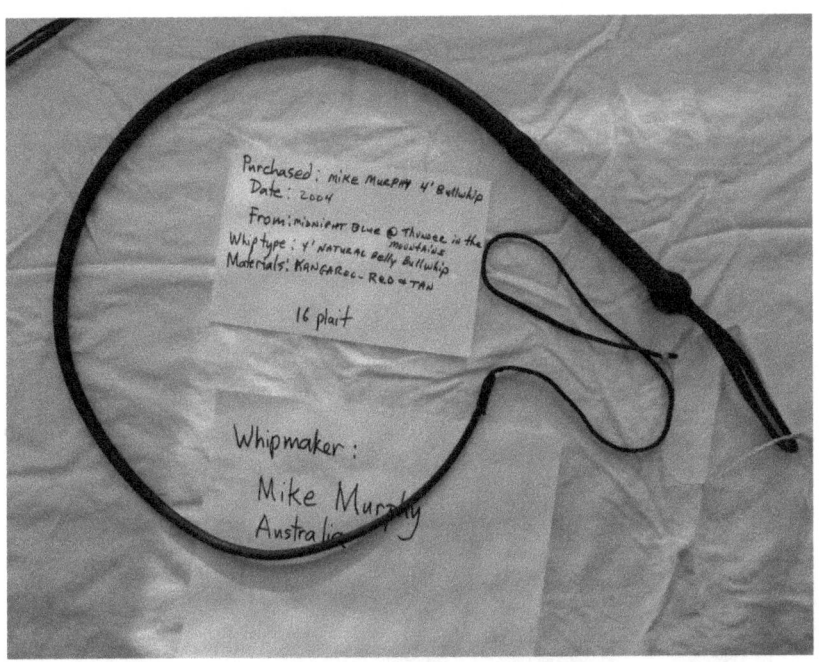

Photo 74 4' 16 plait red and saddletan 2 belly naturally loaded Mike Murphy bullwhip with a latigo fall. (2004)

This Old Whip
December 21, 2023

(Adapted from the lyrics of This Old Guitar by John Denver)
This old bullwhip taught me to sing a love song
It showed me how to laugh and how to cry.
It introduced me to some friends of mine
And brightened up my days
And helped me make it through some lonely nights. Oh
What a friend to have on a cold and lonely night
This beloved whip gave me my lovely lady
It opened up her eyes and ears to me
It brought us close together
And I guess it broke her heart
It opened up the space for us to be

What a lovely place and a lovely space to be.
This old whip gave me my life, my passion
All the things you know I love to do
To serenade the stars at night
From a dimly lit dungeon, sacred space
And most of all, to dance my dance for you
I love to dance my dance for you.
Yes, I do, you know
I love to dance with my whip with you.

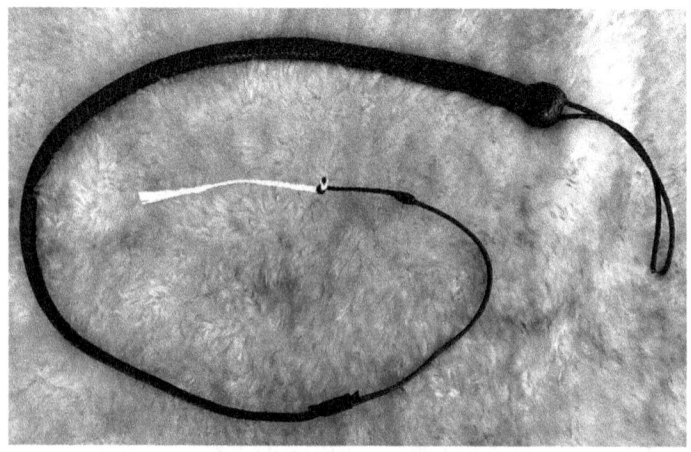

Photo 75 Old Faithful. My first singletail. 3'
16 plait Happy Tails snake whip.

Part of your leather journey and finding the art of the whip will be to find the whip maker you "love." The whip maker whose whips are gold in your hands. I can say that along my journey, I've owned and thrown whips by some of the greatest whip makers who have ever lived or are still alive. I may, of course, by fault of memory, leave someone out.

John (last name unknown) plaited for Happy Tails flogger makers and made signals, snake whips and tomcats (hybrid cat o nines) for them. His snake whip was my first singletail. Roddy Williams,

Mike Murphy, Benton Cassaday, Blake Bruning, Casey Tyler, Bill Glasgow, Si Davies, Bernie Wojcicki, Simon Martin, Blake Gorey, Desert Minx, Viper, Skip San Soucie, Bill Stevenson, Victor Tella, Steve Koliski, Tyler Blake, Peter Thorndike, Evan Fava, Bill Nones, Torrance Fisher, Bobby Holyoak, Joe Strain, Axel, Giovanni Celeste, Alyssum Iris, and Peter Jack; each one of these whip makers have contributed to my leather journey. Most are leather whip makers, and a few are paracord or nylon ribbon whip makers, but all have contributed.

As I near the end of my journey, most of my herd has been sold and passed on to other 'scene' whip throwers. Part of this is so Moodstone doesn't have to figure out who made what, how many plaits it is, and how much the leather is truly worth.

So, what remains and what do I recommend for advanced whip throwers who do not want to collect but want to be able to play in a wide variety of settings? Try out other whip throwers' whips if they will let you every chance you get. But when you do, be very respectful of their whips; do not loudly crack them or stress the leather out in any way. Throw the whip gently and let the leather speak to you.

Recognize that if you like the whip and order your own from that same whip maker, the whip you receive will not throw and feel exactly like what you tried out that night in the dungeon. Not all whip makers' whips and even different classes of whips from the same maker will fit everyone's throwing style or preferences. Unless you are willing to spend your life savings and every spare penny you have on collecting leather whips as I have, utilize the resources you come across along your journey and thank, thank, thank anyone who lets you throw their whip to try it out.

Of ALL the whips in my herd that I've sold and passed on, I have not had a single person anywhere come back to me and tell me they didn't like the whip I sold them or that it was not a good one. Those whips were all from good whip makers; their whips will feel good in many hands.

Of all of these makers, the ones whose whips have adapted to my style of throwing the best are Skip San Soucie's woodies, Mike Murphy's shot-loaded and natural belly bullwhips, Joe Strain's pocket snake whip and Peter Jack's bullwhips (all of his bullwhip builds). I usually do not throw signal whips outside workshop presentations. Still, if I have to do so in a dungeon session, I prefer Desert Minx's and Bill Stevenson's (_Maker_ on Fetlife) signal builds over all others. If you are looking for a "hybrid signal whip" (a hybrid bullwhip), this whip has a bullwhip handle and thong but is finished like a signal whip. Desert Minx has the best "scene" friendly hybrid signal whip build.

These are whips that I believe every whip lover should own: A galley whip, a cat o' nine tails, a dragontail, a signal whip, a snake whip, and a bullwhip. If you throw two-handed, then a matched set of all of them. Your arsenal needs a three-foot signal whip and a three-foot bullwhip for small dungeons and house parties. My standard single-hand toy bag loadout is a galley whip, tomcat, three-foot snake whip, and two four-foot bullwhips. My two-handed toy bag holds a matched set of cat o' nines, four-foot dragontails, three-foot snake whips, and four-foot bullwhips.

I own matched sets of three-foot and four-foot signal whips for house parties. For outdoor play, everyone should own one whip (either snake or bullwhip) that is six feet or longer for doing wraps. I have two six-foot kangaroo bullwhips, a six-foot kangaroo snake whip, and an eight-foot kangaroo black snake. I have a six-foot paracord snake and a six-foot paracord bullwhip for inclement weather. Most of my outdoor play relates to doing wraps with the eight-foot black snake whip, but in recent times, I've been interested in learning contact play with the six-foot bullwhips. For whip painting with acrylics, I use three-foot or four-foot inexpensive paracord whips.

So, in all of that, who do I consider my whip maker? Peter Jack, The Whip Man, is my whip maker. Peter began plaiting when he was 15 years old. As of this writing, he is in his 48th year of plaiting.

Peter once wrote me, "The proper tools in the right hands will change the world." I wrote back that his tools in my hands had changed my world. Moodstone's back tattoo immortalizes Peter Jack's handle plaiting pattern on my four-foot latigo y dago whip. This whip earned the name "Jesus Jack" because when I pulled it out of the box and threw it for the first time, it flew right where I pointed it, and I exclaimed, "Jesus Jack." It is my only named whip.

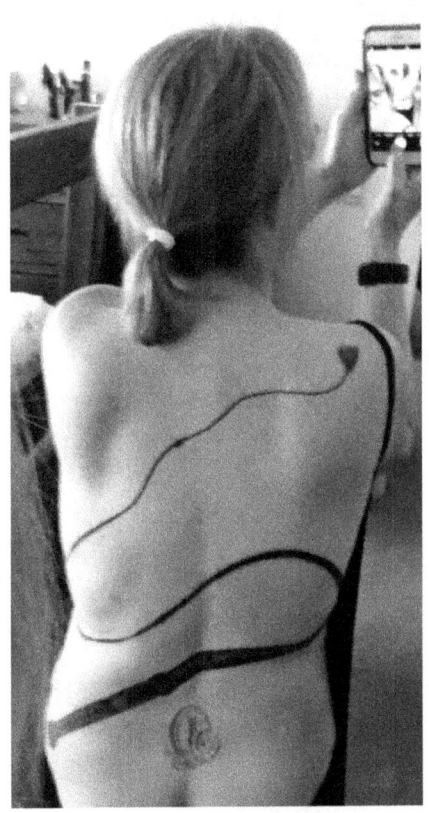

Photo 76 Full Back Tattoo of 4' Peter Jack Latigo y Daga Bullwhip—The Jesus Jack Whip.

In the US scene, most signal whip throwers are probably throwing horizontal style. So, when someone asks me about purchasing a signal whip, I ask if they are throwing it primarily horizontal or East

Coast Swing style. If horizontal is the primary dynamic technique someone uses when throwing, then a signal whip with a heel-loaded medium to heavy shot load will help this throwing style. I point folks toward Desert Minx at Mohave Outliers or Maker (Bill Stevenson). At EF Whips, Evan Fava makes a good signal whip, but his price point is significantly higher[29].

If someone runs across a Roddy Williams or Joe Wheeler signal whip and you throw horizontal then you should empty your bank account, offer your slave up for play for a week, get on your knees and beg, and essentially do anything to acquire the whip.

For overall signal throwing between horizontal style and overhand style, Desert Minx's signal whip build with the extra handle binding, and also _Maker_ have my recommendations.

When we move into bullwhips, Peter Jack truly is The Whip Man. His bullwhips roll out like a ripple on a quiet pond and finish on target. Johnny Öhgren (Witchcraft Whips), Blake Gorey (Smokey Mountain Whips), and Alyssum Iris (Iris Whips) all make excellent bullwhips. Whip tops with different throwing styles will prefer different whip makers; eventually, everyone will have their favorite.

---

[29] Now Peter Jack, as a master whip builder, makes great snake whips. I own a matched set of his pocket snake whips. My Joe Strain snake remains my primary snake for single-handed work. Peter Jack makes an excellent signal whip if you throw overhand, as his signals have exceptional rollout and finish on point.

References

Bean, J. W. (2000). *Flogging.* Emeryville, CA: Greenery Press.

Budworth, G. (2002). *The ultimate encyclopedia of knots & ropework.* London, UK: Hermes House.

Conway, A. (2000). *The bullwhip book.* Emeryville, CA: Greenery Press.

Dante, R. (2016). *"Let's get cracking!": The how-to-book of bullwhip skills.* 2nd ed., with Sylvia Rosat. Middletown, DE: Dante (self-published).

Dante, R. (2024). *Bullwhip: The Dante method.* NP: Dante (self-published).

Dex. (2019). *Whips in the dungeon: Singletail techniques for play.* Tampa, FL: Joan's Books.

Edwards, R. (1997). *How to make whips.* Centreville, MD: Cornell Maritime Press.

Goriely, A., & McMillen, T. (2002, June). *Shape of a cracking whip. Physical Review Letters, 88*(24). Retrieved from https://www.researchgate.net/publication/11315556_Shape_of_a_Cracking_Whip

Merriam, S., & Birerema, L. L. (2014). *Adult learning: Linking theory and practice.* San Francisco, CA: Jossey-Bass.

Miller, P., & Devon, M. (1995). *Screw the roses, send me the thorns: The romance and sexual sorcery of sadomasochism.* Fairfield, CT: Mystic Rose Books.

Morgan, D. W. (1972). *Whips and whipmaking: With a practical introduction to braiding.* Centreville, MD: Cornell Maritime Press.

Pawson, D. (2004). *Handbook of knots*, expanded edition. New York, NY: DK.

Stohlman, A. L., Patten, A. D., & Wilson, J. A. (1969/1984). *Leatherwork manual.* Fort Worth, TX: Tandy Leather Company.

Bio

Dex in Full Leathers.

Dex is a covered Master who began his journey in the leather lifestyle over 25 years ago on an educational and self-reflective path of discovery. For several years, he led an extended leather family in upstate NY. His hospitality in his house of D/s, complete with dungeons in the attic and cellar, became legendary in the northeast. He has since moved on but continues to hone his skills and grow as a Dominant. As a college professor (now retired), he loves teaching and sharing his knowledge. That, coupled with his love of learning in the lifestyle, naturally led to presenting. Dex taught his first lifestyle workshop within his first year in the D/s community. He has since presented at numerous events and venues including: Anchor, T.I.E.D., Rose & Thorn, A.P.e.X., Albany Stocks & Bonds, A.K.P.C., Summer Bash, Spring Fling, Feel Me Breathe, The Floating World 2008, 2013 & 2014, Ohio SMART, Southeast Leatherfest 2009, 2010, 2011 & 2023, Kinko de Mayo 2011, SINSations in Leather 2010, Beyond Leather 2010, 2019, Thunder in the Mountains 2009, South Plains Leatherfest 2011, LeatherFET 2011, Lupercalia MMXIV, Edmonton, Canada, Feel Me Breathe (FMB), Western Mass Power Exchange; E-P-I-C Lifestyle Conference 2016, Whips in Oakland Park, The Woodshed, Orlando, Tampa Phoenix Club, Sadovarius, Academy of Fetish Arts, Fetish Con 2017, The Society (Hartford, CT), Sin in the City 2019, TESfest 2019, Weekend of Wickedness 2019/2022/2023/2024, Jax FetFest 2019/2022/2024, Savannah Underground 2022, the Vulgarians 2023/2024, Arizona Power Exchange 2024, Leather Culture Club N.E. 2024, and Carolina Coastal Fetish Fair 2024. His first passion is the whip, but he does not confine himself to one love. His other interests include canes, the violet wand, bastinado, urethral sounds on females, and food play. He produces two lifestyle YouTube channels: The Leather Journey and Whips in the Dungeon. His instructional videos that compliment *Whips in the Dungeon* and *Variations and Vignettes* are hosted at http://witd.houseofgraves.com

www.ingramcontent.com/pod-product-compliance
Lightning Source LLC
Chambersburg PA
CBHW070632160426
43194CB00009B/1442